Outsourcing Repression

Studies of the Weatherhead East Asian Institute, Columbia University

The Studies of the Weatherhead East Asian Institute of Columbia University were inaugurated in 1962 to bring to a wider public the results of significant new research on modern and contemporary East Asia.

Outsourcing Repression

*Everyday State Power in
Contemporary China*

LYNETTE H. ONG

OXFORD
UNIVERSITY PRESS

OXFORD
UNIVERSITY PRESS

Oxford University Press is a department of the University of Oxford. It furthers
the University's objective of excellence in research, scholarship, and education
by publishing worldwide. Oxford is a registered trade mark of Oxford University
Press in the UK and certain other countries.

Published in the United States of America by Oxford University Press
198 Madison Avenue, New York, NY 10016, United States of America.

Library of Congress Cataloging-in-Publication Data
Names: Ong, Lynette H., author.
Title: Outsourcing repression : everyday state power in
contemporary China / Lynette H. Ong.
Description: New York, NY : Oxford University Press, [2022] |
Includes bibliographical references and index.
Identifiers: LCCN 2021056065 (print) | LCCN 2021056066 (ebook) |
ISBN 9780197628768 (hardback) | ISBN 9780197628775 (paperback) |
ISBN 9780197628799 (epub) | ISBN 9780197628782 (UPDF) |
ISBN 9780197628805 (Digital-Online)
Subjects: LCSH: Political persecution—China. | Social control—China. |
Government, Resistance to—China. | Power (Social sciences)—China. |
Urbanization—Political aspects—China. | Gangs—Political
aspects—China. | China—Politics and government—2002-
Classification: LCC JC599.C6 O58 2022 (print) | LCC JC599.C6 (ebook) |
DDC 323/.0440951—dc23/eng/20211210
LC record available at https://lccn.loc.gov/2021056065
LC ebook record available at https://lccn.loc.gov/2021056066

DOI: 10.1093/oso/9780197628768.001.0001

3 5 7 9 8 6 4 2

Paperback printed in Canada by Marquis Book Printing
Hardback printed by Bridgeport National Bindery, Inc., United States of America

To all those who received the short end of the stick in
the state's ambitious scheme

Contents

Figures

Tables

Preface

Outsourcing Repression addresses strategies put in place by the state to seize farmland and demolish houses when its actions lack legitimacy. The strategy of outsourcing repression to nonstate violent and nonviolent agents has proven expedient and largely effective. Authorities in China have figured out that by hiring street hoodlums and patron-trusted local influentials, they can get the job done expeditiously. Thus, *Outsourcing Repression* is a study about how to repress the right way—and minimize the costs of backlash and resistance at the same time. Examining these issues empirically, using urbanization as a window of observation, I elaborate on how they can be further applied to other areas similarly devoid of legality.

At a fundamental level, I demonstrate the ways that outsourcing repression redraws the boundaries between state and society and the topography of state power, surpassing state repression or even social control—and animating a new creature of the state.

This research has brought to the fore the prominence of violent and nonviolent repressive strategies in different times. As I moved to field sites in the inner core of metropolitan cities over time, I gained an appreciation of the increased salience of nonviolent coercion under the guise of the official discourse of "harmonious demolition." From 2011 to 2019, I conducted on-the-ground ethnographic research before and after President Xi Jinping's ascendancy to power. The case studies speak to the unique challenges a field researcher faced in the respective periods. While those in disciplinary and China studies conscientiously debate how future field research can and should be carried out in this rapidly deteriorating political environment, this book offers the fruits of my labor in the not-so-distant past.

Research conducted in the early 2000s for my last book, *Prosper or Perish*, provided the basis for this book, in which I analyze the search by local authorities in China for alternative revenue sources to meet unfunded mandates created by a semireformed fiscal system. When revenue from township and village enterprises dried up in the late 1990s and early 2000s, local authorities enthusiastically bet on land sales and urban development as new revenue sources. Even though the end product of this monograph involves repression and state power instead of the political economy I initially envisioned, I draw implications in appropriate places throughout the book for what this type of coercive distribution means for the state's role in economic development.

Acknowledgments

Given the long and arduous process that research entails, this book would have been impossible without the many people who have accompanied me at various stages of this journey. I stand on the broad shoulders of scholars and colleagues who have contributed to the field of authoritarian politics, the study of the state, and China studies.

My China-based colleagues and friends have helped me tremendously in understanding the country—both its allures and idiosyncrasies. With wise advice and good humor, many went out of their way to open doors for me and helped me navigate the field. Their tenacious capacity to survive, and even thrive, in an increasingly challenging environment has always been a source of inspiration.

I extend my gratitude to Dave McBride, my editor at Oxford University Press, who has enthusiastically supported this project from the outset, steering it in the right direction.

Over the decade during which this research was conducted, numerous colleagues and friends have taken time to discuss ideas and invited me to conferences, workshops, and seminars to present working papers, from all of which I have benefited tremendously. Among them were Ben Hillman, David Goodman, Shan Wei, Qian Jiwei, Peter Lorentzen, Xiaobo Lü (Columbia), Mary Gallagher, Christian Davenport, Yuen Yuen Ang, Cai Yongshun, Ray Yep, Feng Cheng, Ting Gong, Chen Chih-Jou, Jean Hong, Li Lianjiang, Pierre Landry, Stephen Noakes, Elena Meyer-Clement, Jesper Zeuthen, Genia Kostka, Patricia Thornton, Xin Sun, Kerry Brown, Hyun Bang Shin, Tim Hildebrandt, Federico Varese, Jean Oi, Andy Walder, Lizhi Liu, Melanie Manion, Dan Slater, Kimberly Marten, Sheena Greitens, Suzanne Scoggins, Dimitar Gueorguiev, Victor Shih, Kristen Looney, Jenn Pan, Iza Ding, Blake Miller, Peng Wang, Yanhua Deng, and Yang Zhong.

I am thankful for the support of the Weatherhead Center for International Affairs at Harvard University under the leadership of Michelle Lamont and subsequently Melani Cammett for generously offering me a fellowship to host my writing for this book.

I have also drawn on the generosity of colleagues and friends who provided insightful comments on earlier drafts and chapters, including those circulated at a book manuscript workshop. They are Liz Perry, Kevin O'Brien, Ben Read, Meg Rithmire, Jenn Earl, Brian Taylor, David Cunningham, Xu Xu, Martin Dimitrov, Xiaobo Lü (UT Austin), John Fitzgerald, Anita Chan, Andy Kipnis, and Charles

Crabtree. My colleagues at the University of Toronto, including Ed Schatz, Seva Gunitsky, Lucan Way, Yoonkyung Lee, Yiching Wu, and Adam Casey, also offered critical comments on earlier versions of this manuscript.

Carolina de Miguel, my department colleague who passed away in 2020, was someone who always made time to chat, read my work, and discuss it over lunch or coffee. Her generous and humane spirit remains a source of inspiration and is sorely missed. The intellectual communities of scholars in political science, global affairs, and Asian studies at the University of Toronto have provided me with the inspiration and advice I needed: Antoinette Handley, Ryan Balot, Peter Loewen, Ron Levi, Joseph Wong, Rachel Silvey, Diana Fu, Sida Liu, Greg Distelhorst, Tak Fujitani, Frank Cody, Melissa Williams, Aisha Ahmad, Phil Triadafilopoulos, Ludovic Rheault, and Kenichi Ariga.

I would have been unable to write this book without the team of dedicated students who have given me incredible support, often under tight deadlines. Although naming them all would be impractical, the following are a few whose help was critical in the final stages of the writing: Kevin, Alex, Alissa, Hao, Zhouyang, Minghan, Brodie, Jasper, Yifan, and Yitian.

Much of the writing was done during the COVID-19 lockdown. Weaving together the stories my interlocutors shared over the course of the research provided much comfort and ameliorated to some extent the toll taken by the extended lockdown in Toronto. I am most grateful for the trust of my interviewees and interlocutors, allowing me to tell their stories. This book is dedicated to them.

Lynette H. Ong
Toronto
July 1, 2021

1

Bulldozers, Violent Thugs, and Nonviolent Brokers

> The worst crime committed by totalitarian mind-sets is that they force their citizens, including their victims, to become complicit in their crimes. Dancing with your jailer, participating in your own execution, that is an act of utmost brutality.
>
> —Azar Nafisi, *Reading Lolita in Tehran*

In July 2010, I stood at the Shanghai Expo's main national pavilion on the banks of the Huangpu River, marveling at the grandiosity of the architectural juggernaut before me. Much like the 2008 Beijing Olympics, the ostentatious Shanghai Expo was intended to display China's raw economic and political ambitions as well as to mark its arrival on the world stage. The Expo's theme of "Better City—Better Life" underscored these messages, intended for domestic and global consumption.

Fast forward six years. In the summer of 2016, my field research for this book led me to interview a group of Shanghai residents who had lost their homes because of the Expo. "My home was situated right where the main national pavilion stood!" an evictee in his 60s told me.[1] After his forced removal in the early 2000s, he was never properly resettled or compensated. He and a group of other evictees from Shanghai have paid monthly visits to the Beijing Petition Bureau for nearly two decades in the hope of having their housing grievances addressed. Nevertheless, all efforts to reassert their property rights and regain their dignity have been nearly futile.

That summer I interviewed another group of Shanghai residents, who shared with me their experience engaging with market brokers to bargain with local governments for even more lucrative compensation over and above the brand-new apartments and handsome cash payments they had been promised and given.[2] The juxtaposition of the two groups of Shanghai residents, who faced similar eviction pressures, albeit at different times—but ended up receiving diverging treatments by the state—is instructive. Their stories encapsulate in miniature the varied configurations of the power of the state and the distinctive means through which it coerces compliance.

Outsourcing Repression. Lynette H. Ong, Oxford University Press. © Oxford University Press 2022.
DOI: 10.1093/oso/9780197628768.003.0001

1.1 The Puzzle: Balancing Coerced Compliance
with Minimized Backlash

Economic growth necessitates the redistribution of resources—including land, labor, and capital—from one group to another. Autocracies may be more effective than democracies in forcibly redistributing resources by means of coercion or the imposition of rules and subsequently withstanding the pressure exerted by the losers (Wintrobe 1998),[3] yet wielding the stick comes with a cost. Persistent coercion may invite backlash, provoke resistance, and delegitimize the regime (Davenport and Inman 2012). If a regime bent on growth enacts a policy that redistributes resources and subsequently causes dissent among the losers, how the regime balances coerced compliance with minimized backlash remains a question.

In this book I use urbanization as a window of observation for state policies that entail immense resource reallocation to study the practice of state power to gain compliance and mute dissent. Rapid urbanization, by its very nature, involves vast population relocation and resource redistribution among groups. In China, property owners have been coerced into compliance, their voices muffled as the state tries to fast track the urbanization process. To be sure, popular resistance has arisen against land taking and housing demolition,[4] yet no country has ever pulled off the spatial transformation and relocation of people on the scale achieved by China while simultaneously maintaining social stability.

To capture the essence of the monumental scale of China's urbanization, consider this: an estimated total of no fewer than 52 million peasants were displaced between 1987 and 2010 (Han 2009; Shengsan Jiang, Liu, and Li 2010). An estimated increase of 10.4 million acres in land used for urban construction purposes occurred from 2010 to 2017—equivalent to 125 percent of the land mass of the U.S. state of Maryland.[5] If we compare China with India, another large developing country similarly fixated on pursuing growth through industrialization and urbanization, the contrast is stark. State efforts to requisition farmland in India are frequently met with strong peasant resistance and are mediated by a range of brokers who hold significant bargaining power.[6]

In this book China serves as a case study to exemplify a state that practices vigorous *everyday state power* over society by outsourcing repression to nonstate agents who use violent and nonviolent strategies to extract compliance and stifle dissent. The authoritarian nature of China's political system, led by the Chinese Communist Party (CCP), serves to strengthen this power; but it is not a necessary condition. Theoretically, everyday engagement of third-party agents by the state to coerce pushes the boundary on what scholars currently understand as state repression. Because the repressive capacity of the state is a central element of its strength, I also invite readers to reimagine what constitutes the notion of state power.

1.2 The Theory and Arguments: Outsourcing Repression to Augment Everyday State Power

Advancing two major arguments, this book presents a theory about outsourcing repression which lies at the core of *everyday state power* over society.[7] First, the state implements unpopular policies effectively and swiftly by using the "everyday repression" of outsourced violence.[8] Carried out by "thugs-for-hire" (TFH), it is an expedient state strategy to impose its will on society.[9] Although violent repression usually incurs costs, outsourcing violence to third-party agents provides the pretense for plausible deniability and evasion of political accountability. Second, the state extracts citizen compliance and resolves state–society conflicts by mobilizing the masses (MTM), which involves marshalling a small segment of society—the brokers—to gain acquiescence from the larger society. Because mass mobilization is conducted through social networks, brokers with social capital legitimate state repression, in turn minimizing resistance and backlash.

An unconventional autocratic tool, outsourcing violence to TFH serves as a proverbial stick. When outsourced to third parties, however, violent repression is a stick with no identifiable wielding agent, allowing for plausible deniability and the evasion of political accountability that is a major cost of violent repression. I call this strategy "everyday repression," denoting the banal, low-grade violent repressive acts of coercion, deployed when formal state coercive acts are impractical (Ong 2015b). It is most effective in minimizing costs when the hiring authority can effectively distance itself from the illegitimate violent acts and serious casualties caused by it.

Meanwhile, MTM is a political strategy that shapes citizen behavior through persuasion, an authoritarian tool independent of the proverbial carrots and sticks, often carried out alongside rewards and punishments with the similar intention of extracting compliance. MTM via persuasion is carried out by political, social, and economic grassroots brokers, who persuade citizens through mobilization of affective emotions like love, trust, and respect. Critically, because persuasion is lubricated by social relations and their attendant emotions, it is not commonly perceived as state repression—thus allowing for lower-cost state extraction of consent.

Figure 1.1 illustrates the agents and mechanisms through which outsourcing repression augments *everyday state power*. The nonstate agency of TFH and brokers enables the state to exercise low-level violent everyday repression and to

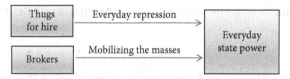

Figure 1.1 Agents and Mechanisms that Lead Outsourcing Repression to Augmentation of Everyday State Power

mobilize the masses with socially embedded emotions. The elusive private identity of TFH makes possible plausible deniability and the evasion of state accountability, and brokers with social standing legitimize the state's mass mobilization. Collectively, these strategies minimize the resistance and backlash typically associated with state repression.

Everyday state power is not, however, a guaranteed outcome of engaging non-state agents. Outsourcing repression works to the state's advantage only under certain conditions, leading to variation in the successful practice of *everyday state power* over society, the outcome variable of this study. Untrained TFH can exert undisciplined violence that results in excess casualties, making the evasion of responsibility a challenge. When government officials are seen as endorsing TFH explicitly, the agents' illegitimate violence is then associated with state sponsorship. As with brokers, they bring net benefits to the state insofar as they remain legitimate in the citizens' eyes. When they are corrupt or prioritize personal interests at the citizens' expense, they cease to legitimate state mobilization. Under these circumstances, outsourcing repression is costly, and *everyday state power* is diminished accordingly.

I illustrate these arguments through a study of the Chinese state's efforts to spearhead urbanization as an engine of growth. Most governments face formidable challenges in land redistribution, but the Chinese state has been far more successful in imposing its will on society and forcing citizens to acquiesce to state orders—thanks to its engagement of nonstate agents. Beyond urbanization, the state also engages TFH in areas of illegitimate or illegal actions, such as the rural exactions of the 1990s, and the intimidation of protestors, petitioners, dissidents, journalists, and other troublemakers. To appreciate how ubiquitous the strategy of mobilizing the masses is, simply consider the role of neighborhood committees and the nationwide army of volunteers in controlling people's movements during the fight against SARS and the COVID-19 pandemic. Grassroots brokers not only contribute enormous manpower to state pursuits, but they also invoke affective emotions to persuade citizens, a strategy that is often overlooked.

In addition, temporal and regional variations in China are noteworthy. In general, the prevalence of violent repression by TFH diminished from the

2000s to 2010s, the period covered by this study; but nonviolent, brokered mass mobilization has increased in prominence over time. In a regional variation, people living in the inner core of metropolitan cities, such as Shanghai and Chengdu, tend to see significantly less or no violence, whereas those in the city peripheries and the rural areas still experience violent repression. Using in-depth case studies, I show that the violent repression prevalent in Zhengzhou, the provincial capital of the mid-income Henan province, in the mid-2010s had already occurred in metropolitan Shanghai a decade earlier in the mid-2000s. By the mid-2010s, however, Shanghai had "progressed" into the nonviolent mass mobilization era.

Despite these variations, outsourced violent coercion can be deployed alongside nonviolent mobilization. As the case studies will illustrate, much depends on the availability of thuggish agents and trustworthy local volunteers willing to do the state's bidding and the extent to which they can effectively repress or mobilize the society. These considerations are location specific.

In this book, the state refers to the Party-state, notwithstanding the occasional bifurcation of the central-local state interest.[10] Using "state" in this volume, I refer to local governments that have direct agency, not the central leadership. But some of the outsourced repressive strategies, such as mobilizing the masses, have been actively promoted by the central government as in the "Fengqiao Experience" (Z. Zhu 2018). Overall, local governments' outsourcing of repression has been either explicitly promoted or tacitly approved by the central authority. Condonation by the center is palpable in the case of "black jails," where petitioners are illegally detained.[11]

To what extent do these arguments apply beyond China? *Everyday state power* is the state's exercise of power *through* society, or via society itself. To exercise this power, the state must be strong enough to control the behavior of the violent agents or nonviolent brokers with whom it engages. In the absence of state domination over agents, the latter should normatively believe that doing the state's bidding contributes to the collective public good. Furthermore, that authoritarianism is not a necessary condition for the outsourcing of repression deserves emphasis. The arguments advanced here could be applied to other autocracies as well as democracies, subject to the scope condition that I will elaborate in Chapter 2. I illustrate in Chapter 8 the prevalent use of criminals and gangsters by the authoritarian South Korean regime under Park Chung Hee and Chun Doo Hwan to conduct mass evictions. This violent practice continued after the country transitioned to a democracy in 1987, albeit less blatantly and more tacitly. In democratic India, *goondas*, or neighborhood gangsters, lend their "muscle power" to local politicians to intimidate political rivals, gather campaign budgets, and win elections in return for political protection for their illegal business pursuits.

1.3 Challenges to Conventional Wisdom: State Power, Repression, and Authoritarian Control

1.3.1 Reimagining State Power

What constitutes state power? I consider its three key dimensions—state–society relations, state capacity, and obedience to state power (vom Hau 2015)—and appraise outsourcing repression for its capability to shine new light on the traditional construct and contours of the power of the state.

The repressive strategies discussed in this book reconstruct state–society relations because they allow the state to mobilize nonstate actors to pursue state objectives.[12] When TFH are engaged in state projects, they become part of the state's army of foot soldiers, whose goal is to intimidate and coerce citizens. Similarly, when brokers are mobilized, they are effectively transformed into state extensions that conduct persuasion or "thought work" on the citizenry. State–society boundaries are then blurred and shifted against the society. In other words, TFH and brokers become complicit in the state's repression of society, using violent and nonviolent strategies, respectively.

Outsourcing repression to nonstate actors heightens the presence of *everyday state power* throughout the society. This augmented state power is not acquired through repression in the conventional sense; instead, it involves a two-step process. First, the voluntary participation of proxies—impossible with brute repression—must be secured. Second, the elusive nonstate nature of violent proxies (TFH) or legitimation by nonviolent proxies (brokers) then allows the state to control society, simultaneously managing dissent and minimizing backlash. Brokers who serve as legitimizing vehicles help to change the perception of repressive acts, thereby blunting resistance to them. In *Outsourcing Repression* I invite readers to reimagine state power—the state occupies new ground with augmented penetrative capacity, through which it can unconventionally acquire societal approval of its very power.

1.3.2 Cost-Minimizing Repression

State repression typically involves trade-offs between increased control and loss of loyalty, giving rise to what Ronald Wintrobe (1998) called the "dictator's dilemma." This is the reason that no regime can survive through naked coercion alone. I argue, however, that reconstituted *everyday state power* makes possible the state's enforcement of compliance, which is met with minimal backlash. Thus, I theorize a *counterintuitive* form of repression—when carried out by nonstate agents, outsourced repressive acts lower the costs of state repression.

This book is a study of outsourced violent and nonviolent repressive acts, the former conducted by TFH, such as street gangsters, hooligans, or hoodlums, who render their muscle power as a for-profit service. As opposed to armed state coercive agents, namely the military, paramilitaries, or the police, capable of committing massive violence (Alvarez 2006; Geddes, Wright, and Frantz 2018; Mazzei 2009), TFH deploy low-level violence or threats of violence to carry out coercion. They are an integral part of the state's "everyday repression," denoting banal, ordinary repressive acts expediently imposed on marginalized citizens who defy everyday state directives (Ong 2015b). Critically, the concealed identities of TFH allow the state to maintain an arms-length relationship with them and their illegitimate violent acts. This provides the pretense for plausible deniability and evasion of accountability, which lowers the costs associated with violent repression accordingly. As untrained agents, TFH may, however, commit undisciplined violence in excess of what is necessary to execute the tasks assigned to them. The latitude for deniability improves when serious casualties, including deaths, are absent and when the hiring authority can effectively distance itself from the agents.

In contrast, outsourced nonviolent repression is exercised through the engagement of brokers who mobilize the masses for state pursuits. By connecting the two disparate parties of state and society, brokers facilitate information gathering, surveillance, public goods provision, and mobilization (Baldwin 2013; Koter 2013; Mares and Young 2016, 2019; McAdam, Tarrow, and Tilly 2001; Stovel and Shaw 2012). I divide brokers into political brokers, whose brokerage power stems from the state, namely residents and village committees; social brokers, who draw on social capital to exercise brokerage, such as volunteers and community enthusiasts; and economic brokers, who have connections with political insiders and who have gained the trust of state and society, allowing them to use their informational advantage to seek profits by bridging trust deficits, such as the *huangniu* in my case study.

In general, MTM is a political strategy that mobilizes the people for state pursuits. When organized into a movement, it becomes a state-organized social movement (Ekiert, Perry, and Yan 2020) like Mao's Red Guard Movement or Nashi, the youth movement organized by Putin (Hemment 2020). In the present context, MTM refers to mobilization on an individual basis to gain citizens' compliance. Because ideology holds less appeal in post-Mao China than it once did, contemporary brokers mobilize through emotion-lubricated social relations or *guanxi* networks, cultivated over a lifetime to serve the dual purposes of sentimentality and instrumentalism (Kipnis 2002). In effect, social brokers who invoke *guanxi* for the purpose of persuasion serve to legitimate the state's mobilization of society for statist goals. Because of social capital they possess, brokers' actions are not usually perceived as state repression; hence, nonviolent brokered repression is more likely to be accepted by society, significantly reducing the likelihood of resistance and backlash.

1.3.3 A New Tool in the Autocrat's Toolkit

I also introduce some tools new to the autocrat's toolkit—third party-wielded sticks and persuasion—and argue that they enhance state control of society largely without the fear of backlash.[13] Both falling under the ambit of outsourced repression, they correspond to everyday repression via TFH and MTM through brokers, respectively. Sticks wielded by private agents allow for plausible deniability insofar as the hiring authority can effectively distance itself from the TFH and the illegitimate violence does not result in severe casualties. If these conditions are met, outsourcing violence is superior to the conventional stick of violent state repression because it allows the state to keep perpetrators of violent acts at arm's length.

Meanwhile, persuasion is an autocrat's tool, wielded by brokers who command social capital, with which they mobilize the masses for state pursuits. Social brokers thus legitimize the repression and blunt the resistance and the backlash that would have otherwise occurred. Even though persuasion can serve as an independent tool, it is often facilitated by carrots (inducements) and made credible by sticks (emotional coercion). With the declining traction of ideology, the Party-state sometimes uses carrots to induce the participation of brokers to extract acquiescence from the larger society, which in turn, as the target of mass mobilization, is coaxed by inducements, cowed by psychological coercion, or simply admonished by thought work (思想工作) in the parlance of Chinese politics. Brokered persuasion thus serves an important legitimating function to state repression.

Like propaganda, persuasion is a mass communication tool designed to influence people and change their behavior (Jowett and O'Donnell 2014; O'Shaughnessy 2016). Notably, persuasion and coercion are often nondichotomous; "even as some forms of coercion are more or less violent, some forms of argument are more or less coercive" (Crawford 2009). Put differently, persuasion can have the intended and actual effect of coercing acquiescence from message recipients. Although propaganda has received much attention in the literature of authoritarian politics, persuasion has not received nearly as much. The effectiveness of persuasion in enforcing obedience underscores the primacy of legitimacy. This stands in contrast to the much celebrated *Ambiguities of Dominance*, in which Lisa Wedeen argues for the symbolic effects of propaganda in bolstering the Asad regime even though few Syrians bought into the actual messages behind the grandiose spectacles (H. Huang 2015; Loveman 2005;

Wedeen 2015).[14] In Wedeen's words, "Asad's cult is a strategy of domination based on compliance rather than legitimacy" (2015, 6). In contrast, persuasion—unlike propaganda—does not produce the spectacle effect; and thus, without legitimation, it is nothing more than empty words.

When is the autocrat more likely to use persuasion vis-à-vis carrots and sticks? Broadly speaking, persuasion and carrots are nonviolent means of control; sticks are violent measures. Regimes adopt nonviolent repressive measures if given an underlying normative preference[15] or when violent measures become too costly. Persuasion is the least costly of all the tools in material terms and in backlash minimization. Carrots draw directly on material resources, and as citizens' income levels rise, the threshold for material inducements also increases. What constituted carrots to the urban citizenry in the 2000s would certainly not qualify as financial inducements to the urban middle class in the 2010s. Meanwhile, sticks impose the highest costs in terms of the potential resistance and backlash they may invite; therefore, we should expect persuasion to be deployed when one of the following conditions is met. First, the material costs of carrots are too high; second, carrots have lost their appeal to the targeted citizens; third, the costs of sticks are unbearably high; or fourth, legitimacy is of utmost importance to the state.

Condition 1 accurately describes the Maoist period, during which the scarcity of financial resources meant that Mao could not dole out carrots to induce compliance. In other words, the masses, that is, the people, who were in relative abundance—not guns or money—became Mao's greatest resource. Mao's revolutionary experience of drawing on the relatively abundant resource gave rise to the tradition of relying on the masses to act as internal security agents. This stands in contrast to the secret police institutions in other socialist countries, such as the KGB in the former Soviet Union and the Stasi in East Germany. In contemporary China, however, persuasion is deployed because compliance from the targeted citizenry cannot be easily bought with material inducements (Condition 2) and in some regions, especially in metropolitan cities, and the cost of using sticks or overt repression is too high for the regime (Condition 3). Critically, persuasion assumed primacy in China under Mao and continues to dominate under Xi because both political leaders recognized the importance of preserving legitimacy amidst the regime's widespread suppression of the society (Condition 4).

This study is inspired by the existing literature on repression in China. Notably, Yanhua Deng and Kevin O'Brien's (2013) "relational repression" and Elizabeth Perry's (2002b) "moving the masses" have informed much of my understanding of how mobilizing the masses works. Separately, Ching Kwan Lee and Yonghong Zhang's (2013) "bargained authoritarianism" underscores the state buying stability from aggrieved citizens. This book, however, diverges from the existing work on state repression in that it is the first to bring together the gamut of violent and nonviolent strategies (or sticks, carrots, and persuasion) and demonstrate their temporal and regional variations.

This book builds on my earlier work on the state's outsourcing of violence to TFH as a means of implementing unpopular everyday policies and dealing with protestors and dissidents.[16] It is the first book-length manuscript that devotes attention to the use of thugs and criminals as repressive agents, an important area of state repression that has received little attention.[17] State-sponsored violence no longer takes place in the metropolitan cities of China on an everyday basis today. Why and the conditions under which nonviolent measures are substituted for violent repression is a key inquiry of this research. To that end, I have carefully assembled and analyzed the outsourced violent and nonviolent repressive measures that have been previously unexamined or have hitherto been studied separately in the existing literature.

1.4 Empirical Strategy

I have employed various methodological tools, including field interviews, quantitative media-sourced data, and content analysis of government regulations, to capture temporal and regional variations in state repressive actions and the ensuing conflicts. My first empirical strategy drew on more than 200 field interviews conducted annually over the span of nearly a decade from 2011 to 2019 with householders, petitioners, activists, Party cadres, and lawyers in both rural and urban areas in China.

I visited a total of eight provinces or provincial-level municipalities that encompassed dozens of rural farming villages, villages-in-a-city (城中村), and residential compounds on the outskirts of cities as well as urban communities in the inner-city cores. As illustrated in Figure 1.2, the field research locations were Anhui's provincial capital, Hefei; Beijing municipality; Yunnan's provincial capital, Kunming; Sichuan's provincial capital, Chengdu; Henan's provincial capital, Zhengzhou; Shanghai municipality; Guangdong's provincial capital, Guangzhou; and Tianjin municipality. I also visited Mumbai and New Delhi in 2015 to interview activists, lawyers, and academics whose work delved into land conflicts in India. All the interviews are annotated in Appendix B.

Each of these field research trips typically lasted between two and four weeks. I had the opportunity to participate in the everyday activities of the communities, observe activists' speeches and rallies, and interact with village and urban grassroots cadres on a daily basis. These largely semistructured interviews were conducted in paddy and corn fields, teashops, public squares, street-level corridors of shophouses, private residences, and community and grassroots

City	Year of visits
Hefei	2011
Beijing	2011, 2014, 2015
Kunming	2012
Chengdu	2013, 2014, 2015, 2019
Zhengzhou	2014
Shanghai	2016, 2018
Guanzhou	2017
Tianjin	2017

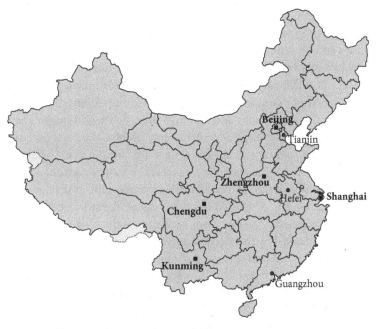

Figure 1.2   Field Research Sites and Year of Visits

Note: Square markers represent locations of detailed case studies in Chapters 4 and 6. Circle markers identify visited sites not covered in the case studies but are the sources of interview quotations, sprinkled throughout the book.

government offices as well as half-demolished villages with debris surrounding me and my interviewees.

In each of the interviews, I adopted a common structure that began with warm-up questions about the interviewees' basic household information, occupations, and economic conditions before broaching relatively sensitive topics, such as their encounters with government repression and activism. This interview technique allowed me to build the trust of the interviewees over the course of one lengthy session, and, not infrequently, over multiple sessions in repeated follow-up visits. Some interviewees, nevertheless, still preferred to deflect my queries and regurgitate government propaganda. I attempted to corroborate controversial evidence from multiple sources instead of accepting it at face value. Sometimes, for reasons of personal safety, I could not revisit the field sites for follow-up investigations as I had desired. Some of the field interviews yielded sufficient data to weave together detailed case studies as covered in Chapters 4 and 6, but others amounted to scattered data, in which case the interview quotations are sprinkled throughout the manuscript.

The long decade over which the field research was conducted has provided me with some unique observations. At the beginning of the research in the early 2010s, I encountered the pedestrian nature of thuggish violence in forced land grabs and housing demolitions. Over time, as I moved to field sites in the inner core of metropolitan Shanghai and Chengdu, I discovered the increased prominence of mobilizing the masses as a state strategy under the guise of the official discourse of "harmonious demolition." Without a doubt, the preponderance of violent repression has declined over time, but that of nonviolent coercion has risen correspondingly. Another deeply felt observation is the changing nature of field research in China—certainly a turn for the worse—particularly the challenges posed by increased self-censorship, state surveillance, and even outright prohibition of the subjects of intellectual inquiries. The number of red lines has increased, and what used to be grey zones of research has moved into the space defined by the red lines. Not accidentally, the progression from grey to red was also marked by the ascendancy of Xi Jinping's presidency. I offer my thoughts on the issue of field research in China in the concluding Chapter 8.

To complement field observations, my second empirical strategy was the construction of an event dataset, consisting of forced land-taking and demolition cases sourced from Chinese and English media. The dataset contains more than 2,000 cases from the 1990s through to the late 2010s. The data quality is subject to the usual caveats associated with media-sourced data favoring large-scale, violent, newsworthy incidents. To address the selection-bias issue, I triangulated alternative sources, including smaller civil society-run websites that draw on reports filed by independent citizen–journalists and victims throughout the country. The independent reporting complements the large and widely publicized cases reported by commercial media. Quantitative data analyses are covered in Chapters 3 and 6. A detailed discussion of the dataset construction and its caveats is elaborated in Appendix C.

Furthermore, to supplement these two largely society-centric methodologies, I collected regulations on land-taking and housing demolitions issued by the central government and the Shanghai, Chengdu, and Zhengzhou municipalities from the 1990s through to the 2010s. These cities hosted the detailed case studies in this book. I applied content analysis to the regulations to analyze discernible patterns in government discourse and changes in state strategies to gain compliance, resolve conflicts, and promote social stability. The findings from content analysis appear in Chapters 2, 3, and 6. Taken together, the varied empirical strategies were designed to address the research questions from the perspectives of both the state and society. They also complement each other because in-depth contextual case studies reveal what statistical analyses do and do not inform.

1.5 Roadmap

The next chapter situates the book's findings in the relevant bodies of theoretical literature on repression, state power, and authoritarian politics. The findings push the boundaries of the traditional conception of state repression held by political scientists and sociologists. When outsourced to third-party agents, state repression can realize the intended effect of extracting compliance while minimizing dissent and backlash. Thus, when state–society boundaries blur and relationships change, *everyday state power* is reconstituted and augmented. This book therefore reenvisions the traditional conception of state power. Even though this study does not center on the question of growth, I draw implications for the state's role in economic development at the chapter's end.

Important temporal and regional variations occur in the use of rewards, coercion, and persuasion in urbanization projects. Incidents of forced evictions by thuggish violence have declined over time and are less common in urban than in rural areas. Concomitantly, the frequency in the use of nonviolent strategies, particularly persuasion, has risen over time; these strategies are more prevalent in metropolitan than in smaller inland cities. Evidence for these temporal and regional patterns is borne out in qualitative case studies and media-sourced quantitative data from Chapters 3 through 6. Chapters 3 and 4 cover the violent strategy of everyday repression; Chapters 5 and 6 pertain to the nonviolent strategy of mobilizing the masses. Relevant literature about China and context-specific information are engaged and discussed in these four empirical chapters while the intent of Chapters 1 and 2 is to speak to broader disciplinary readers.

In Chapter 3 I conceptualize a novel form of repression—everyday repression carried out by TFH—as a state response to foot-dragging and banal noncompliance captured in what James Scott called "everyday forms of resistance." It provides quantitative evidence from media-sourced data to support the argument that everyday repression is a lower-cost repressive strategy, pointing to its negative or lesser effect on the likelihood of street protest and violent backlash, particularly in comparison with police and government officials.

Chapter 3 presents quantitative and qualitative data to detail the profile of typical TFH and the conditions under which they operate, but the chapter that follows does the opposite. Drawing on detailed primary case studies, I turn in Chapter 4 to exceptional cases of outsourced violence that resulted in death or large-scale contention or that received official government sponsorship. Under those circumstances, TFH were no longer a lower-cost repressive measure; instead, they became a liability to the hiring authority. The case studies also demonstrate the negative consequences for governance when the relationship between local governments and thugs transformed from principal-agent to patron-client, heightening the risk of usurpation of government authority by criminal groups. In effect, they demonstrate the rare practical consequences of violating the unspoken conditions of outsourced violence.

Chapter 5 covers nonviolent brokers who are part of the state's networks of infrastructural power. Political brokers, such as members of urban residents' committees and rural village committees, who derive their brokerage power from state appointments, are perceived as grassroots state or quasistate agents. Social brokers, such as local elders, community enthusiasts, or long-time volunteers, derive their brokerage power from the social capital they possess in the community, drawn from years of relationships, or *guanxi*, cultivated with members with attendant emotional ties, or *ganqing*. Economic brokers are private individuals but with connection to political insiders. They are trusted by both the state and society and who seek profits by bringing the two parties closer in negotiations and facilitate deal-making between them. Compared to the political brokers, social brokers who exploit their social capital to mobilize the masses encounter significantly less resistance. Their standing in the community helps to legitimate the repressive acts, thereby blunting resistance, enforcing compliance, and lowering the cost of state repression.

Drawing on thick case-study evidence, I demonstrate the repression-legitimating social brokers in action in Chapter 6. Their use of persuasion as a control instrument, underpinned by *guanxi* and *ganqing*, helps to reduce citizen resistance to state policy. In practical terms, their social standing legitimates their repressive acts and reduces the likelihood of backlash. This chapter also illuminates how economic brokers help resolve state-society disputes by bringing together disgruntled citizens and government officials to negotiate an agreement. This prevents disputes from becoming protracted and contributes to the maintenance of social stability. Nonviolent repressive measures have gained prominence as the costs of violent coercion have escalated over time particularly in metropolitan cities, yet as the case studies illustrate, even though they are nonviolent in nature, they are not necessarily less coercive than violent repression.

In Chapter 7 I contextualize the experience of China with two comparative cases: South Korea (the most similar case study) and India (the most dissimilar case). I trace how the changes in state-criminal and state-civil society relationships affect the exercise of *everyday state power* in these two countries.

Authoritarian South Korea in the high-growth era most closely resembles that of contemporary China, where the principal-agent relationship meant that the state wielded power over criminal groups, allowing it to engage and direct violent agents' behavior to its advantage. After its transition to a democracy in 1987, overt state-sponsored violence might have disappeared; but the state still turns a blind eye to covert private violence insofar as it attains societal compliance. In the post-1987 era, the increased strength of organized civil society has posed the greatest challenge to state power in South Korea.

In contrast, the Indian state and criminals are entangled in a patron-client web. Criminals or *goondas* become informal sovereigns who provide public services in housing settlements and deliver vote banks to local politicians because of the state's lack of penetrative capacity into slums. The state's interactions with rural society are also mediated by local influential brokers, hampering the state's capacity to penetrate and influence voting or political behavior directly. State power in India is further checked by a raucous organized civil society. The cases of democratic South Korea and India demonstrate that authoritarianism is not a scope condition for my argument of outsourcing repression even though autocracies can generally exercise tighter control over society.

Chapter 8 concludes the book, and in it I draw implications for thinking about state-society relations in China and the country's political future under President Xi Jinping. I also discuss the ramifications for field research in China, given the tightening political environment.

2

The Theory

State Power, Repression, and Implications for Development

Power is of two kinds. One is obtained by the fear of punishment and
the other by acts of love. Power based on love is a thousand times more
effective and permanent than the one derived from fear of punishment.
—Mahatma Gandhi

This book is about how an authoritarian state acquires power *through* society. The
state does not exercise power through naked coercion or brutal oppression that
sparks revolts and hardens aboveground or underground rebellion. It is a form
of state power attained by outsourcing coercion to nonstate agents and mobilizing society through the masses. Critically, exercising this form of state power
minimizes backlash and thus lowers the cost of repression. This book engages
and contributes to bodies of literature on state power and repression, and it draws
implications for the state's role in economic development. It prompts readers to
revise their traditional conception of state repression and reimagine new ground
that state power can credibly and actively occupy at the society's expense.

This research has broader implications for the study of comparative politics.
My argument brings scholars of repression and state power into closer dialogue
with one another, generating significant new insights for both. On one hand, this
study impels scholars of state control to reconsider what constitutes repression
when nonstate agents are engaged to do the state's bidding. On the other hand,
it urges scholars of authoritarian politics and the state in general to grapple with
new boundaries and topography of state power when the Leviathan could penetrate deeply into the society to mobilize the masses within.

2.1 Everyday State Power

Everyday state power is the quotidian exercise of state authority to lead, govern,
and rule society, but how it is manifested in a state with strong capacity deserves

Outsourcing Repression. Lynette H. Ong, Oxford University Press. © Oxford University Press 2022.
DOI: 10.1093/oso/9780197628768.003.0002

attention. Although state capacity is recognized as essential for development, democratization, and political stability, what constitutes state power remains poorly delineated (Albertus and Menaldo 2012; Bellin 2004; Gerschewski 2013). "State power" typically denotes the following: first, in Weberian terms, it is the state's monopoly of the legitimate use of violence in its territory (Weber 1965). For example, "stationary bandits" use violence to defend citizens from "roving bandits" (Olson 1993). Second, in Michael Mann's (1993) conceptualization, despotic power comprises the actions a single leader can take without routine or institutionalized negotiations with other regime members, whereas infrastructural power involves the capacity to implement policies. Third, Joel Migdal (1988) has defined "state capabilities" along the lines of the state's ability to penetrate society, regulate social relationships, extract resources, and appropriate resources in determined ways.[1] These definitions are, however, limited in facilitating an understanding of the extent to which state power is unopposed or accepted by society. One can say a strong state has the capacity to get jobs A, B, and C done, and a weak state does not; but saying so does not indicate whether the incapacity results from a lack of state capability or the presence of societal resistance. Although distinct, both are constitutive elements of state strength.

More broadly, writing about complex organizations, Amitai Etzioni has argued for three types of power: coercive power, utilitarian power, and normative power (Etzioni 1975).[2] Different types of power, Etzioni argues, in turn yield their corresponding compliance: the use of physical force yields coercive compliance; the use of material means, such as salaries, yields remunerative compliance; and the use of normative means, such as prestige symbols, yields normative compliance.

2.1.1 Operationalizing State Strength

Building on earlier works, I propose a different way of thinking about state strength—by theorizing *everyday state power* in terms of the following constitutive elements: participation, acquiescence, and legitimation.

"Participation" connotes a certain degree of voluntarism by societal members to take part in state undertakings. "Acquiescence" denotes acceptance of state orders. Often, though not always, societal acquiescence is accomplished with state sanctions, the use of force, or threats of punishment. Finally, "legitimation" denotes what unequivocally undergirds societal acceptance of state directives without the use of force. It allows for the granting of consent to the state to set the rules of the game and the subsequent societal approbation of state rules as legitimate.

Participation and acquiescence entail the state's ability to regulate social behavior with a degree of voluntarism in the former and some forms of coercion
in the latter; however, it is legitimation—an oft-neglected dimension of state
strength—that facilitates citizen participation and acquiescence in the state's
ambitious endeavors or mundane activities. For instance, the value-based legitimating belief in the government effectiveness leads to citizen's quasivoluntary
compliance in tax payment (Levi 1988). The scope of legitimation extends beyond what is purely lawful to what is perceived as rightful in the eyes of citizens (Gilley 2006). Légitimation allows for state control over society without the
use of overt violence or coercion. In its absence, social control may still be attainable but coercion will be required to minimize dissent.[3] Put differently, by
altering the society's frame of what is or is not repressive and what constitutes
unfair or unequal treatment, legitimation can powerfully forestall grievances,
demands, and the ensuing conflicts. The most classic means of gaining legitimacy include invoking ideologies, like Marxism-Leninism; cults of personality,
for example, that of the Great Leader Kim Il-Sung of North Korea (Lim 2015;
Suh 1995); building trust in government and procedural justice (Levi, Sacks, and
Tyler 2009); and having nominally democratic institutions, like elections and
legislatures, which claim to represent the interests of the people (Gandhi 2008;
Gandhi and Lust-Okar 2009; Schedler 2002). I argue that these three constitutive—and complementary—elements of power make for a more comprehensive
understanding of state prowess.

2.1.2 Everyday State Power and the Dictator's Toolkit

As a corollary, the dictator's toolkit comprising the traditional tools of carrots and
sticks needs replenishing. I argue that to effectively exercise *everyday state power*,
a dictator needs to acquire persuasion as a tool, in addition to carrots and sticks.

The stick, or repression, is central to how most autocrats control society
(Arendt 1958), but repression is costly because it breeds resentment and could
invite backlash (Baldwin 2013; Davenport 2007a; Davenport and Inman 2012;
Lichbach 1987; Mares and Young 2019; Rasler 1996). Taking the shape of state
employment and state provision of social welfare, carrots that serve to co-opt citizens are vital to the way Communist states garner social support. They are also
a crucial vote-buying strategy in hybrid regimes. Persuasion has received insufficient attention as a dictator's tool in controlling society.[4] In my conceptualization, persuasion must be conducted by state-society intermediaries or brokers,
who are trusted by both the state and society. The value of brokered persuasion
lies in its capacity to solicit compliance without appearing to be a social control
strategy. Social buy-in, made possible by the legitimation of brokers trusted by

both the state and society, is what distinguishes persuasion from the dictator's other tools. As I will demonstrate, persuasion resembles propaganda, which communicates with the intention of influencing mind and shaping behavior; yet it also differs from propaganda in that it requires legitimation to achieve the intended outcome.

2.2 When Everyday State Power Can and Cannot Be Exercised

2.2.1 The Arguments in Brief

Everyday state power cannot be exercised in every political context. All rulers want to control their people and yearn for their support at the same time. But why is it that only a select few have managed to achieve both? Assuming that a state holds permanent *everyday state power* throughout the country's history would be erroneous. Political control and support, which are often trade-offs, cannot be taken for granted as a political outcome, even in the same polity. This section lays out the scope condition of the argument.

For a state to exercise *everyday state power*, it must have the capacity to marshal a segment of society to serve as agents to repress or mobilize the rest of society for state pursuits. This involves a two-part action. First, the marshalling of some societal members to become state proxies, which is the essence of participation. Societal participation could be bought, literally, by paying some non-state agents to do the state's bidding. Participation can also occur when societal members believe they are doing the right thing by becoming state proxies. Thus, participation gives rise to the complicity of proxies in the state's actions.

Second, these recruited state proxies in turn help to obtain compliance from the broader society or mobilize the masses. This is the essence of acquiescence, which has a higher threshold than participation,[5] yet the participation of a smaller group of societal members as state proxies makes possible the acquiescence of the wider society. Why is participation of a small group a necessary prelude to the acquiescence of the broader society? The answer is related to the costs of extracting compliance directly from society; that is, the state directly repressing the people.

Typically, the mobilization of society conjures up an image of modern European states mobilizing the people to form a standing army and pay taxes for state-building purposes (Migdal 2001; Levi 1988). In the present context, however, mobilizing the masses (MTM) is used to secure acquiescence to everyday state policies. As in state building, however, the state must render the society legible (Scott 1998) and extend penetrative roots into it, and with that emerges the potential of MTM. Legibility and penetration, which are important dimensions of a state's infrastructural power (Mann 1993), are the preconditions for MTM.[6]

To mobilize society, the state competes with a hodgepodge of social organizations, some of which are organized civil society groups and others are unorganized or informal social groups, such as clans, tribes, gangs, and mafias. Why should street gangsters and underground "black societies," who set up their own internal codes of conduct, obey the rules set by the state? Why should lineage and religious organizations, who adore and worship their own leaders, be loyal to the head of state? Because of the tensions inherent in these situations, the state must be strong enough to render subservient all civil society organizations and social groups so that they will observe and comply with the rules set by the state. The citizens of countries like India, Indonesia, and Kenya, which are highly fractionalized along various identity cleavages, are more challenging to mobilize than those in more homogeneous societies. Countries like Sierra Leone and Afghanistan with numerous competing local strongmen, sometimes a consequence of their colonial legacies, are also more challenging to coalesce and mobilize (Migdal 1988).

The other means of mobilizing society is hiring agents directly and compensating them monetarily. In wartime, states hire private security companies, militias, and paramilitaries, compensating them or paying them in kind to borrow the coercive force they lack or to use the violence that they cannot overtly deploy. To put the state firmly in control, outsourcing coercion must adhere to the condition of principal-agent: the state must remain resolutely the principal, and the people it hires are the agent. In addition, the state outsourcing of coercion implies ceding the monopoly of territorial violence to some degree. In the selection of repressive agents, states are better off working with those who can follow their orders closely. In Chapters 7 and 8 I explore the manner and the extent to which outsourcing repression applies to areas beyond urbanization projects in China and to other country contexts, contingent upon meeting the scope condition.

2.2.2 Scope Condition

Figure 2.1 is a schematic representation of outsourcing repression through the exercise of *everyday state power*; it lays out the scope condition and dimensions of power involved. The two-step process of outsourcing repression involves marshalling a small group of society as proxies and then motivating them to conduct repression or mobilization on the state's behalf. The scope condition is the complicity of proxies. Participation is required of the proxies with the intent of acquiring the acquiescence of the larger society. Notably, complicity is required of the proxies—but not of the society. The latter is a much higher bar that necessitates the assumption of a society subservient to the state to begin with.

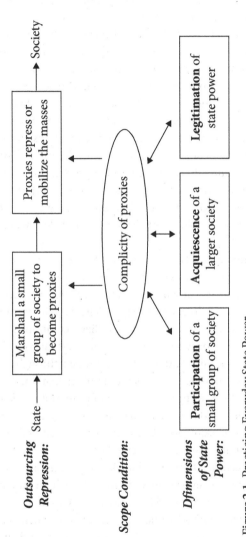

Figure 2.1 Practicing Everyday State Power

The third dimension of state power is legitimation, which enables the state to acquire the acquiescence of the populace without resorting to the use of force. Legitimation of state power is attained only when the nonviolent instrument of persuasion is applied through brokers who can legitimate repressive acts.

Proxy complicity is based on either witting or unwitting participation. Complicity under witting participation is a function of state strength over proxies, or the capacity to control proxies' behavior, which is the essence of the principal-agent relationship. When states engage coercive forces, such as the military and the police, to surveil and repress domestic population, or hire private security companies to fight in wars on foreign soils, these agents wittingly participate in states' actions domestically and abroad, respectively.

Unwitting participation occurs when proxies hold the normative belief that they are contributing to the public good by doing the state's bidding. Normative beliefs may arise out of ideological convictions, cultish myths of political figures, trust in government, and information control or propagation. Unwitting participation or the sense of obligation and willingness to obey and participate is attributable to "value-based legitimacy" in Margaret Levi's terms (2009). It explains why people willingly vote, volunteer to be drafted, and participate in community activities pro bono.

Historically, Chinese society has not always met the scope condition; it did so only with the rise to power of the CCP in 1949. After its rise, the CCP installed and assembled in rural and urban areas many grassroots brokers, on whom the state relied to carry out ordinary everyday policies as well as ambitious political campaigns. They include political brokers (village committees, rural production teams, urban neighborhood committees, block captains) and social brokers (volunteers and community enthusiasts) positioned throughout the country. With extensive party building and ideological indoctrination, the CCP was able to solicit witting and unwitting participation of grassroots brokers by asserting firm control over them and then marshal them to mobilize society.

The same cannot be said about China prior to the rise of the CCP, namely during either the Kuomintang (KMT) Republican period or the Qing dynasty. By the end of the 18th century, the gradual weakening of the Qing state had bred secret societies, bandits, and eventually warlords, all of whom grew more powerful vis-à-vis the state (Kuhn 1980, 37–64; Rowe 2009). With declining fiscal and bureaucratic powers, local authorities had to engage bandits to fight powerful landowners and to collect taxes (Averill 2006, 53–75; D. Wang 2018, 49–127; P. Wang 2017, 21–34). The more local state elites relied on criminal groups for everyday state functions, the more state power was chiseled away by these groups. In addition, the lack of control over nonviolent brokers also defined the Qing era. In the 19th century, when the weak Qing state faced challenges in collecting taxes, it relied on state-appointed brokers to do so. Many of the state-appointees were predatory, collecting taxes only to enrich themselves, prompting some rural peasants to organize their own brokers to protect them from the state appointees (Duara 1988, 42–57).

The KMT government co-opted regional warlords on one hand, and used secret societies to destroy its political nemesis, the CCP, on the other (Marten 2006, 50–52). Because the KMT had only weak control over secret societies, it had to forge clientelist ties and share power with them (P. Wang 2017, 34–50). In particular, the KMT gave the Green Gang, a secret society in Shanghai, political protection in legal businesses as a quid pro quo for violently suppressing CCP organizations (Martin 1995). The relationship between the KMT state and secret societies was one of patron-client rather than principal-agent (Averill 2006, 53–75; D. Wang 2018, 49–127; P. Wang 2017, 21–54). In other words, the proxies engaged by the Qing and KMT governments were not perfectly complicit because the states had incomplete control over them.

In contrast, the CCP adopted from its predecessors a different approach in dealing with secret societies. During the Revolutionary period of the 1940s, the Party was fundamentally more interested in consolidating its power instead of forging clientelist ties for the sake of expediency. Thus, the Maoist state powerfully asserted itself over secret societies and bandits, resulting in a strategy of either coopting secret society members into its fold (Perry 1980, 1–4), replacing them with Party organizations, or suppressing them altogether (Lieberthal 1973).

Party building under the CCP came at the expense of societal capacity to provide for itself and to organize collective actions against the state. Through control over political and social brokers, the state can penetrate deeply into society and marshal these proxies to mobilize the masses. The pre-Mao historical trajectory has implications for the political cultural dimension of the scope condition. It suggests that unwitting participation by proxies is not exclusive to the Confucian political culture that promotes obedience to the state,[7] and the cultural factor is not nearly as critical as state strength (evident only in the CCP era) in rendering proxies subservient. In China under the Communist rule, unwitting participation of proxies is partly a result of the socialist legacy that fosters communal trust and prioritizes collective interests above those of one's own.[8]

In the next two sections I discuss the two key mechanisms of outsourcing repression—everyday repression and MTM—carried out by TFH and brokers, respectively, to bring about *everyday state power*.[9]

2.3 Everyday Repression and Thugs-for-Hire

Authoritarian regimes rely on a range of coercive agents to carry out repression and preserve their rule. The military is indispensable for a regime's survival, but it requires training, discipline, and costly resources to maintain. Overreliance on the military can threaten the regime with defections and coups d'état (Svolik

2012). Autocrats also establish internal security agencies, such as the paramilitary, militias, secret police, and police, to deal with internal dissent (Geddes, Wright, and Frantz 2018; Greitens 2016). Militias receive less training than the army or paramilitaries and are thus less costly to set up (Decalo 1998), but they are subject to agency problems.[10]

If these coercive agents were ranked for their professionalism and capacity for violence, the military occupies the top position, followed by the paramilitary forces, the militias or vigilantes, and the police. TFH who carry out everyday repression rank below the militias and the police. Distinguished from the other coercive violent agents in these dimensions,[11] TFH are private individuals or nonstate agents who wear no uniform and carry no badge. They deploy low-level or merely the threat of violence—bare hands or fists and at times iron rods, knives, and other low-intensity weapons—in carrying out coercive acts. Even when equipped with light weapons, militias are better armed than TFH (Alvarez 2006; Mazzei 2009), who lack the organizational structure that characterizes formal coercive agents. TFH are loose gangs of individuals who sell muscle power for profit. On most occasions, their acts are intended to be concealed from public view; these include acts carried out late at night or in dark alleys as opposed to overt repressive acts like police arrests.[12]

In the context of the repression-dissent nexus, if foot-dragging by citizens, for example, delays in complying with eviction orders, is viewed as routine dissent or resistance, the term "everyday repression" refers to state actions taken in response to those defiant acts. They constitute defiance per James Scott's (1985) notion of everyday forms of resistance, which are small-scale, piecemeal, and mundane acts. Analogously, everyday repression consists of routinized repressive acts that require no strong organizational capacity, disciplined agents, or sophisticated weapons. Typically targeting marginalized citizens on the fringes of society, everyday repression is deployed to compel obedience in routine policy implementation, to handle political dissidents, and to suppress small-scale protests, diverging from repression carried out by internal security or secret police designed for the purpose of either coup-proofing or preventing mass uprisings (Greitens 2016).

TFH are ruffians, hooligans, hoodlums, street gangsters, and legalized professionals who render violence as a for-profit service or in exchange for in-kind benefits. They usually comprise the unemployed, those lacking regular salaried jobs, or people who "make trouble" for a living. They are distinct from mafias, which are crime groups defined by complex organizations and specializing in the provision of private protection and seeking to monopolize territorial protection (Varese 2010). Recruited from the street, TFH lack specific codes of conduct, rules, and admission rituals that bind mafia members. Their nature also differentiates them from the Sicilian mafiosi, who were previously disbanded soldiers; the Japanese yakuza, who were formerly samurai; or the Russian "violent entrepreneurs," who were largely ex-KGB officers (Gambetta 1993; Hill 2003; Volkov 2002a).

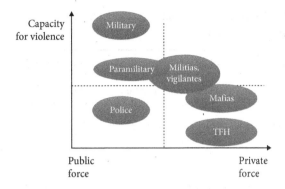

Figure 2.2 Capacity for Violence and Public vs. Private Force

Figure 2.2 situates various violent agents along two dimensions: their capacity for violence and the public vs. private nature of their acts. Values on both axes are nondichotomously scattered along a continuum. On one hand, TFH, along with mafiosi, vigilantes, and members of militias (to some degree) are perpetrators of private—and by implication—illegitimate violence. The state can potentially prosecute them for their illegitimate and illegal use of force. On the other hand, when the military, the police, and the paramilitary (to some extent) use a justifiable degree of force to maintain domestic order or protect national borders, they are public agents who carry out legitimate violence.

2.3.1 Benefits of Everyday Repression via TFH

2.3.1.1 TFH as Perpetrators of Illegal or Illegitimate Acts

Since the introduction of fiscal decentralization in China in the 1980s, local authorities have suffered from unfunded mandates, resulting in a proliferation of local "money pots."[13] The sources of these extrabudgetary revenues range from illegal rural fees and exactions before their abolition in 2003, to fines for the one-child policy violations before it was abolished in 2015, to rapacious revenues from land-expropriation and demolition projects since the late 2000s.[14] Land taking, demolitions, illegal rural exactions, and population control fines—in each of these local practices, local authorities face determined resistance because of the lack of the legitimacy or legality of the policy. Thus, because of expediency, local governments have consistently relied on TFH to carry out these challenging everyday policies.[15]

Also a matter of expedience is engaging TFH in illegitimate or illegal local government pursuits in general, such as threatening protestors and petitioners into withdrawing their complaints (Human Rights Watch 2009; Lianjiang Li and O'Brien 2008), silencing human rights activists, journalists, and other "troublemakers" (Biddulph 2015; Radio Free Asia 2013).

Table 2.1 State and Nonstate Agents vs. Observability of Repressive Actions

Actions	State Agents	Nonstate Agents
Observable	Police arrest, military crackdown on civilians	TFH beat civilians in broad daylight
Unobservable	Intelligence agent phone tapping	TFH kidnap victims in dark alleys

2.3.1.2 Nonstate Identity Offers Pretense of Plausible Deniability

The concept of TFH contributes to existing repression literature by adding a new dimension to agent identity and the observability of repressive actions. As nonstate agents, TFH augment the range of state coercive agents, namely the military and the police. Figure 2.2 indicates that paramilitaries and militias fall between state and nonstate agents, but they conventionally have greater associations with the state than street gangsters do. Repressive acts by state agents are either observable, such as police arrests, or unobservable (concealed), such as phone tapping and intelligence gathering (Earl 2003). By way of contrast, repressive acts carried out by TFH are more likely to be unobservable, such as kidnappings in dark alleys, than observable, such as beating people in broad daylight.[16] These distinctions are made clear in Table 2.1. Although scholars have given much attention to repression by state agents in the left-hand quadrants, this book shines the spotlight on the understudied right-hand quadrants that nonstate agents occupy.

The consequences of hiring nonstate agents are substantive. Nonstate agents who assume no official identity can evade responsibility for their actions more easily than state agents can. Their elusive nature offers them plausible deniability unafforded to the police or other uniform-wearing repressive agents. In the literature of civil war and ethnic cleansing, similar arguments have been advanced to provide the rationale for some states' preference for privatized violence—instead of their own coercive agents—in fighting political enemies.[17]

2.3.2 Costs of Outsourcing Violence to TFH

2.3.2.1 Agency Problems and Accountability

Despite its expediency, outsourcing repression to nonstate violent agents is subject to the agency problem of undisciplined violence over and above what is necessary to get the job done. When excessive violence results in deaths, sparking public outcry or large-scale protests, TFH become a liability—rather than an asset—to the hiring authority. Punishment of government officials for political accountability is rare in China, but mass protests and intense public pressure, including from the media, have arisen in some exceptional cases, leading to the firing of local government officials.[18] Usually, the punishment of officials takes place not because of one or two violent incidents but a series of large-scale protests and severe casualties.

2.3.2.2 Risks Usurpation of State Authority

The decline in local state capacity in China since the mid-1990s has resulted in a rise in collusive local government-criminal relationships (Pei 2006);[19] however, the proliferation of criminal groups in China has not been accompanied by an emergence of organized mafia groups that threaten central state power. The TFH with whom local authorities engage in the practice of everyday repression are street gangsters who lack the organizational sophistication, codes of conduct, and viciousness that typically characterize mafias. By outsourcing violence to third parties, however, the Chinese state has voluntarily ceded its monopoly on violence to some degree, which risks feeding the "dark forces" of society that could potentially usurp its power. In Chapter 8 I examine how Xi Jinping's *saohei* campaign had aimed to wipe out these criminal groups that posed threats to grassroots authorities.

2.4 Mobilizing the Masses and Brokers

How is MTM a political control strategy? When organized into a movement, MTM becomes a state-organized (social) movement like the Red Guard Movement, made up of various youth factions organized by Mao and the Party elites, or Nashi, the youth movement organized by the Russian authorities to thwart the Orange Revolution in Ukraine (Atwal and Bacon 2012; Wales 2016). Although social movements are organized from the bottom up to express people's collective grievances, MTM is a top-down strategy that similarly mobilizes the people—but to the end that the state's will is imposed on the masses. In state-organized movements, states play a premeditated and proactive role in shaping the agenda and form of movement actions (Ekiert, Perry, and Yan 2020); however, MTM does not necessarily have to be organized into a movement. It could be a strategy of MTM on an individual basis or simply mobilizing individuals for state pursuits. This is how the concept is applied in the present context.

2.4.1 The Octopus and Its Tentacles: State, Brokers, and Society

MTM presupposes a strong state with penetrative capacity that allows it to reach deeply into the society's roots. Because of the cost of mobilizing every single individual, a state needs brokers to connect it with the masses. This conjures up an image of an octopus with its many tentacles ensnaring prey and fending off attackers. If the state is conceived as an octopus, the brokers are the tentacles with which the state penetrates society and influences citizen behavior.

In general, brokers fulfill the following functions when connecting the disparate actors of state and society: information gathering, reducing information asymmetry, surveillance, provision of public goods, mobilization, and creating new contention (Baldwin 2013; Koter 2013; Mares and Young 2019; McAdam, Tarrow, and Tilly 2001). The CCP has relied on three types of grassroots brokers—political, social, and economic—to reach rural and urban populations since its establishment. The power of political brokers, such as urban communities (社区), neighborhood committees (居委会), block captains, and rural village committee and production team leaders, derives from the state. Neither village nor community is a formal level of government but part of the state's grassroots organization. Not state agents, they are brokers with the agency to act on behalf of the state, society, or their own interests (J. Wang 2012). An overwhelming majority of, but not all, political brokers are grassroots party cadres or members of the rank and file. Although party rank and file may be effective in implementing state policies at the grassroots level (Koss 2018), they are not as capable in improving citizens' reception and abating resistance to the state's coercive acts as social brokers are, which I will turn to next.

Social brokers draw on their social capital to conduct brokerage. The existing literature has focused much attention on the role of leaders of informal civil society organizations, such as rural lineage and temple associations, in bridging the gap between the state and society or controlling society (Tsai 2007; Mattingly 2019). In contrast, I place emphasis on the individuals who do not lead any registered or unregistered civil society organizations yet possess considerable social capital because of their longstanding voluntary service to the community. Social capital in this context more closely approximates Bourdieu's theory of individual social capital rather than Putnam's concept of collective social capital (Bourdieu 1986; Portes 2000; Putnam, Leonardi, and Nanetti 1993). The exclusive nature of the former implies that only members with access to social networks can enjoy the benefits—to the exclusion of nonmembers. Command of social capital makes them part of the grassroots elite social structure, providing them with access to social networks despite their nonleadership positions.

Local social-elite status imparts social brokers with legitimacy in the community, and the source of legitimacy does not derive from the state. They construct their brokerage power by using their social capital to mobilize the masses and facilitate negotiations to resolve conflicts. Social relationships, or *guanxi* (关系), become an important means by which they mobilize the masses. Social brokers are the volunteers and community enthusiasts who collect intelligence, keep surveillance, mobilize the masses, and conduct thought work (思想工作) on the citizenry.[20] The most iconic among them are the legendary red armband-wearing Chaoyang Masses (朝阳群众), who volunteer to patrol their neighborhoods and zealously sniff out intruders.

Economic brokers, or *huangniu* (黄牛), are private individuals with connection to political insiders. Having gained the trust of the state and society, they profit from bringing the two disparate parties to agreement. The need for economic brokerage arises from information gaps or trust deficits between the parties. In corrupt transactions, citizens often do not know whom to bribe and how much they should pay. In cases of housing demolition, economic brokers who can bring the state and aggrieved citizens to agree on relocation deals help to prevent the aggrieved from taking their grievances to the street and thus contribute to maintaining social stability.

Delegating authority to brokers, however, is subject to risks. With intense party institution building and ideological indoctrination, the CCP is better able to mobilize and exert firm control over political and social brokers and to materially incentivize economic brokers compared to its predecessors. Nevertheless, brokers can still prioritize their own interests, for example, engaging in corruption to enrich themselves at the state's expense. Chapters 5 and 6 will demonstrate that as ideology loses its appeal with market reforms, the state is challenged to mobilize social brokers and increasingly relies on material incentives to motivate them.

2.4.2 The Masses as Internal Security Agents

A central feature of the Chinese internal security system is its reliance on the masses for collecting information and intelligence, monitoring, patrolling, and executing collective punishment. Despite the myriad internal security apparatuses that deal with political opposition at the elite and grassroots levels,[21] China has never developed a powerful secret police equivalent to the KGB in the former Soviet Union, the Stasi in East Germany, or the former South Korean Central Intelligence Agency (X. Guo 2012). Instead, Mao relied on the "mass line" (群众路线), the political strategy intended to arouse the enthusiasm of the masses—as well as his personality cult—to maintain his dominance. In contrast to the secret police-inflicted mass terror in place in many Communist states, mass mobilization was the key strategy behind public denunciation and individual self-criticism during Mao's political campaigns that similarly afflicted the masses (Brehm and Niou 1997). When family members were asked to spy on one another and neighbors were expected to monitor one another's behaviors, "mass line" politics resulted in psychological wreckage fed by mutual distrust and oftentimes communal killings (Perry 1985; Y. Su 2011). A historical study has uncovered evidence of Mao's recruitment of covert agents from the masses to spy on those

with bad "class backgrounds," peasants who failed to show sufficient political enthusiasm, and members of ethnic minority groups (Schoenhals 2012).

In comparison, the internal security agents in the former Soviet Union were
members of the police or militia, which drew relatively few resources from the
masses. Reporting to the Ministry of Internal Affairs (MVD), the militia were
the everyday coercive agents in Soviet society, complementing the powers of the
KGB and the military (Taylor 2011, 45–46). The involvement of mass organizations in the militia's work in the Soviet Union was nowhere near the level seen
in China (Shelley 1996, 3–17).[22] Local mass organizations in China, namely
political brokers like neighborhood committees or village committees, administer and enforce the household registration system, which resembles the Soviet
citizen registration system, while registration records are kept by local police
stations (Read 2012). In both the pre- and post-Mao eras, the Chinese police
persistently lean on neighborhood committees, work units, and other mass organizations to keep tabs on local populations (Scoggins 2018). The recruitment
of volunteers is another point of contrast as the Soviet militia persistently faced
challenges in this area (Russia Update 2015; Shelley 1996, 86).[23]

To appreciate the tenacious presence of MTM in Chinese society today, simply
consider the nationwide army of volunteers and neighborhood committees
mobilized in the fight against the COVID-19 pandemic. Interestingly,
responding to Xi Jinping's call for a "people's war" against the coronavirus, local
communities did not necessarily view the human surveillance and privacy intrusion imposed as coercive (Kuo 2020).

2.5 Theoretical Contribution

Figure 2.3 illustrates the two mechanisms of outsourcing repression: everyday
repression and MTM as well as their corresponding agents and strategies, what
they represent as autocrats' tools, and the respective effects of repression.

2.5.1 Reimagine the Contours of State Power

What does outsourced repression imply for state power? How does it change
the way state power is traditionally conceived? Revisiting the analogy of the octopus and its tentacles now that the physical shape and reach of these tentacles is
known prompts one more question: How does the analogy reveal the nature of
the creature (state) and its relation to its prey (society)?

Outsourcing Repression reenvisions state power by challenging the existing
conceptions of these notions: first, state-society relations, or boundaries between
state and nonstate actors; second, state capacity, or its ability to reach, penetrate

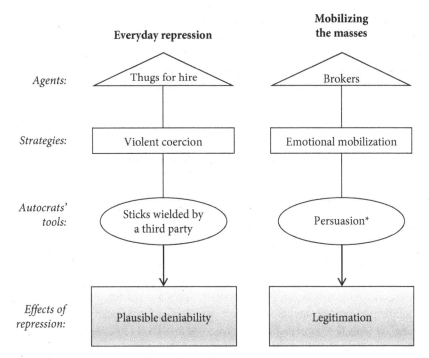

Figure 2.3 Mechanisms of Outsourcing Repression
* Used in tandem with carrots and psychological coercion.

society, and implement policies (vom Hau 2015; Soifer 2008; Soifer and vom Hau 2008); and third, what amounts to state repressive acts from the citizen's perspective. Revisions of these concepts in turn heighten consent to state power.

In Joel Migdal's state-in-society approach, states that comprise a mélange of social organizations must compete with these organizations seeking to dominate (Migdal 1988, 2001). Thus, strong states emerge only when they can successfully impose control on societies. In Peter Evans' notion of embedded autonomy, the state is autonomous insofar as it is not captured by powerful societal groups.[24] Placed in these contexts, the Chinese state is strong not only because it is autonomous, but more importantly, it is able to overstep the state–society boundary to hire nonstate actors and marshal brokers to mobilize the society for state pursuits. In other words, the state pushes against society, blurs the boundaries between them, and extends its tentacles into society to mobilize the masses within.

State capacity can be viewed through the lens of infrastructural power, its territorial reach, and its effects on society.[25] Some states have stronger reach because of varying "authority over distance,"[26] and uneven penetration throughout the country.[27] Vivienne Shue (1988) argues that the Chinese imperial state's reach was limited by the rural honeycomb structure made up of the gentry. I argue that the CCP-state has strong capacity because it engages and mobilizes nonstate actors, who are part of society. Thus, with enhanced reach, it can penetrate the grassroots and implement unpopular everyday policies, imposing its will on society. More importantly, social brokers whom the state engages serve to legitimate state repressive acts by altering the citizens' conception of state repressive acts, thereby improving their receptions and blunting resistance accordingly.

Consent to state power thus becomes a necessary product of redrawn boundaries between the state and society. When a strong state encroaches upon society and mobilizes the masses within it, it is capable of extracting compliance from the citizenry. Consent comes in varying shades, ranging from consent to registration and legibility, everyday policy compliance, and obedience extracted by state repression to violent oppression. The consent to state power explored in this book covers the medium shades of everyday policy compliance and acquiescence to state repression. By redrawing the boundaries between state and society and by augmenting state capacity to secure societal consent, I invite readers to stretch their imagination on how state power has been reconfigured as a result.

Figure 2.4 illustrates graphically how state power is bolstered by engaging and mobilizing nonstate agents to extract compliance from society. The left-hand panel denotes the state hiring thugs who use low-level violence against society. The right-hand panel indicates the state's engagement of brokers with the social networks to mobilize members within them. Graphically, the state pushes the state–society boundaries against the society, and recruits TFH and brokers within it as proxies to do its bidding. Thus, TFH and brokers become complicit in the state's repression of society, albeit using different means; furthermore, the nonstate identities of TFH and brokers enable them to enforce obedience while minimizing the risks of strong backlash.

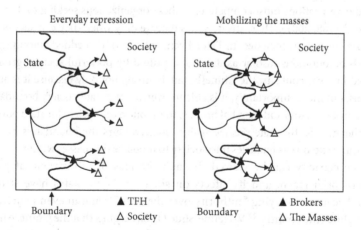

Figure 2.4 How Outsourcing Repression Enhances State Power

Once the contours between state and society are redrawn, state power is significantly strengthened. Beyond urbanization projects, the state engages TFH in other areas where its involvement similarly lacks legitimacy or legality, such as silencing petitioners, protestors, dissidents, and journalists as well as collecting illegal fees and exorbitant fines from marginalized members of society. The ability of the state to hire muscle power that provides it with plausible deniability as and when it requires dirty jobs to be done—as opposed to the alternatives of sending its own legitimate coercive agents to do the job, not carrying out the repressive actions, or not extracting compliance from the marginalized—speaks to the state's augmented power vis-à-vis society.

By the same token, the Chinese state's capacity to draw on grassroots brokers, many of whom command social legitimacy, during normal and emergency times alike is another testament of its augmented state power. In times of crisis, such as during the battle against SARS and the COVID-19 pandemic, the state has relied on its nationwide army of neighborhood committees and volunteers in the cities and village committees and "activists" in the rural areas to implement strict measures and control people's movement. During normal times, the enthusiasm of urban community volunteers, such as the Chaoyang Masses and Xicheng Aunties, in patrolling alleyways to keep crime rates low, is an integral part of the Party's mass policing. Social brokers not only contribute manpower to state endeavors, but they are also legitimizing vehicles of state repression. Taken together, these means of outsourcing repression allow for the practice of *everyday state power* to mobilize and repress society in a wide range of areas—well beyond urbanization—that minimizes the costs typically associated with state repression.

2.5.2 Novel Contribution to the Repertoire of State Repression and Authoritarian Control Strategy

In what is commonly referred to as the law of coercive responsiveness, or threat-response theory, states retaliate with repressive actions when they face challenges to their power (Davenport 2007a; Earl, Soule, and McCarthy 2003). State repression is "actual or threatened use of physical sanctions (taken by the state) against an individual or organization . . . for the purpose of imposing a cost on the target as well as deterring specific activities" (Davenport and Inman 2012, 620). This begs the question as to why states do not repress or mete out punishments whenever they face challenges. The reason is simply that repression incurs costs. Regimes that rely heavily on the military to maintain their grip on power risk being overthrown by the same security forces that may grow to be too powerful (Svolik 2012; Greitens 2016). Beyond the risk posed by the military, repression is also subject to the costs of citizen backlash and demand for government accountability. The effort to understand the repression-dissent nexus has spawned a rich body of literature but with little consensus on how government coercion affects dissent.[28]

In defining authoritarian control, I adopt a broad scope similar to Mai Hassan's (2020) scholarship on bureaucratic management as a means of social control by the Kenyan state. The scope of social control in this and Hassan's work is broader than the traditional conception of state repression in that it includes distribution (or withdrawal) of local public goods, administration of the population, and maintaining social compliance.

Outsourcing Repression augments the existing repertoire of repressive agents by studying the state's delegation of coercion to nonstate agents—a research area that has received limited attention to date. Repressive acts carried out by the nonstate agents—TFH and brokers—entail different dynamics: the former deploy violence whereas the latter do not, but they both help to lower the costs of repression and enhance state power. Thus, outsourcing repression presents an attractive option for autocrats who wish to minimize the costs of controlling society. The rest of this section explains how this book makes a novel contribution to the existing literature on state repression and authoritarian control strategies.

2.5.2.1 Everyday Repression and Sticks Wielded by a Third Party

Everyday repression comprises banal repressive acts that require no strong organizational capacity or disciplined agents. They occur in response to small defiant acts, captured by James Scott's conception of everyday forms of resistance. Its counterfactuals are a) nonenforcement resulting from the lack of state capacity to penetrate or carry out policies; b) nonenforcement because the state cannot justify the cost of deploying formal agents to deal with small defiance, resulting in a case of selective policy implementation; and c) forbearance: the state purposely chooses nonenforcement to elicit support from selected societal groups.[29] Instead, I argue that everyday repression offers a viable alternative to nonenforcement, which arises from the absence of state capacity, cost justification, or political will.

Everyday repression helps to lower the costs of repression in several ways. As an on-demand service, nonstate agents can be employed on a contract basis at the beginning of projects and dismissed when projects are completed. They require no training, organizational setup, or maintenance costs, resulting in a direct reduction of the material cost of engagement.

More importantly, given the elusive identity of nonstate agents, states can maintain an arms-length relationship with them and the violent acts they commit. Thus, states stand a better chance of plausible deniability for violent repression that typically provokes backlash. Deniability of responsibility in turn allows for the evasion of accountability to citizens as well as to higher-level authorities in a multilevel government system.

Furthermore, when unidentified nonstate agents wearing no uniform or badge perpetrate low-grade violence, the result is often the minimization of citizen backlash relative to similar state agent-deployed violence. TFH offer this benefit so long as their violent acts do not result in severe casualties, such as death, and the state can effectively distance itself from the illegitimate violence committed. When TFH are led by government leaders or sent alongside state coercive agents instead of being deployed on their own, the latitude for plausible deniability narrows at the outset, reducing the pretense of the evasion of accountability. Furthermore, when the state is perceived as the explicit sponsor of the illegitimate violence of TFH against citizens, the nonstate agent becomes a liability.

As an autocrat's tool, everyday repression amounts to a stick wielded by a third party. Thus, it offers a range of benefits associated with maintaining an arm's-length relationship with the perpetrator of violence so long as the autocrat can effectively distance himself and the violence does not result in severe casualties.

2.5.2.2 Mobilizing the Masses and Persuasion

This study advances the argument that persuasion is a powerful third pillar sustaining the capacity of regimes to control society in addition to the conventional tools of carrots and sticks. More importantly, unlike the other autocrats' tools, persuasion is undergirded by legitimacy. Persuasion is like propaganda insofar as both are means of communicating to the masses and are aimed at influencing citizen behavior. A persuasive message brings with it the intention of voluntary acceptance by the recipient (Jowett and O'Donnell 2014, 37–45). Propaganda—which is organized persuasion—acts as psychological artillery alongside military weaponry and material enticements to court sympathizers and demoralize political enemies. Although propaganda has received ample attention in the literature, persuasion has not.[30]

Propaganda was essential to the rise of Hitler's Nazi Germany. Communication expert Nicholas O'Shaughnessy (2016) argues that Nazism was about selling a conspiracy theory of Jewish malice and nihilism through myth, symbolism, and rhetoric. Similarly, China scholars have argued that official Chinese propaganda bolsters the regime's power by selling the merits of market reforms and a nationalist discourse (Brady 2009; Zhao 1998). Another line of argument similarly underscores the role of propaganda in enhancing regime power but suggests that doing so is possible even if it is not perceived to have legitimacy. Political scientist Lisa Wedeen (2015) underlines the role of rhetoric and symbols in creating the spectacle effect of projecting authoritarian prowess despite the absence of a committed ideology in Asad's Syrian regime. Propaganda worked even when the ruled did not believe in it and had no emotional connections with the ruler. Others highlight the signaling effect of propaganda in projecting the state's capacity and resolve in maintaining political order (H. Huang 2015).

Like government propaganda, persuasion can similarly draw on symbols and rhetoric to solicit social buy-in, but it does not produce spectacle effect that propaganda does. Thus, unlike propaganda, persuasion hinges on legitimacy, or legitimation by the actor who persuades. Then, what is the basis on which persuasion is communicated? The currency of persuasion, I argue, is emotions lubricated by *guanxi*. Unlike propaganda that is communicated en masse to the public, persuasion is conducted on an individual basis via brokers capable of evoking affective emotions of like-dislike, love-hate, trust-distrust, respect-disrespect among the targeted audience (Jasper 2018). When brokered by those with appropriate social networks, persuasion can achieve the intended effect of engineering compliance. Fundamentally, it undergirds thought work（思想工作）in China. Neta Crawford (2009) has argued that coercion and persuasion are often nondichotomous: some arguments can be coercive, and coercion can be nonviolent. Persuasion can have the intended and actual effect of coerced consent. Even though persuasion exists independently as an authoritarian tool, it is often used in tandem with material inducements, or carrots, and backed by the threats of psychological coercion, or sticks.

Emotional mobilization is a well-recognized instrument of MTM in China. During the Maoist years, evoking Maoism (毛泽东思想) alone was sufficient to mobilize the masses to violently rebel against the imagined enemies of "counterrevolutionaries" (Y. Liu 2010; Perry 2002b). Ideology has lost much, though not all, of its allure among the post-Mao Chinese citizenry;[31] therefore, emotion-lubricated social relations have become the Party's wand to mobilize the masses. Enabled by one's *guanxi* network, emotions allow for persuasion and MTM to take place. Cultivated over a lifetime, *guanxi* serves the dual purposes of sentimentality and instrumentalism, writes the anthropologist Andrew Kipnis. The dual dimensions can reinforce each other. Instrumentalism carries with it reciprocal obligation, and *guanxi* could be repaid in material or nonmaterial terms. The practice of *guanxi* often generates sentimentality or *ganqing* (感情), which can be strategically exploited to manipulate obligations (Kipnis 2002). The repressive strategy of MTM relies on moving people using the emotions and *guanxi* that bind members of a network together. Given the binding social-network ties, this form of authoritarian control is generally accepted by network members and by extension, society at large. This gives rise to the new territory that *everyday state power* credibly occupies and one that requires a revision of the notion of state power.

In *Ambiguities of Domination*, Wedeen (2015) argues that in the absence of legitimacy, propaganda can still achieve the goals of projecting state power. My book, however, takes the opposite position: persuasion sustains authoritarian power in China precisely because it is underlined by legitimacy. Legitimation serves to enhance order, stability, and the effectiveness of government rule (Beetham 1991). With very few exceptions, no regime can survive on repression alone, thus accentuating the importance of legitimacy in enhancing regime rule. MTM has proven to be an enduringly effective state repressive strategy in China because grassroots brokers with *guanxi* networks, who serve as legitimizing vehicles, are the implementors.

By drawing on affect to move and using relations or acceptable norms within community cultures to shame and blame, the likelihood of dissent is significantly lowered. Accordingly, persuasion or MTM minimizes the cost of backlash usually associated with repression. Since Hu Jintao's era and through to Xi Jinping's years, the state has placed increased emphasis on MTM as a political strategy, harking back to the stratagem prevalent during Mao's years.

In the existing literature insufficient attention has been paid to how social networks and the attendant emotions are explicitly exploited by the state to legitimize its rule and to empower the regime's stranglehold on society. This book is not the first study in which MTM is examined; however, I make a bold and novel attempt to bring into dialogue mass mobilization in Chinese politics and the social science literatures on state repression and social movements.[32] To be sure, I do not study state-mobilized movements; instead, I examine state-mobilized individual persuasive efforts. In other words, the state mobilizes the masses to persuade the masses without organizing them into a collective movement. The difference between the collective and individual dimensions of MTM is nontrivial.

The two types of nonstate agents diverge on the use of violence in their repressive strategies, so one may ask whether TFH merely constitute another form of broker. In Chapters 5 and 6 I will provide further detail on the categories of brokers into which the TFH do not squarely fit. The rationale for the engagement of for-profit TFH by the state vastly differs from the reason it draws on brokerage power. Hence, combining TFH and brokers into a single analytical category serves to cloud rather than provide greater clarity.

2.5.3 Social Control in China

In this study I build on existing literature on repression in China. Elizabeth Perry (2002b) studies the Party's use of emotions to move the masses during the revolution, emphasizing the Maoist roots of this strategy. Ching Kwan Lee and Yonghong Zhang argue that China's brand of bargained authoritarianism is premised upon the state's buying stability with funds set aside to minimize social dissent.[33] In relational repression, Deng and O'Brien (2013) discuss the state's use of workplace ties to demobilize protestors. Scholars who study the police force recognize the prioritization of protest control above other objectives, such as crime fighting (Scoggins and O'Brien 2016; K. Zhou and Yan 2014). Others look at the state's cooptation and infiltration of informal organizations in civil society to exert control over it (Mattingly 2019) and the state's use of social welfare to preempt protest (Pan 2020). Given the wide array of repressive strategies, one may ask how the state chooses one over the other and under what conditions. These questions remain unanswered in the existing literature.

In other words, what are the scope conditions for the autocrat's tools—carrots, sticks, and persuasion—in China? Under what conditions is the use of one tool preferred over the other? Doling out carrots (buying stability) is conditioned on the availability of material resources. Sticks are subject to citizen backlash, imposing significant costs on the regime. However, if sticks are wielded by third parties—as in outsourced violence—plausible deniability and the evasion of accountability are possible, thereby reducing the cost of repression.

With persuasion an existing structure of infrastructural capacity is presupposed, but it is the least costly in material terms among the autocrat's tools. It is thus more likely to be deployed when a) material resources are scarce, b) material resources have lost their appeal among the targeted citizens, c) the costs of repression or violence have become too high to bear, or d) the state desires to legitimate its repressive acts. The first and last conditions fit the times of Maoist politics, when the PRC in its early days lacked the material capacity it now has in the postreform era to dole out carrots or buy stability. But more importantly, mobilizing the masses was prevalently deployed in the Maoist era because of the ruler's desire to appear legitimate in the face of the regime's massive suppression of the population.[34]

The second, third, and fourth conditions fit some time periods and regions in contemporary Chinese society. Carrots have lost their appeal among some in the middle and especially upper-middle classes; not everyone with a grievance can be placated with financial compensation in China today. In the age of commercialized media and the proliferation of social media platforms, the costs of using sticks or violence are high for the state. Local governments are scrutinized by the public if they use blatant and unjustified violence against citizens. Viral videos on Chinese social media of beatings of farmers or residents are a manifestation of the cost of using overt violence. Intense public pressure can in turn result in reprimands of local officials by higher-level authorities. Under these circumstances, persuasion becomes an increasingly attractive strategy. Moreover, its increased prevalence since Xi Jinping's rule, as will be discussed in Chapter 6, is similarly driven by a desire to maintain the regime's legitimacy amid the widespread political crackdown in the society. Even though MTM has been similarly deployed as a social control strategy in the pre- and post-Mao periods, it was used for similar but also different reasons. In Mao's times, the Party-state could not afford to give financial payoffs, but three decades into the postreform era, payoffs no longer work as effectively. The cost of using violence has, furthermore, become too exorbitantly high in some regions, especially in the inner core of metropolitan cities. In addition, Xi's regime is similarly preoccupied, as Mao's was, with legitimacy-preserving state repression—and this is an attractive benefit of persuasion. To be clear, despite its attractiveness, few autocratic regimes can draw on the tool of persuasion because, unlike China, they lack either the infrastructural capacity of complicit proxies that I have alluded to earlier or the army of masses willing to serve as the state's internal security agents, as per the discussion in section 2.4.2.

Despite serving as distinct tools for control, in reality carrots, sticks, and persuasion are often deployed in tandem or in sequence. For autocrats to isolate the use of any of these tools is impracticable. That said, as I illustrate in the next section, the predominance of sticks—and to a lesser extent, carrots—has been overtaken by persuasion over time.

2.6 Temporal Distribution of Carrots, Sticks, and Persuasion, and Preemptive vs. Ex-Post Measures

For a glimpse into the official thinking behind urbanization, I collected and conducted content analysis of relevant government regulations. The methodology is further discussed in Appendix A.[35] Based on central government-issued documents, Figure 2.5 shows that rewards and punishments have become considerably less important over time, persuasion, more significant.

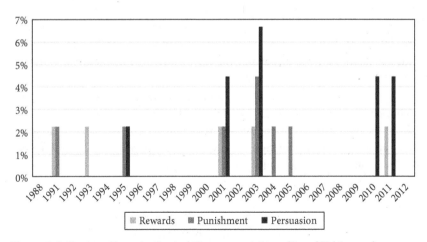

Figure 2.5 Strategy Types in Central Government-Issued Land Taking and Demolition Documents

Note: The percentages in the figure indicate the number of documents mentioning these means as proportions of total central documents.

Source: Author's analysis of data collected from *Beida Fabao*.

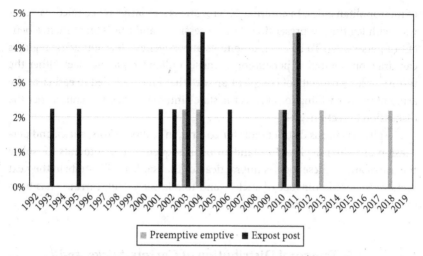

Figure 2.6 Stability Maintenance Measures in Central Government-Issued Land Taking and Demolition Documents

Note: The percentages in the figure indicate the number of documents mentioning these means as proportions of total central documents.

Source: Author's analysis of data collected from *Beida Fabao*.

To preserve social stability, the central government has placed more emphasis on preemptive—as opposed to ex-post—measures over time as shown in Figure 2.6. It suggests that 2011 was a turning point, after which the central authority emphasized conflict prevention in enforcing social stability. The year 2011 saw the passing of a major central government policy, the National Ordinance on the Requisition and Compensation of Houses on State-Owned Land (国有土地房屋征收和补偿条例), designed to better protect citizens' rights and to regulate demolition activities. The National Ordinance declares illegal demolition work conducted by private real estate developers, designating local authorities as the only parties able to carry out lawful housing demolition. An accompanying regulation also bars public security and the police from taking part in demolitions (C. Wang 2012).

2.7 Implications for the State's Role in Economic Development

Urbanization has been promoted as an engine of growth in China. What are the implications of my arguments for the state's role in economic development? What lessons does China offer to the rest of the world?

China's growth has defied many cross-national trends because it lacks what economists Daron Acemoglu and John Robinson (2012) call "inclusive institutions," namely the rule of law, secure property rights, and democratic and pluralistic institutions that are often considered essential for economic growth. In *Why Nations Fail*, the authors argue that inclusive institutions make economic opportunities available to a broad segment of society beyond selected elites and limit the state's role to enforcing law and order, securing property rights, and providing public services.[36] The pattern of coercion and state expropriation of properties described in this book, however, suggest that the protection of property rights is anything but secured in China. This implies that more than four decades of uninterrupted Chinese economic growth since the early 1980s have been achieved despite—not because of—the lack of inclusive institutions.

China's development experience, as this book shows, offers poignant lessons for the role of the state in economic development. To stimulate growth, such as driving an ambitious urbanization project, a state must be strong enough to resist vested societal interests and defeat dissent aimed at its policy directives. Urbanization and development projects in general often necessitate resource redistribution between societal groups. In China, local jurisdictions have varying property rights rules depending on the bargains made between local governments and society (Rithmire 2015). China's model of state-led urbanization can be described as one of coercive distribution, where the state intervenes to coercively distribute resources, in this case land, from one group to another group.[37] Analyses in this book suggest rural residents and those living on the fringes of cities are relative losers compared to those living in city centers, simply because the former are more likely to be short-changed and thus resist, finding themselves subject to sticks. In contrast, carrots or persuasion is more likely to be applied to the latter group. In the counterfactual situation that the state lacked the capacity to take land or demolish existing structures as it wished, urbanization would have stalled.

State endeavors in land distribution have redistributive consequences—along rural-urban divides, between city cores and peripheries, and between capitalists and property owners (Hsing 2010). Insecure property rights allow state authorities to act in cahoots with capitalists or real estate developers to extract rents at the expense of property owners. Hardly surprising, real estate has consistently been the major source of corruption in China (J. Zhu 2012), and collusion between the state and capitalists has negative implications for growth. Urbanization experiences, however, in other populous developing countries like India and Brazil suggest the state's lack of capacity to redistribute land according to housing needs also has significant welfare implications. One palpable example is the prevalence of urban slums in Mumbai and Sao Paolo and slum dwellers' uneven access to basic public goods (Auerbach and Thachil 2018; Donaghy 2018; Yu Zhang 2018).

The state's penetrative capacity and its ability to mobilize the society for development purposes, therefore, cannot be taken for granted.[38] Despite its equity implications, this book shows that the state's ability to redistribute resources by outsourcing repression can spearhead economic growth. The strong capacity of the CCP-state in this respect stands in stark contrast to weak states incapable of overcoming powerful vested interests, let alone mobilizing society, for the state's developmental goals. These weak states can be found in India, Brazil, and Indonesia in the developing world and the United States in the industrialized world. Leviathans proven incapable of escaping from the cage of (societal) norms in tribal arrangements or corporate structures suffer compromises in prosperity as well as liberty (Acemoglu and Robinson 2019). The ineffectiveness of the U.S. federal state in overcoming big corporations' too-big-to-fail impunity that resulted in the 2008–2009 Great Recession or organizing a consistent and effective public health response to the COVID-19 pandemic, provide ample illustration of this point (Cassidy 2009; Micklethwait and Wooldridge 2014, 2020; Stern and Feldman 2004; The Economist 2020).

2.8 Alternative Explanations

Existing literature has provided partial explanations for the success of state coercion in China from the perspectives of contentious politics and government responsiveness. Notably, Ching Kwan Lee has argued for the Chinese state's adeptness in fragmenting aggrieved citizens' interests, even among those advocating for the same labor grievance (C. K. Lee 2007). Fragmentation of interests divides groups and prevents collaboration among protesters, thereby precluding individual protests from growing into a mass labor movement (Perry 2002a). This argument of cellular activism can potentially be applied to land and housing contention because most protests take place locally with no sign of an emerging nationwide movement. Most land-related protests also take place in short duration and lack sustainability except for the Wukan incident in Guangdong (L. Lee 2017). Sociologist Yao Lu has attributed Wukan's exceptionality to its geographically expansive migrant worker network that acted as a vehicle for information transmission and a medium for consciousness-raising among villagers (Lu, Zheng, and Wang 2017).

On government responsiveness, land-related protests have been found to lead to improved policy outcomes. Protests affect the career incentives of local officials, making them more responsive to local demands, which are then translated to more favorable policy outcomes at the central level. Recent works highlight the Chinese government's use of technology in allowing for limited grassroots inclusion (Gueorguiev 2021), as well as the significance of state capacity in policy implementation through penetration of grassroots Party institutions (Koss 2018) and through its control of informal civil society organizations (Mattingly 2019). All these studies have contributed to an understanding of how policies are implemented in China, yet neither cellular activism, government responsiveness, nor the building of Party institutions or informal civil society can on their own account for the Chinese state's ability to coerce, maintain stability, and achieve strong growth at the same time. This book represents a serious effort to address this very question by bringing together a gamut of repressive measures, previously unexamined or studied separately, to provide explanations for this important political outcome.

3

Outsourcing Violence

Everyday Repression via Thugs-for-Hire

> Privatized state violence, as a subset of state violence, is coercion
> orchestrated by the state . . . but carried out by nonstate actors, such
> as vigilantes, paramilitaries, and militias, who are directly or indi-
> rectly supported by the government. (Roessler 2005, 209)

In Chapters 3 and 4 I take up the subject of outsourcing violence to third-
party agents. This chapter conceptualizes everyday repression, a banal
and mundane form of repression in which low-level violence is used to coerce citizens into compliance with state policies.[1] In the context of the
repression-mobilization nexus, everyday repression can be seen as the state
response to citizen foot-dragging and other small-scale acts of delayed compliance—or everyday forms of resistance as James Scott calls it. It is a repressive strategy that requires no coercive apparatus or trained agents and thus
incurs lower material costs than conventional repressive measures of police or
military crackdowns.

I then introduce the logic behind state preference for outsourcing violence to
thugs-for-hire (TFH) under certain conditions. Outsourcing repression to nonstate agents helps to bolster state capacity in the implementation of vexatious
everyday policies; furthermore, the third-party nature of the agents allows for
plausible deniability and evasion of accountability from the masses and higher-
level authorities. Outsourcing is, however, subject to agency problems, which
could result in the undisciplined use of violence—more violence used than necessary and violence used for reasons other than getting the job done—that causes
unnecessary harm to the subjects.

This chapter presents empirical evidence from a media-sourced dataset to illustrate that deployment of thugs was positively associated with the acts aimed to
injure and kill, yet the presence of thugs produces a negative marginal effect on
the likelihood of collective action and results in less violent backlash relative to
the police, quasistate security, and government officials, subject to some caveats.
To explain these findings, I offer tentative reasoning drawn from the literatures

Outsourcing Repression. Lynette H. Ong, Oxford University Press. © Oxford University Press 2022.
DOI: 10.1093/oso/9780197628768.003.0003

on the legal psychology of the legitimacy of police violence and the sociology of emotions when citizens encounter violent repression.

The empirical evidence in this and the next chapters suggests everyday repression via TFH is a lower-cost repressive measure because it incurs less material cost, offers the possibility of plausible deniability, and minimizes the likelihood of collective action and violent backlash relative to agents who represent the state to varying degrees. In addition to the media-sourced event dataset drawn upon in this chapter, the next chapter provides further detailed case-study evidence to illustrate these arguments.

3.1 Conceptualizing Everyday Repression

Charles Tilly (1978, 100) defines repression as "any action by another group which raises the contender's cost of collective action." The scope of repression has since been broadened beyond protest control, however, to encompass "a wide variety of coercive efforts employed by political authorities to influence those within their territorial jurisdiction: overt and covert; violent and nonviolent; state, state-sponsored (e.g. militias), and state-affiliated (e.g. death squads); successful and unsuccessful" (Davenport 2007a, 10). The notion that states usually undertake repression as a response to internal dissent is supported by an extant body of literature (Earl, Soule, and McCarthy 2003; Francisco 1995; Gartner and Regan 1996; Poe 2004; Tilly 1978). When faced with internal threats, states can either repress or accommodate; the latter, which works through concession or co-optation, is considerably costlier to the regime than repression (della Porta 1995; Pierskalla 2010, 117; Ritter 2014).

Although repression usually conjures up the image of police arrests, tear gas, rubber bullets, and military tanks deployed by state coercive agents in uniform, I argue that scholars have neglected banal and ordinary acts of repression. I call these acts "everyday repression." They require no detailed strategic planning, high-level coordination, or disciplined or trained agents. Strong organizational repressive capacity and sophisticated technology are not prerequisites for their execution either, in contrast to state repressive acts, such as military crackdowns on activists, police arrests, Internet surveillance, and restrictions on civil society organizations.

3.1.1 Everyday Repression and Everyday Forms of Resistance

Everyday repression takes on many characteristics of James Scott's everyday forms of resistance. The latter include acts such as "foot-dragging, dissimulations, false compliance, feigned ignorance, surreptitious assault, murder, and anonymous threats" (Scott 1985, 35). These quiet, piecemeal, and prosaic techniques are used when "open defiance is impossible or entails mortal danger" (Scott 1989, 34). The small scale of the actions makes them relatively safe, but in the aggregate, they are capable of producing results far beyond that of a single large-scale act. As opposed to social movements or organized collective actions, everyday forms of resistance consist of unorganized and uncoordinated actions. Analogously, everyday repression involves the use of low-level violence to coerce citizens into complying with the state's policies and orders. If situated on the spectrum of repression with large-scale organized and coordinated repressive acts placed at one end, everyday repression lies at the opposite end as shown in Table 3.1.

According to Scott, those who engage in everyday forms of resistance have no intention of staging a revolution, in contrast to those involved in open confrontation. These everyday actions imply their accommodation—rather than challenge—of existing power arrangements (Scott 1989, 51). The same could be said of everyday repression: prosaic repressive acts are intended to suppress, not to exterminate, those who defy government policies or challenge its authority, people like squatters, "nail household" dwellers, petitioners, and protestors. The state seeks to regulate their activities, coerce them into compliance, and prevent them from challenging its authority on an everyday basis.

Nevertheless, the target of everyday forms of resistance necessarily differs from that of everyday repression. Everyday forms of resistance are "stratagem[s] deployed by a weaker party in thwarting . . . [the one] who dominates the public exercise of power" (Scott 1989, 52). Resistance is always staged by the weaker against a stronger opponent. Everyday repression represents the opposite in this respect. All repressive acts, no matter how banal or mundane they may be, are always adopted by a stronger party against the weaker one. The weak targets are marginalized citizens living on the fringes of societies, such as lower-income peasants and urban residents living in precarious housing conditions with insecure property rights. Urban middle-class and political elites are rarely the targets of everyday repression. Put simply, everyday forms of resistance are weapons of

Table 3.1 Organizational Capacity vs. Target of Repression and Resistance

		Organizational capacity–Agent training	
		Low	High
Target	Strong against weak	Everyday repression	Open violent repression
	Weak against strong	Everyday forms of resistance	Organized collective action

the weak, but everyday repression derives from a repressive authority with power over the repressed.

Table 3.1 classifies various types of resistance and repression by their targets and organizational capacity or agent training required. On one end, organized collective actions require a high-level of organizational capacity and coordination among activists (Tarrow 2011; Tilly 1978). They are actions organized by the weak against the strong repressive authority. On the other end, diagonally across from organized collective action lies everyday repression, which is imposed by the strong on the weak and marginalized but requires little organizational capacity or training of repressive agents. Thus, everyday repression can be an attractive repressive action compared to open violent repression.

3.1.2 What Incentivizes Everyday Repression?

If state repression is generally viewed as a response to dissent, what incentivizes the deployment of everyday repression? When authorities view foot-dragging by citizens—such as delays in tax payments and compliance with eviction orders—as acts of dissent, everyday repression is state action taken in response to defiance of routine state orders. Defiance not only takes the form of demonstrations and protests but also small-scale and prosaic everyday forms of resistance (Scott 1985). The state exercises everyday repression when it cannot efficiently deploy its formal coercive apparatus, namely the police or military, or when the targeted subjects or acts are too small to justify any coordinated repressive effort. Like everyday forms of resistance, the exercise of everyday repression reflects the state's tactical wisdom (Scott 1989, 35) of an expedient alternative when formal coercive means are not practical.

What are the alternatives to using everyday repression against citizens? When confronted with citizens' routine defiance, states can instead choose nonenforcement for any of the following reasons: a) the state may lack capacity to penetrate or carry out policies; b) the cost of deploying formal agents to deal with small defiance cannot be justified, resulting in selective policy implementation; or c) the state purposely chooses nonenforcement to elicit support from selected societal groups, also known as forbearance.[2]

My argument here is that everyday repression offers a viable alternative to nonenforcement arising from any of these circumstances. In fact, everyday repression is the deliberate—but cost-minimizing—enforcement used to extract compliance from citizens. Everyday repression is a politically expedient strategy compared to conventional repression for several reasons. First, it is less costly in material terms because it requires no establishment or maintenance of a coercive apparatus. Often, it is outsourced to nonstate violent agents, a

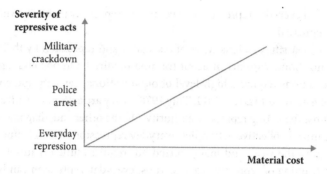

Figure 3.1 Severity of Repressive Acts vs. Financial Cost of Deployment

point further detailed in the next section. In general, third-party repressive agents are less costly because they do not belong to a formal coercive force to whom the state pays permanent salaries and social welfare benefits. Figure 3.1 indicates that the financial cost of repressive actions increases proportionately from everyday to planned and highly coordinated coercion. Because these outsourced nonstate agents are temporary or contract workers, they can be hired and fired easily.

3.2 Outsourcing Violence to Thugs-for-Hire

3.2.1 Benefits and Costs of Outsourcing Violence

3.2.1.1 Benefits
Why do states outsource violence? When carrying out certain policies and repression, some states prefer outsourcing to nonstate violent agents instead of doing it themselves.

A state can outsource the tasks of tax collection, everyday policy implementation, and repression to third-party violent agents. When peasants refuse to pay taxes, cities need to clean up eyesores like illegal structures and vendor stalls; or when the authorities want to quell protesters, outsourcing violence to nonstate agents becomes an expedient strategy. States may opt to outsource violence when they lack the capacity to effectively deploy violence themselves. Weak or weakening states across Europe, Africa, and the Middle East have subcontracted violence to private armies in order to boost their inadequate coercive capacity (Ahram 2016). "If some states, like Serbia, Croatia, Bosnia, and Rwanda, came to depend on irregulars . . . [the reason is that] they are unable to muster an adequate number of recruits to field a real army" (Mueller 2000, 70).

This does not preclude outsourcing violence by strong states, despite the likelihood of their doing so for another reason. Nonstate agents who perform violent acts offer distinct advantages to states. When nonstate agents, instead of uniformed personnel like the military or the police, use violence against citizens illegally, states stand a better chance of evading responsibility. The identity of nonstate agents is often elusive, which allows states to maintain an arm's-length relationship with them and the violent acts they commit (Carey, Colaresi, and Mitchell 2015; Staniland 2012). States can more easily sever relationships with nonstate agents than with state agents if they need to.

> The first obvious benefit to relying on paramilitary groups [in genocide] is deniability ... There is no concealing the fact that they are representatives of the government and their involvement ... makes clear the role of the government in the murder of the targeted population which those regimes are often at pain to conceal. (Alvarez 2006, 17)

A range of countries from the United States to Sierra Leone have engaged private security companies to maintain a distance from the agents' actions. The abuse of prisoners at Abu Ghraib by security personnel working for the U.S.-contracted Blackwater was a case in point (Avant 2005a, 233). Democracies engage with private security companies to reduce the need to work through institutional processes required by their allies or multilateral institutions to which they belong (Avant 2005a, 238). Semidemocratic governments facing voters regularly may also prefer third-party repression to avoid being punished in elections. In addition, countries reliant on foreign aid from democracies engage in privatized state violence to maintain a veneer of legitimacy in the eyes of donor countries (Carey, Colaresi, and Mitchell 2015; Mazzei 2009; Stanley 1996).

In summary, strong and weak states may similarly outsource violence, albeit to further diverging ends—deniability for the former and boosting state capacity for the latter. These two objectives, however, are not mutually exclusive; outsourcing violence can confer the benefits of bolstering capacity and evading responsibility simultaneously. Outsourcing violence is not confined to only authoritarian regimes either; democracies have also similarly contracted out violent repression to third-party agents, especially against nondomestic nationals on foreign soil.

3.2.1.2 Costs

Outsourcing violence is often subject to agency problems as with any subcontracting job (Miller 2005; Spence and Zeckhauser 1971; Weingast and Moran 1983). When states engage private militias to repress, agent-centered human rights violations like excessive violence and the sexual abuse of repressed citizens are commonplace (Brysk 2014; Bohara et al. 2008; Campbell and Brenner

2002; Mitchell 2004). The consequence is uncontrolled and undisciplined violence—with more violence committed than is necessary to get the job done.[3] Privately motivated, this sort of behavior is beyond the state's instruction. Nashi, the youth league sponsored by the Kremlin to crush protestors supporting the Color Revolutions in the mid-2000s, was a case in point. As they became increasingly violent, they became a dead weight, prompting the Kremlin eventually to step in to reform the movement (Atwal and Bacon 2012; Hartog 2016). Excessive violence may also help the victims attract sympathizers, in turn garnering support for citizen actions rather than deterring them.

In other words, when states outsource violence to criminal groups, militias, or paramilitaries, they must firmly ensure they are the principal and the violent groups remain the agent. But not all states can exert tight control over the agents to whom they outsource violence. In general, strong states that can manipulate the proxies to whom they contract out violence are more capable of managing the risks from outsourcing coercion. When weak states hire violent groups, they run the risk of being usurped by the violent agents, further demonopolizing their claim to legitimate territorial violence. Hence, weak states are in general less capable of exerting control over the targets and the intensity of violence exercised by third-party agents.[4]

When violent groups become too powerful, they may end up usurping state autonomy. The Chinese state's relationships with violent criminal groups in the late Qing and Republican periods provide ample evidence to illustrate this point. By outsourcing violence to secret societies and mafias, the Qing and Republican states voluntarily ceded their monopoly on violence, further eroding state power (Campbell and Brenner 2002). Granted, the Chinese states during these periods were weak to begin with; however, a vicious cycle intensified. The more violence states outsourced to these groups, the more powerful they became; and they ended up biting the hands that fed them as was the case with bandits who attempted to overthrow the Qing dynasty. Kimberly Marten (2012, 137) argues that similarly, in Russia, by working with a warlord to exert indirect control over Chechnya, Russia has perpetuated the warlord leader Ramzan's control over the unruly territory and consequently "outsourced a piece of domestic sovereignty."

3.2.2   Thugs-for-Hire in China

TFH in contemporary China are ruffians, hooligans, and unorganized stragglers. Usually the unemployed or those lacking regular salaried jobs who depend on "making trouble" to sustain a living, they stand in contrast to mafiosi with professional identities, complex organizational structures, and rituals typically absent among TFH (Hill 2003; Volkov 2002a, 96–98). Thus, TFH more closely approximate criminal groups than mafias, the latter belonging to a category of organized crime. Notably, TFH is a market exchange—thugs provide violent coercion to the state, which pays for their service—differentiating them from other groups who conduct violence for political purposes.[5]

The thugs are hired by local governments, said my interviewees, to "manhandle villagers," "intimidate residents with vulgar language," "tear down billboards to disrupt business," and "loot stores." Such actions require no specific skills aside from physical strength and hooliganism.

An interviewee from a Yunnan village noted:

> The thugs hired to do dirty work in this village are recruited from other villages or towns in the same region. They are relatively familiar with the area and speak the local dialect, yet they have an escape route if they get into trouble. The local authorities will never hire local villagers to beat up their own people.[6]

Why did the village authority not hire local villagers to do the job?

> Of course, they dared not do so. If the victims found out the neighbor's son had carried out intimidation and beating, the neighbor's family would be in trouble. Few locals would want to do the dirty work for fear of getting their own family members in trouble. Outsiders, however, have an advantage of not being recognized by the locals under attack.[7]

As a politically expedient strategy, TFH in China fulfill several functions, in accordance with the literature reviewed earlier. First, they help augment local authorities' lack of capacity to implement policies, execute day-to-day tasks, and subjugate citizens; but TFH, who are not precluded from being hired by private individuals or companies, primarily serve as an extension of the local state's capacity.

Second, and more importantly, because of their third-party nature, they provide opportunities for plausible deniability for violent acts committed. In postreform China, local governments engaged thugs to assist in the collection of rural taxes and other illegal exactions before their abolition in the early 2000s.[8] Not unlike demolition and land grabs, compliance was vexatious for local officials. Thuggish violence had also been blatantly used against women in forced abortion cases before the abolition of the one-child policy in 2015 (Hardee-Cleaveland and Banister 1988). In a decentralized authoritarian one-party state, the performance of local leaders in China is subject to periodic evaluation by higher-level governments. Social instability in local jurisdictions, indicated by severe casualties in land taking or housing demolition, large-scale violent protests, or rising petition cases, could invite reprimand by higher-level authorities (Yongshun Cai and Zhu 2013). In addition, local leaders in China are also under institutional pressure to appear responsive to the populace (Heurlin 2016; Z. Su and Meng 2016). Outsourcing violent repression to nonstate agents thus offers local leaders the pretense of the evasion of accountability in the eyes of both higher-level governments and the local population. Thus, for local authorities who require extra capacity to implement everyday policies and are also under pressure to maintain a veneer of legitimacy, outsourcing violence can confer these twin benefits.

Outsourcing violence, however, can also incur considerable costs. As the case studies in Chapter 4 will illustrate, engaging with TFH may result in agency problems of excess violence and inflicting harm on citizens beyond what is required to extract compliance. When death or a violent large-scale confrontation ensues from excess violence, the attention it attracts may put pressure on higher-level authorities to punish local officials, and TFH can become a liability accordingly. The pretense for plausible deniability also operates on the presumption that TFH are deployed exclusively. On occasions where government officials lead a group of thugs to demolish houses, their co-presence defeats the purpose of outsourcing violence for the sake of avoiding accountability. Illegitimate violence conducted by TFH is then seen as sponsored or endorsed by the government. Persistent reliance on TFH for the implementation of everyday policies also risks devolving power to nonstate violent agents and ceding part of local authority accordingly. When a gang of thugs evolves to become a powerful mafia group, it may eventually usurp local state power.

3.3 Repertoire of Violence: Agents and Violent Strategies

Building on the notion of the repertoire of violence that Charles Tilly and Elisabeth Wood have developed (Tilly 2003; Wood 2008), this section maps the array of violent strategies deployed to take land and housing forcibly from citizens as well as the agents most likely to carry out the respective acts. In studies of civil wars, the repertoire of violence includes, for example, kidnapping, assassination, massacre, torture, sexual violence, and forced displacement (Kalyvas 2006; J. M. Weinstein 2007; Wood 2008).

Drawing on my original hand-coded dataset consisting of more than 2,000 land-taking and demolition events, I classify the violent strategies into the following actions:

a) Disrupt. This category includes disruption of water and electricity supplies to households and physical damage to properties, including breaking glass windows and kicking down doors. This is the first set of strategies that violent agents typically use before resorting to more severe ones.

b) Injure. With this category of strategies, intimidation, threats, and injuries are inflicted on citizens, including verbal abuse, beating people up, and throwing feces, all verbal and physical attacks short of killing.

c) Kill. Violent acts constitute this category and include the taking of lives, regardless of intent. Burying people alive, running people over with a heavy vehicle, or hacking people to death are examples.

d) Restrict liberty. Kidnapping, forced detention, and house arrest are included in this category.

e) Covert. Actions in this category are carried out in a covert manner or with covert (hidden) intentions. Examples include setting ablaze a house or conducting demolitions under the guise of taking down an illegal construction. These are typically carried out deceptively or furtively without the full knowledge of residents. More egregious examples include buying residents dinner to take them away from their home and sending in a bulldozer in the meantime and bulldozing a home in the middle of the night.

As Tilly has argued, the repertoire of violence could be carried out by violent specialists, such as military personnel, police, security guards, executioners, judicial officers, militias, and paramilitaries, as well as political entrepreneurs, whose specialties comprise organizing, dividing, and representing constituencies (Tilly 2003, 30–54). These entrepreneurs could be government agents or actors who compete or bear no relationship with the state.

Along a similar line of reasoning, agents who conduct violent demolitions or land grabs far surpass official state agents, encompassing an entire array of state, quasistate, and private actors. Specifically, I have grouped them into the following categories:

a) State security, namely the police (警察 or 公安);

b) Quasistate security officials, such as street patrols (城管), assistant police (协警 or 辅警), and joint "law enforcement" teams (联合执法队);

c) Government officials, namely, urban street officials (街道干部), rural township officials (乡镇干部), officials from demolition or expropriation offices (拆迁办, 拆迁指挥部, 征收办), construction committees (建设委员会), and the court (法院);

d) Grassroots government officials, such as village committees and officials (村委会 or 村干部), urban communities (社区), neighborhood committees (居委会);

e) Grassroots nongovernment officials, who are primarily volunteers and "activists"; and

f) "Thugs," who constitute two categories: agents sent by private companies and hired agents. Examples of private companies include demolition companies (拆迁公司) and developers (开发商). Instances of hired agents are unidentified agents (来历不明人员), hooligans (流氓打手), gangsters (黑社会), ruffians (暴徒), scoundrels (歹徒), exconvicts (刑满释放分子), the socially idle (社会闲散人员), and illegal security personnel (黑保安).

These categories are drawn from media reports filed by reporters and citizen journalists, often accompanied by interviews with victims or eyewitnesses. The "agent" categories listed above were, therefore, as described by citizens, that is, direct victims of violence or those who bore witness to the events.

3.3.1 Methodology and Datasets

3.3.1.1 Media Sources and Potential Biases

Media-sourced protest-event data are generally subject to selection bias and description bias (Earl et al. 2004; Weidmann 2016). Selection bias can arise from a lack of media freedom, censorship by the authorities, and event coverage by particular media or reporters.[9] Many events are unreported with information never reaching the reporters because of the remote location in which they occur (Davenport and Ball 2002) or their small size (Biggs 2016). Description bias pertains to the veracity of reporting, which may result in information omission and misrepresentation as well as event framing (McCarthy and McPhail 1998).[10]

Given these potential biases, I discuss below the sources of the media data use and how they help address some of these concerns. The quantitative data are drawn from two sources. One is the Social Unrest in China (SUIC) dataset I have constructed, which is an original media-sourced dataset spanning the early 1990s to the late 2010s. The range of media sources is wide-ranging, from the *Southern Weekly* (南方周末) and Boxun, to English-language media outlets, such as Reuters and the *South China Morning Post*. The multiple sources address both selection and description biases to some extent. English-language Western media may be more inclined to cover larger events because of the reach of reporters and the interests of their readership. U.S. government-sponsored websites, such as Boxun, might be more interested in violent events that involve human rights abuses. Some Chinese newspapers, such as the liberal *Southern Weekly*, were considerably bold in their reporting of social issues that exposed the plights of marginal citizen groups in the late 1990s and early 2000s but had to occasionally self-censor when pressured by propaganda authorities (Kaiman 2013).

Because SUIC is a protest-event dataset, it focuses on land- and housing-related events that involve collective actions. Events were captured and reported at the point of protest, but protest is not the only outcome of interest; I am also interested in the repertoire of repressive strategies deployed by agents, which may not have necessarily resulted in collective actions. Thus, I also drew on cases from the China Human Rights Defenders (CHRD; 维权网), a non-profit organization focused on highlighting human rights abuses in China, in order to supplement protest events. The NGO records the events at the point where citizens' rights have been infringed, usually the time when their land has been illegally taken or houses demolished without their consent, even when they did not protest in defiance. The two independent datasets thus complement each other, capturing events at different points in the repression–mobilization cycle.

The complementarity between SUIC and CHRD data also helps address concerns on biases against rural-based, smaller, and less violent events to a certain extent. As a result of limited resources for coverage and reporting bias on what captures readers' attention, SUIC data that relies on reporters' filings may favor violent incidents with greater numbers of protest participants in urban or peri-urban areas. Meanwhile, because the CHRD events are filed by independent citizen-journalists or the victims themselves, they are either unconstrained or less constrained by resources or commercial considerations. That said, events involving thugs or covert strategies might still conceivably be systematically underreported compared to those where formal security agents or government officials were deployed and more overt strategies were used. Given the data constraints in studying a politically sensitive subject, however, I believe the triangulation of data sources provides a far more comprehensive view of the events of interest here than if I were to rely on a single source. For further details on the data and methodology, see Appendix C.

3.3.2 Descriptive Statistics

3.3.2.1 Distribution of Violent Cases by Year

Figure 3.2 indicates temporal trends in the data. The number of violent cases rose steadily throughout the 2000s and then rose sharply after 2009, when the central government launched the 4 trillion-RMB fiscal stimulus package to avert an economic slowdown amidst the Great Financial Crisis in the United States. The fiscal stimulus was largely financed by regional and local governments, which raised funds by setting up financing vehicles that used land as collateral. This gave rise to fervent efforts by local authorities to take farmland and demolish houses.

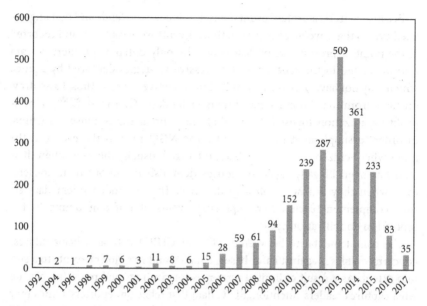

Figure 3.2 Distribution of Violent Land Taking and Demolition Cases by Year (1992–2017)

Source: Author's violent land taking dataset.

Violent cases peaked in 2013, two years after the passing of a national ordinance in 2011 regulating housing demolitions on state-owned land (国有土地上房屋征收与补偿条例), which was aimed at reducing violent land conflicts (China Daily 2011; The State Council of the People's Republic of China 2011). Violent cases have declined since 2013, also partly the result of a slowing economy that curtailed the appetite for land transactions.

3.3.2.2 Repressive Agents—Violent Actions

Government officials, comprising mostly urban street (街道) and rural township (乡镇) bureaucrats and those from demolition offices (拆迁办), were omnipresent among all the agents (appearing 1,028 times out of a total of 5,067).[11] The agents who followed closely were state security or the police (1,002 times) and thugs (973 times). More than two-thirds of the thugs were unidentified private agents (hired agents, 760 times); the other one-third made clear they were sent by demolition companies or real estate developers (private companies, 331 times). In smaller numbers were grassroots government officials, such as village committee and urban community officials; grassroots nongovernment officials, namely volunteers and activists; and quasistate security agents, such as street patrols (see Figure 3.3).

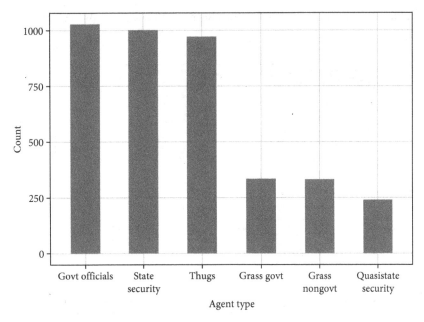

Figure 3.3 Number of Times Present for Each Agent Type (N = 5,067)

Source: Author's violent land taking dataset.

N.B. Counted presence exceeds the total number of events (2,209) because multiple agents could be present at one event.

Table 3.2 shows a heatmap of the cross-tabulation of repressive strategies vs. agent types. The shading in the boxes indicates the frequency of strategies used: darker shades correspond to higher frequencies. The percentages in the boxes represent the number of times the strategy was carried out by a specific agent as a proportion of the sum of the specific strategy. For instance, thugs account for 26 percent of the total disrupt strategy used, 29 percent of injure, 30 percent of kill, 20 percent of restrict liberty, and 23 percent of covert.[12]

The most common strategies were disruption of utility supplies (disrupt, N = 2,592) and causing bodily injuries (injure, N = 2,551), followed by forced detentions or arrests (restrict liberty, N = 1,589), covert actions (N = 621), and kill (N = 181). Government officials (27 percent), thugs (26 percent), and state security or the police (23 percent) were the agents who most frequently conducted disrupt acts. Acts that caused bodily injuries were most often carried out by thugs (29 percent), the police (27 percent), and government officials (22 percent). Acts that ended lives were most frequently carried out by thugs (30 percent), followed by the police (27 percent), and government officials (22 percent). Restrict liberty actions were most often conducted by the police (33 percent), followed by government officials (25 percent), and thugs (20 percent). Finally, covert

Table 3.2 Heatmap of Cross-Tabulation: Repressive Strategies vs. Agent Types

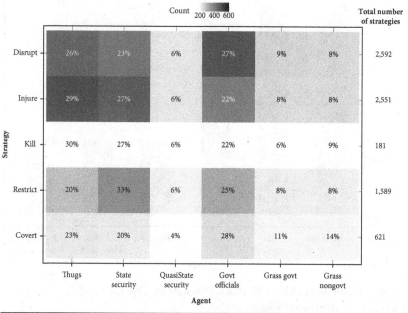

Source: Author's violent land-taking dataset

N.B. (a) Shading indicates frequency, higher numbers represented by darker shades. The percentages represent the strategies accounted for by specific agent as proportions of a particular strategy type; (b) This table counts the number of times present at events. Because multiple agent types could be present at a single event, the total count here of 7,534 is greater than the total number of events of 2,202.

strategies were most regularly conducted by government officials (28 percent), thugs (23 percent), and the police (20 percent), followed by grassroots nongovernment officials (14 percent), grassroots government officials (11 percent), and quasistate security (4 percent). In the thugs category, unidentified hired agents, rather than those sent by private companies, accounted for most of the actions.

Among these agents, the police are the most well-trained coercive agents carrying out violent acts or making arrests. As agents of state security, they are the enforcers of legitimate violence, along with the military. Quasistate security agents, who are the urban patrols or enforcers of bylaws (城管), assistant police (协警，辅警), or village "joint law enforcers" (联合执法队，联合巡防), are the least frequently deployed; but they are among the agents most likely to provoke a violent backlash, a point revisited in section 3.4.2. Many quasisecurity agents are hired on a contractual basis and are poorly trained and ill-equipped to do the demanding job of dealing with citizens daily. They lack the professional training and job security given to the police, who are officially on the government payroll (编制) (Hanser 2016). The backgrounds of some of these quasistate agents are not too dissimilar from TFH in that they are also unemployed street ruffians hired to fill temporary positions (Ong 2018a). The only notable distinction is that quasistate security agents wear uniforms and are, therefore, perceived as representing local authorities (municipal or village) to some degree. TFH may be remunerated by and perceived to be paid for by local authorities, but their unidentifiable nature does not make for automatic association with the state—at least not in what counts as evidence for accountability tracing. (See Chapter 4).

Among the three types of nonviolent agents, government officials from urban street offices, township governments, demolition offices, or the court are formal representatives of the state, who command government prerogatives, in comparison with grassroots government officials from the semistate organizations of village or neighborhood committees. Grassroots nongovernment officials, such as volunteers and activists, are typically individuals living within communities who have social ties with citizens. The last two agent types infrequently engage in violent acts, but they commonly deploy nonviolent strategies to persuade citizens to comply, a subject of investigation in Chapters 5 and 6.

3.3.3 Propensity for Violence: The Effects of Agent Type on Repressive Strategies

To predict agents' propensity for violence, I simulated the marginal probability effects of agents on repression based on the binomial logit models. The models control for rural-urban location and the year 2012, when the national ordinance governing housing demolition on state-owned land came into effect.[13] Because more than one agent is often present at an event, I simulated the expected probability under the condition of agent mutual exclusivity; that is, the probability that thugs or other agents are exclusively deployed on their own.[14]

Figure 3.4 illustrates the marginal probability effects with a 95 percent confidence interval.[15] Substantively, the coefficients convey the marginal likelihood of repressive measures when thugs or other agents were exclusively deployed. As it suggests, all agents, except the police (security), raise the expected probability of the disrupt strategy. All three violent agent types—thugs, the police, and quasistate security—increase the expected probability of the injure strategy, most notably thugs, who raise it by 0.294, followed by the police (0.180), and quasistate security (0.086). Meanwhile, all the nonviolent agents reduce the expected probability of the injure strategy. As for kills, thugs raise the expected probability by the largest extent (0.022), whereas grassroots government officials reduce it by the most (-0.011). The police are far more likely than any other agents to engage in restricting liberty as they raise the expected probability by 0.300. Interestingly, but perhaps unsurprisingly, covert strategies are most likely deployed by nonviolent agents. Grassroots nongovernment officials raise the expected probability

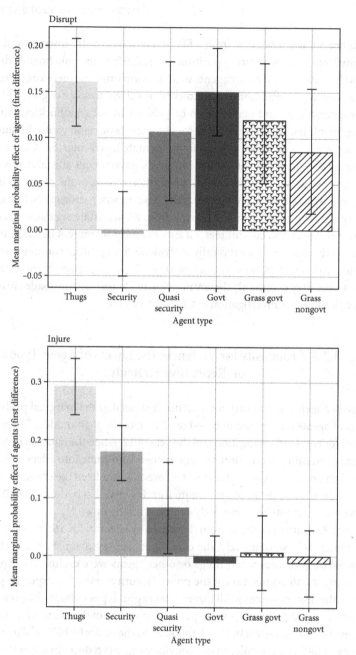

Figure 3.4 Comparing the Marginal Effects of Agent Types on Repressive Strategies (Panel A = Disrupt; B = Injure; C = Kill; D = Restrict; and E = Covert)

N.B. The line on each bar represents the 95 percent confidence interval about the estimate. Figures are based on the regression analysis presented in Table D.3 in the Appendix D. The first difference occurs between the treated and untreated exclusive presence of agent x; the probabilities appear in Table D.7 in Appendix D.

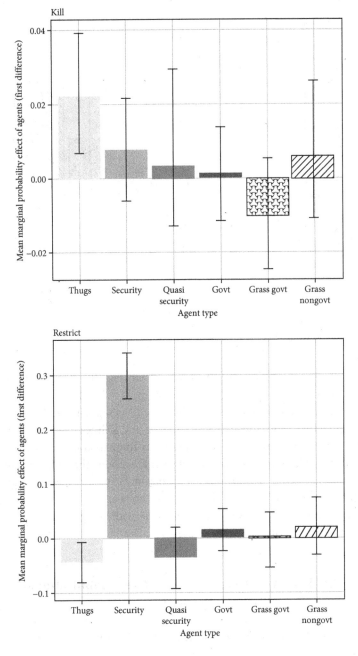

Figure 3.4 Continued

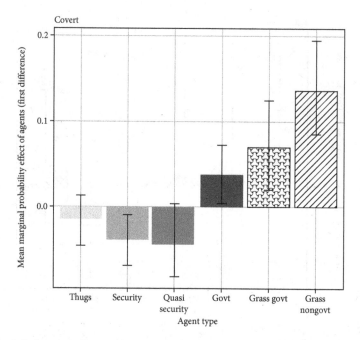

Figure 3.4 Continued

by 0.135, followed by grassroots government officials (0.068) and government officials (0.036).

Taken together, these marginal probability effects suggest that thugs have the highest propensity for violent acts of injuring and killing. The police have the highest proclivity to restrict citizens' liberty. In comparison, quasistate security agents have the lowest propensity to injure or kill among the violent agents, but they are just as likely to disrupt as other agents do. Meanwhile, even though non-violent agents do not deploy explicit violence, they are most likely to carry out covert acts hidden from the eyes of the public or with deceptive intentions, such as bulldozing homes in the middle of the night.

3.4 How Agent Types Affect Citizen Mobilizational Responses

3.4.1 Nonviolent Citizen Responses

The range of nonviolent citizen-mobilizing responses include protest, petition, and legal mobilization. Petition and legal mobilization are institutional channels of conflict resolution that involve lengthy and time-consuming bureaucratic or legal procedures.[16] Because access to government institutions requires resources, we should expect less educated citizens and those living in rural areas to enjoy less access. Meanwhile, protest offers an extra-institutional route of taking one's grievance to the street; however, organizing collective action in China is challenging because of the lack of land or housing-related civil society organizations found in India, South Korea, and other democratic societies (see Chapter 7 for a comparative perspective). In addition, by engaging in street protests, protestors incur considerable risks to their personal safety and professional lives. Petitioners can also face physical harassment by local authorities as a case study in Chapter 4 will illustrate.

Given the presence of multiple agents at each event, I simulated the expected probability for each type of agent under the condition of mutual exclusivity, based on the binomial logit models.[17] These models identify agents as the first movers, the presence of which triggers certain citizens' responses. Most media reports contain a description of events with agents being the first movers, and citizens being the second. For example, thugs or quasistate security arrived at residents' homes and broke glass windows and tore down doors. How did the residents respond to those actions? Coders were instructed to code only the first set of events in the reports with that initiator-responder sequence.

Figure 3.5 indicates the marginal probability effects of agents for nonviolent mobilizing responses with a 95 percent confidence interval.[18] Substantively, the coefficients indicate the marginal likelihood of citizen mobilization when thugs or other agent types are exclusively deployed. Among the violent agents (thugs, the police or security, and quasistate security), thugs are rather effective in deterring street protest, second only to quasistate security. Thugs reduce the expected probability of protest by 0.037, compared to the police, who increase it by 0.198 (see Table D.8). Quasistate security agents reduce the likelihood of protest by even more (0.049). Thugs are, however, not so effective in deterring citizens from taking institutional routes of mobilization, namely petition and legal mobilization.

Government officials, grassroots government officials, and grassroots non-government officials all have negative marginal effects on street protest but positive marginal effects on petition and legal mobilization. This suggests that when citizens encounter illegal land taking or demolition by nonviolent agents, they are more likely to pursue their grievances through institutional channels instead of taking them to the street. The effect of government officials (those from urban streets, townships, or higher authorities; demolition offices; and the courts) on the likelihood of street protest is worth probing further. When control variables are held at means (instead of zero), government officials raise the expected probability of protest by 0.254.[19] This suggests two conditions. First,

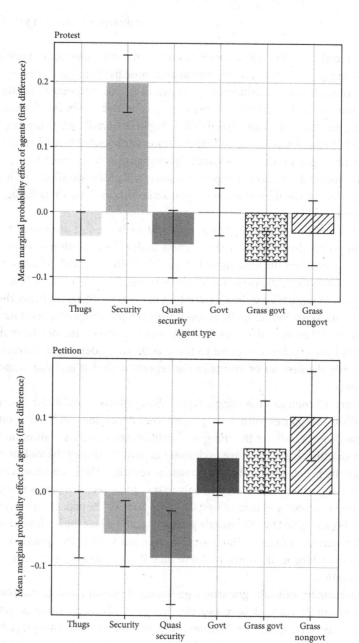

Figure 3.5 Comparing the Marginal Effects of Agent Types on Nonviolent Citizen Responses (Panel A = Protest; B = Petition; and C = Legal Mobilization)

N.B. The line on each bar represents the 95 percent confidence interval about the estimate. Figures are based on the regression analysis presented in Table D.4 in the Appendix D. The first difference occurs between treated and untreated exclusive presence of agent x, the probabilities can be found in Table D.8 in Appendix D.

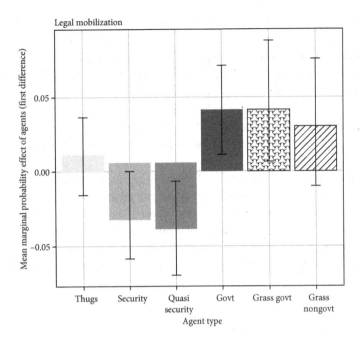

Figure 3.5 Continued

the controls of rural–urban location and the year 2012 are important to predict the marginal effects of government officials for citizen mobilization. Second, the marginal effect of government officials (0.254) for street protest is higher than those of all the other agents, except the police (0.449).[20] In other words, government officials' presence raises the probability of street protest more than any other agent, except the police.

The binomial regression models indicate that petitions and legal mobilization are more likely to take place in urban areas, (see Table D.4 in Appendix D), as per earlier predictions as a result of the higher costs of institutional access rural citizens face. Legal mobilization is also more likely to take place after 2012; however, neither of these control variables has any significant effect on protest.

Taken together, these findings imply that even though thugs are most associated with violent acts of causing bodily injury and death, they do not cause citizens to mobilize through street protest as much as the other agents do. Instead, the formal representatives of the state—the uniform-wearing police officers and government officials—are more likely to prompt citizens to pursue the high-risk option of street protest. Quasistate security may be more effective than thugs in deterring nonviolent mobilization, but they are far more likely to provoke violent backlash, the subject of the next section.

3.4.2 Violent Citizen Responses

In the dataset, citizens' violent responses are categorized as damage to property, self-harm, and harm to the agent. Violent property damage, such as breaking glass windows and destroying doors, is the least costly of all violent responses. Inflicting self-harm most often takes the form of self-immolation (自焚),[21] but it also includes ingesting poison and suicide by hanging. Harming an agent is a very costly response because of the heavy penalty that could result from criminal conviction.

Figure 3.6 indicates the marginal effects of agents for the likelihood of violent backlash under the condition of agent mutual exclusivity.[22] Similar to the models in Figure 3.5, agents were the first movers, who predicted citizens' violent responses as per the first set of event description in media reports. The marginal effects of thugs are considerably weaker, compared to the police and quasistate security. Although thugs reduce the marginal probability of citizen self-harm by

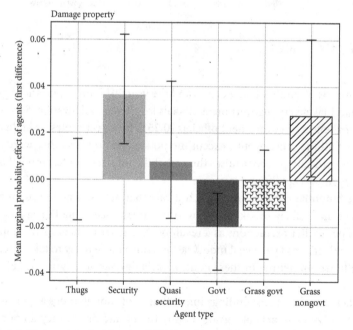

Figure 3.6 Comparing the Marginal Effects of Agent Types on Violent Citizen Responses (Panel A = Damage Property; B = Self-harm; and C = Harm Agent)

N.B. The line on each bar represents the 95 percent confidence interval about the estimate. Figures are based on the regression analysis presented in Table D.5 in Appendix D. The first difference is calculated between treated and untreated exclusive presence of agent x.

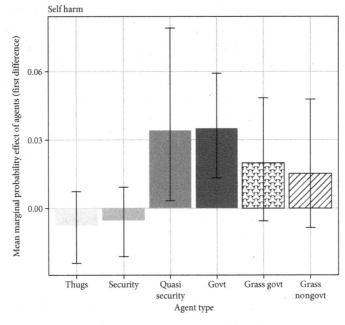

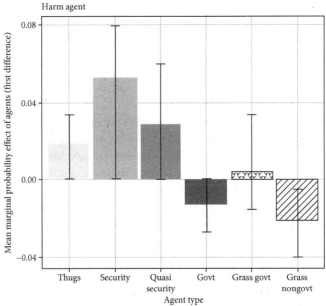

Figure 3.6 Continued

0.007, the police reduce it by 0.005, and quasistate security increases it by 0.034 (see Table D.8). As for citizens harming agents, quasistate security and the police both raise the marginal probabilities by 0.027 and 0.052, respectively, compared to 0.017 for thugs (see Table D.8). Meanwhile, quasistate security and the police both raise the likelihood of citizens damaging properties, but thugs produce no such effect. Subject to the caveats of media-sourced data discussed above, these findings suggest TFH is a lower cost repressive measure—relative to other violent agents—because it reduces the likelihood of violent backlash.

All the nonviolent agents were more likely than thugs to cause citizens to inflict self-harm but less likely to provoke citizens to harm agents. In particular, the presence of government officials (officials from urban streets, townships, or higher; officers from the demolition office or the court) raises the probability of citizens harming themselves by 0.035, compared to thugs, who lower it by 0.007 (see Table D.8). Similarly, government grassroots officials (village officials, urban community, and neighborhood committee members) and nongovernment grassroots officials (volunteers and activists) increase the probability of self-harm by 0.020 and 0.016, respectively (see Table D.8).

The binomial regression models suggest harming agents was more likely to take place in rural areas, whereas all three types of violent backlash were more likely to occur prior to 2012 (see Table D.5 in Appendix D). This implies that violent backlash is on the decline after the passing of the national ordinance.

3.4.3 Discussion of Findings

This section provides some tentative explanations for these findings. In summary, the empirical findings suggest "thugs" were associated with lower likelihood of collective action, compared to the police and government officials. But thugs were not so effective in deterring citizens from taking the institutional channels of petition and legal mobilization. In provoking violent backlash, the presence of thugs was correlated with lower likelihood of property damage, self-harm, and harming agents, compared to the police and quasistate security. The nonviolent agents all raised the likelihood of self-harm, and almost all lowered the probability of harming agents.

Citizens' nonviolent resistance, including collective action, is likely to be driven by cost considerations. Typically, street protests incur higher costs to participants than other institutional forms of mobilization because they may pose greater personal and professional risks. For instance, Chinese citizens with higher educational attainment have been found to be less likely to protest because they face greater income loss should they be punished by the authorities (Ong and Han 2019). Even though protest participants and petitioners face

similar risks of being physically harassed by the authorities, being an extra-institutional channel—protests are by definition illegal—whereas the right to petition is protected by law.[23] In addition, collective actions in China are challenging
to organize given the absence of civil society organizations that typically serve as
mobilizing structures in democratic societies (Ong 2019b), despite the potential
of lineage temples and senior associations to foster collective resistance among
members in a small number of situations (Lu and Tao 2017; Tsai 2007).[24] Thus,
among the range of mobilizational channels available to them, street protests
should be seen as the last resort for citizens.[25] In this context the police comprise the only agent type that raises citizens' risk tolerance sufficiently to make
them pursue the high-cost option of collective action (see panel A in Figure 3.5).
Hence, deploying thugs is a lower-cost repressive measure than the police because of its likelihood in minimizing the occurrence of collective action.

Citizens' violent acts of self-harm and harming agents are not infrequent, but
they have been on the decline since 2013–2014 (see Figure 3.7). Self-immolation
rose from 2009 through 2011, peaking in 2011 with 17 cases registered; however,
deadly attacks on agents exhibit a less consistent pattern. The number of cases
began climbing in 2006, rose significantly after 2009, and peaked in 2010 (28
cases), but remained consistently high throughout the first half of 2010s.

Self-harm and harming agents both incur extremely high costs but for different reasons. Self-harm in the form of self-immolation is an act of protest,
performed in a public place in view of other people (Biggs 2005). Distinct from
terrorism, it belongs with demonstrations, strikes, and sit-ins, not bombings or

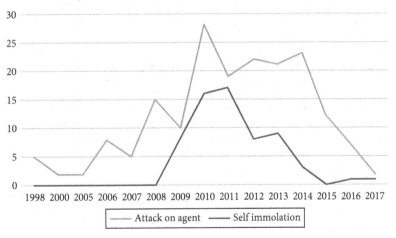

Figure 3.7 Frequency of Self-Immolation and Deadly Attacks on Agents
(1998–2017)
Source: Author's violent land taking dataset.

assassinations.[26] Self-immolation is motivated by the desire to appeal to the sympathy of others by means of a costly signal of self-sacrifice. Harming agents, by contrast, is also a very costly response since criminal punishment may result in loss of freedom or life. It also serves the instrumental purpose of drawing attention to one's desperate plight against a powerful authority—such that pursuit of the agent-provocateur's death becomes the only escape route. These arguments about violent backlash are revisited in the case studies in Chapter 4.

Why are the police and quasistate security far more likely to provoke violent backlash than unidentified thugs? The literatures on the legal and criminal psychology of police violence and the sociology of emotions provide some insights useful in answering this question. That the following are only explanations provided by the existing literature requires emphasis. Without further data collection and empirical testing, which lies beyond the scope of the book, the arguments below are indicative at best.

The legitimacy of state-sanctioned violence rests on the perception among the civilian population that violence used is right or appropriate (Schoon 2014, 782). Studies on police violence have shown that only when procedural justice is observed, that is, when police decisions to use violence are made through fair procedures, the use of force is seen as legitimate (Tyler 2006a, 2011a, 2011b; Tyler and Huo 2002). The perception of the legitimacy of violence in turn shapes citizens' compliance with the law (Tyler 2006b) and their views on the right to use violence for self-defence or other purposes (Jackson et al. 2013). In almost all land expropriation or housing demolition cases in the dataset, the definition of procedural justice was not observed: this was the reason the events were reported in the first place. As such, force used by the uniform-wearing police and quasistate security is more than likely deemed as illegitimate violence, which invites more violent backlash accordingly.

The sociology of emotions highlights three types of emotions useful for understanding motivation for protest and violent backlash.[27] They are reflexive emotions, such as fear and anger, which are quick and automatic responses to events; affective moods, such as solidarity and resentment, which are enduring feelings that encourage continued participation; and moral emotions, such as indignation and injustice, which are feelings of approval or disapproval based on moral principles (Jasper 2011).

When citizens encounter violent repression, they often experience anger and fear at the same time, which simultaneously raises and reduces the likelihood of resistance, respectively (Pearlman 2013). Furthermore, when illegitimate violence is perpetrated by uniform-wearing agents perceived as representing the state—more applicable to the police than to quasistate security but not applicable to thugs—it will provoke moral indignation (Costalli and Ruggeri 2015) and affective feelings of resentment and solidarity. Both moral and affective emotions act in tandem to raise the likelihood of violent backlash and collective action. In other words, because thugs are informal and illegitimate agents to begin with, citizens have no expectation of legitimate violence from them. Thus, the logical implication is that thuggish illegitimate violence does not provoke moral indignation or affective emotions as strong as that perpetrated by the police or quasistate security.

Could the lower likelihood of collective action and violent backlash for thugs be triggered by the fear factor? To investigate this question further, I ran binomial logit models to predict how violent repressive strategies affect citizen responses (see Table D.6 in Appendix D). My earlier findings indicate that thugs are the most violent agent type with the highest likelihood to carry out acts that injure and kill citizens. In the repressive acts–mobilization models, "injure" has no statistically significant effect on protest but a negative effect on petition and legal mobilization and a positive effect on harming agents. "Kill" has a statistically significant positive effect on protest but a negative effect on petition. Taken together, given the positive effects on the more reflexive responses of street protest and harming agents but negative effects on the often-protracted institutional options of mobilization, anger—rather than fear—appears to be the predominant reflexive emotion that drives the positive impact.

3.5 Conclusion

This chapter conceptualizes everyday repression, a novel form of repression carried out by TFH, as a state response to foot-dragging and banal noncompliance captured in what James Scott called everyday forms of resistance. It included empirical evidence for reasons that everyday repression is a lower-cost repressive strategy, showing its negative or lesser association with street protest and violent backlash, particularly in comparison with the police, quasistate security agents, and government officials.

Empirical findings in this chapter are subject to the caveats of biases inherent in media-sourced data. Despite my best efforts at triangulating data sources, the media's propensity for larger and sensational events may leave smaller mundane incidents that involve thugs underreported. I have offered tentative reasons that illegal state-sanctioned violence—perpetrated by the police, quasistate security, and government officials specifically—provoke more violent backlash and collective action than thugs. The reasoning is drawn from existing literatures on the legitimacy of violence in the legal psychology of policing and the sociology of emotions, yet one cannot draw firm conclusions without further data collection and empirical investigation of the role of emotions, a task that lies beyond the scope of this book.

The use of TFH also offers other benefits, namely augmenting state capacity and allowing the pretense of the evasion of accountability; however, it is also subject to costs such as agency problems and erosion of state authority. The next chapter provides substantiation for these arguments with detailed case-study evidence.

4

Case Studies

Thugs-for-Hire, Repression, and Mobilization

> In the process of pursuing efficiency and rapidly transforming the
> city [of Datong], many of Mayor Geng's administrative actions
> broke or even violated conventions. In the massive city-construction
> project in which 50,000 residents were relocated, the Datong munic-
> ipal government played the role of developer and leader. The speed
> of urbanization was simply awe-inspiring.
> —A review of the BBC documentary,
> *The Chinese Mayor* (Song 2015)

This chapter provides thick case-study evidence to illustrate the benefits and
costs of outsourcing violence to thugs-for-hire (TFH). It places everyday repression in the broader context of violent repression carried out by other coercive
agents. Low-intensity, pedestrian violence can be effective in coercing citizens
into compliance, but outsourcing violence may result in agency problems. When
government chiefs are seen to be leading or copresent with a group of TFH, the
pretense for plausible deniability and evasion of accountability that everyday
repression offers is denied. Although outsourcing violence to TFH provides a
means of augmenting local state coercive capacity, doing so allows the gangsters
to grow more powerful, at which point the state risks having its authority usurped
by these dark forces over time. The case studies also demonstrate that everyday
repression is often carried out alongside the nonviolent strategies of mobilizing
the masses (MTM).

4.1 Situating Case Study Evidence in a Broader Theoretical Context

Before turning to field case-study research, this section highlights the ways in
which the qualitative data enhance understanding of the utility of TFH and
how citizens respond to violence perpetrated by them vis-à-vis other agents.
Specifically, I will underscore how field data collected at different points from

Outsourcing Repression. Lynette H. Ong, Oxford University Press. © Oxford University Press 2022.
DOI: 10.1093/oso/9780197628768.003.0004

2012 to 2018 shed light on the nuances of the empirical findings in Chapter 3 and contribute to the conceptual underpinning of everyday repression.

4.1.1 Temporal and Regional Variations

The violent demolition case-study evidence appearing in this chapter, which I collected first-hand in Shanghai in 2005, in Kunming in the early 2010s, and in Zhengzhou in the mid-2010s, represents the patterns of temporal and regional variations in everyday repression. During my field research in Shanghai in 2016 and 2018, I saw that the nonviolent strategies of bargaining and persuasion (covered in Chapters 5 and 6)—although not necessarily less coercive than the violent tactics widespread in the previous decade—were pervasively practiced. What the Shanghai authorities considered socially unacceptable in 2016 (i.e., violent forced demolitions) was, however, ubiquitous throughout Zhengzhou and Kunming, the provincial capitals of Henan and Yunnan, respectively, during the same time period. In other words, Zhengzhou and Kunming were duplicating the violent fast-paced urbanization-driven development that Shanghai had experienced a decade earlier. Table 4.1 indicates the time of the respective violent demolitions and field visits. The violent events of Shanghai in 2005 occurred similarly in Kunming in 2011 and in Zhengzhou in 2012. A map of the geographical locations of the field sites appears in Figure 1.2.

4.1.2 Agency Problems

Outsourcing, a form of delegation of authority, is subject to the principal-agent problem. An incident that took place in the former French Concession in Shanghai in 2005 provides evidence of agency problems when the authorities outsourced a demolition project to thugs who exercised disproportionate violence to get the job done. The thuggish demolition crew set fire to a property in the middle of the night with the intention of intimidating residents but ended

Table 4.1 Location, Year of Field Visits, and Time of Violent Demolitions

Location	Shanghai	Kunming	Zhengzhou	Beijing
Violent Demolitions	2005	2011	2012	Petitioners from all around the country
Field Visits	Summer 2018	Summer 2012	Summer 2014	Summer 2014

up killing an old couple who were sound asleep. Field interviews with long-term petitioners in Beijing also reveal in vivid detail the extent of undisciplined violence TFH hired by local authorities used against their subjects.

Violent demolition was more prevalent prior to the 2011 passage of the National Ordinance that regulates housing demolition on state-owned land; it also bars private real estate developers from taking charge of demolition. The introduction of the law came after a series of highly sensationalized violent cases that drew widespread societal attention to the issue of forced demolition in the 2000s. Since then, local authorities have been put directly in charge of demolition; thus, some degree of government accountability to the process was introduced even though the authorities can still contract out physical work to demolition companies (C. Wang 2016). Suffice it to say, the agency problem of excess violence and callousness still exists after 2012, but their magnitude has been reduced.

4.1.3 Plausible Deniability and Evasion of Accountability

The pretense for plausible deniability and evading accountability for violent acts operates on two levels. By way of its political institutional design, local authorities in China are accountable to higher-level authorities, but they must also appear responsive to the citizenry to some degree despite the lack of popular elections (Heurlin 2016; Qiaoan and Teets 2019). The citizenry in the following case studies consistently experienced low-grade and banal violence covertly exercised by TFH prior to the mass incidents, but it never provoked citizens to rise against the authorities or instigate a violent backlash—until illegitimate violence was explicitly sponsored or condoned by government officials. This often took the form of local political bosses leading a group of unidentified thugs to attack defenseless villagers or residents. Thus, TFH are beneficial insofar as local authorities can plausibly deny their involvement or sponsorship. When it is conducted late at night, early in the morning, in dark alleys, or without serious casualties, thuggish violence can remain detached from public scrutiny.

Instead of offering the opportunity for evasion of accountability, TFH can be a liability when severe casualties result from their violent acts. On one hand, local officials are incentivized to promote urbanization and economic growth; on the other hand, the mass incident is a criterion that receives high priority in the cadre evaluation system, in which failure to prevent such incidents may negatively affect one's career prospects. A study by Yongshun Cai shows that local officials are likely to be punished by higher authorities when local actions result in deaths or large-scale confrontations that attract media attention (Yongshun Cai and Zhu 2013). The political leaders of Kunming and Zhengzhou, two of my field sites, presided over rapid urbanization in their municipalities, but they were later removed from office and are now serving jail sentences for violation of Party discipline. During their tenures Qiu He of Kunming and Wu Tianjun of Zhengzhou ran some of the country's most ambitious demolition campaigns, devastating farmland and razing old housing units at lightning speed, resulting in widespread social unrest and serious casualties.

The case studies here shed light on the nuances of the empirical evidence presented in Chapter 3. They show that outsourcing violence serves its useful purposes of minimizing collective action and violent backlash if local authorities are not seen as explicitly sponsoring or condoning the illegitimate violence perpetrated against citizens. As this chapter will demonstrate, the copresence of government leaders with TFH suggests complicity rather than deniability of responsibility. The resulting outrage against government behavior serves to unite the masses, sustain their collective actions, and provoke backlash.

The qualitative evidence in this chapter shows that the punishment of officials represents the extreme end of the distribution of violence perpetrated by TFH,[1] but a single violent incident does not usually bring down the career of a mayor or provincial leader (Yongshun Cai and Zhu 2013). In Zhengzhou, violent and wanton demolition befell more than 600 villages located across the metropolis, resulting in widespread societal discontent (*The Paper* [澎拜新闻] 2017). Thus, the case studies here largely capture "failed" endeavors of TFH resulting from agency problems and established evidence of government leaders' complicity.[2]

4.1.4 Outsourcing Violence and State Capacity

The case study in Kunming illustrates that although TFH serve the useful purpose of augmenting state coercive capacity, they are also capable of usurping state authority. When a local authority becomes unable to carry out basic functions because of chronic fiscal deficits, outsourcing violence becomes an expedient strategy; yet the greater the reliance on TFH, the greater the risk of being usurped by the thugs, who grow more powerful over time. As I have observed in the field, the village authority became increasingly reliant on the thugs for government functions, ranging from tax collection to maintaining public order. In return for these "services," the local authority had to provide them with the right to collect revenues from local businesses. In *China's Trapped Transition*, Minxin Pei (2006) documents the strength of clientelist ties between local governments and mafias, including buying and selling offices (买官卖官), rampant during the late 1990s and 2000s.

Instead of a principal-agent relationship upon which local authority-TFH relations are premised and in which the principal holds the violent agent on a short leash, these relationships devolve into patron-client ties, in which the two parties forge clientelist relations and become mutually dependent. The nature of this relationship is not without historical precedent in China. An extreme scenario follows. In the early 20th century, the weak and corrupt KMT government had to cede territorial sovereignty to regional warlords in return for their political support. In addition, given its limited capacity, the KMT government enlisted assistance from the criminal Green Gang to defeat its communist enemies in Shanghai.

These are no doubt extreme conditions that China under the CCP will not descend to in any foreseeable future; nonetheless, outsourcing violence to TFH on an everyday basis has sown the seeds for a possible repeat of history. The national campaign against "underworld forces" (扫黑除恶), spearheaded by Xi Jinping, represented the top Party leadership's recognition of the inherent risks these forces posed to state authority and legitimacy. Accordingly, the Party has attempted to sweep them away with the nationwide *saohei* campaign. The gangsters involved in land acquisition and demolition were among the groups the campaign targeted (China Law Translate 2021). The subject of the *saohei* campaign reappears in the concluding chapter of this book.

4.1.5 Interactions Between the Strategies of Everyday Repression and Mobilizing the Masses

The cases of Flower Village in Kunming and Sunzi Village in Zhengzhou demonstrate the synergy between everyday repression in which violence is outsourced to TFH and MTM is coerced by using existing social ties. Local authorities often deploy both violent and nonviolent strategies in the same case at the same time or one after another contingent on several factors. One factor, for instance, is the proportion of the local population on the government's payroll, such as schoolteachers and civil servants, because they are vulnerable to pressure. Another important consideration is the speed at which land taking or demolition must be conducted. In Chapter 6 I show that MTM can be a time-consuming process that requires patience from all parties—local officials, brokers, and the masses. This stands in considerable contrast to the bloody urbanization campaign (血腥拆迁运动) spearheaded by former Party Secretary Wu Tianjun of Zhengzhou. As a result of the project, the homes of 17.5 million people in 627 villages were razed from 2012 to 2015. That said, the number of violent incidents has declined and a corresponding rise in the use of nonviolent strategies has occurred over time across the country.

4.2 Case Studies of Thugs-for-Hire and Other Agents at Work

4.2.1 Arson and Violent Demolition in the Former French Concession in Shanghai in 2005

In the summer of 2018, when strolling in the affluent former French Concession in Shanghai, rich with attractive colonial-style architecture, I stumbled upon a large cordoned-off area of vacant land. Left standing in the compound was a half-demolished dilapidated house. I was puzzled that a neighborhood with some of the country's most expensive real estate and home to many upscale condominiums and restaurants would have a giant vacant lot. I decided to dig a little deeper.

In January 2005, an old couple in their 70s died in their home in the tree-lined neighborhood of Maggie Lane (麦琪里) in the former French Concession. The cause of death was arson. In the early 2000s, this well-off neighborhood, like many others, was zoned for "old city reconstruction" (旧城改造)[3] as Shanghai prepared to host the 2010 World Expo. Located a few streets from Shanghai's premium shopping district of *Huaihai Lu*, land and housing prices on Maggie Lane were among the country's highest and promised strong future growth.

The Chengkai Group, a real estate developer, oversaw the demolition project.[4] Most of the Maggie Lane residents had relocated before the incident happened, but an elderly husband and wife, surnamed Zhu, were among the dozens of people who refused to give in—on principle—because the land had been illegally auctioned off. If it were indeed a renovation project, according to the law, Maggie Lane residents would be allowed to return to the neighborhood once refurbishment had been completed. Instead, they had been forced to relocate to tiny apartments on the outskirts of the city (Schmitz 2016). On the night of the incident, a couple of thugs hired by the real estate developer set fire to the Zhus' residence with the intention of intimidating them into leaving. The elderly couple, who had lived on Maggie Lane for more than 60 years, burned to death in their bed.[5]

In July 2018, I sat down with a former resident of Maggie Lane, Mr. Chen, at an upscale Western-style café in Shanghai's Xuhui District. I ordered black coffee; he ordered a glass of orange juice. Chen, who was in his early 70s, told me his home had been violently demolished a decade ago. One morning in 2009, while brushing his teeth in a T-shirt and boxers, thugs broke into his house. They twisted his arms, violently shoved him and his wife into a minivan, and took them to a faraway site outside Shanghai. While they were gone, a bulldozer came into the compound and razed his two-story residence (see Figure 4.1). When I asked him why he called the assailants "thugs" (地痞流氓), he told me they wore no uniform, appeared rough, and had tattoos, making them look to him like gangsters (黑社会).[6]

Figure 4.1 Chen's Residence in Shanghai's Xuhui District
Photo credit: *Nanfang Zhoumo.*

At the time of violent demolition, five people lived in the household: he and his wife, his elder and younger sisters, and his daughter. His wife died shortly after the demolition as a result of ill health, as did his elder sister. His younger sister also fell ill and passed away after returning from an overseas trip. He described his own plight as one of a "broken family and members deceased" (家破人亡) with very little hope left.

He tried petitioning the Shanghai municipal government and the Central Petition Bureau and had also spoken to officials from the central inspection team (中央巡视组), but all to no avail. He was not giving up his fight, however. When I asked him why, he explained:

> I cannot swallow (咽不下这口气) the fact that my property was taken away from me violently and illegally. This is nothing but state plundering (掠夺) of private properties.[7]

He continued, "The compensation offered was simply unsatisfactory. We had a two-story five-bedroom Western-style stone gate house (石库门小洋房), which I inherited from my father, who bought it in the 1930s for 100 taels of gold. We used to live a comfortable life. My father was a merchant in the Republican era. I have older and younger brothers living in Hong Kong, Australia, and the United

States. The government wants to move us to the faraway Minhang District, which is totally inaccessible. Something like this would never happen in the US, would it?"[8]

Suddenly, he pointed to the Rolex watch on his wrist. Beaming with pride, he said to me, "My brother in Hong Kong bought me this as he knows I like collecting watches!" His watch collection, together with all his other possessions, were violently taken away on that fateful day. Together with 13 other families—out of more than 1,000 households in the neighborhood that underwent demolition—they refused to budge and have become nail households, holding up the project until this day, more than a decade after the attempted demolition first took place.

Chen's story was a middle-class family's struggle against the perceived illegal state plunder of private properties. Monetary compensation was a secondary concern. Their primary grievance was often the violent seizure of their legitimate property rights. Collective action is, more frequently than not, however, framed in terms of inadequate compensation simply because it is more politically palatable than a rights frame.[9]

This case speaks to the agency problem when outsourcing yields excess violence. Undisciplined violence resulting from agent callousness can cost the principal who orders the actions, in this case a real estate developer. The death of the old couple not only attracted widespread attention, but it also hardened the resolve of the remaining residents to hold steadfast against what they perceived as "barbaric demolition" (野蛮拆迁) and the lack of consideration for people's lives.

A new national ordinance promulgated in 2011 declared illegal any demolition conducted by real estate companies. The National Ordinance Regulating Demolitions on State-Owned Land has been credited for the decline since then in extremely violent demolition, such as those involving arson (C. Wang 2012). To a large extent, this case represented what Shanghai was like in the heyday of urbanization in the 2000s in its mad rush to become a world-class metropolitan city and the host of the 2010 World Expo, an international event intended to mark its "arrival" on world stage. Demolition in Shanghai in the most recent past has been conducted using nonviolent strategies, involving the state's mobilization of brokers (see Chapters 5 and 6).

4.2.2 Violent Land Grab and Housing Demolition in a Kunming Village in 2011

In the summer of 2012, I visited Flower Village, located east of Dian Lake (滇池) in Kunming, Yunnan's provincial capital city.[10] At that time Flower Village was the last of the five villages to be razed to make space for the giant 1.46 million square-meter (15.7 million square-foot) Luosiwan International Trade City, modeled after the well-known Yiwu commodity market in Zhejiang province. With 2.6 billion RMB worth of investment, it was positioned to be a key trading hub serving Southeast Asia and beyond.

This massive construction project had been criticized, however, for procedural illegalities from the outset, including land auction collusion between the provincial government and Zhonghao, a large real estate company alleged to have purchased land at only a fraction of the market rate (*Time Weekly* 2011). The project was a hallmark of Qiu He, the former deputy provincial Party secretary, who had an ambitious blueprint to develop Kunming. Qiu was eventually removed from office on corruption charges (Sina News 2015). Although collusion like this between government and private companies is not uncommon in China (J. Zhu 2012), this case was striking because of the sheer scale of capital involved.

Flower Village had 800 households. When the farmland was expropriated in 2003, the villagers were compensated at one third of the price paid by the real estate developer.[11] Their homestead (宅基地), or the land on which village residences stood, was bought off in 2010 for an international trade city project. According to publicly available records, the government sold the land to the developer for 1.8 million RMB/*mu* (4.0 million USD/hectare)[12] but paid villagers only 250,000 RMB/*mu* (562,500 USD/hectare)—a 720% difference between the selling and compensation prices![13] The elderly in the village are entitled to a monthly pension of 250 RMB (38 USD).

The price gap was not a major source of grievance, however. During my visit in 2012, some elderly villagers still lived in the old section, but most families had moved into blocks in the new section or "new village." Most families had built brand new five- to six-story shophouse blocks using the compensatory money and their life savings. Typically, they run small retail businesses on the ground floors, dwell on the first and second, and rent out the other units to migrant workers. Rental income and salaries as drivers, construction workers, and craftsmen were the predominant sources of villagers' income. Flower Village was not a subsistence village.

In fact, their long-standing grievance stemmed from the violence deployed by the local authority to intimidate them into compliance. Here is how my 76-year-old interviewee described his experience with violent demolition:

The first measure taken [by village authorities who were party to the demolition project] was cutting off water and electricity supplies to homes. Then, they sent thugs to spray-paint our houses with intimidating words: "If you refuse to move, the house will be bulldozed while you are asleep!" and "Those who don't vacate, watch out for your safety!"[14]

Both threats were carried out. Some villagers found their homes bulldozed in the middle of the night. Others were beaten:

> At night, they drove trucks through the paddies and farms, destroying our crops and vegetables, killed our poultry, and fed our dogs poison. They set fire to my courtyard, built with teak wood in the nineteenth century. Four generations of my family have lived in this traditional home. My life was spared only because I wasn't at home at the time.[15]

"Those of us who submitted a petition letter were particularly targeted. My eldest daughter, who was one of the petition organizers, was badly beaten by a bunch of thugs when she returned from work late at night. She was left unconscious," lamented another interviewee.[16]

"One fine day, we saw a bulldozer rolling into the village, closely followed by a bunch of thugs. After destroying our newly built village roads, the next target was to demolish the public toilets. But they were met by a group of brave villagers who formed a line and stood in front of the bulldozer, refusing to let it flatten public property"[17] (see Figure 4.2).

Demolition of public toilets is often intended to create an impression of a "dirty, chaotic, and inferior" (脏乱差) village. Once deemed unfit for human living conditions, the authorities can justify village demolition by declaring it a "village-in-a-city" (城中村), a term reserved for dilapidated and poor neighborhoods in need of refurbishment or demolition. Yet another routine tactic is to begin demolition work once a particular family had signed the agreement. This was intended to create chaos. In a village where half the households had signed and the other half had not, the village conditions would become imaginably chaotic, full of debris from partly demolished houses. The overall objective was to render the living space uninhabitable in order to push the remaining residents out.[18]

Villagers were also concerned with the potential harm posed by the massive construction on Dian Lake's ecosystem and its cultural heritage, particularly a 600-year-old Buddhist temple. During my field research, I spoke to a group of elderly volunteers taking turns guarding the temple 24/7 to ensure no covert demolition took place.[19]

The events took a radical turn when the government wanted to forcibly demolish the new shophouse blocks built merely two years earlier. Most families emptied their savings and invested all the compensation received in the new construction. Forcible demolition took the form of looting of villagers' shops in the new village by the "comprehensive law enforcement brigade" (综合执法大队), led personally by the township Party secretary himself.[20] The comprehensive law enforcers are quasistate security agents, who are largely temporary or contractual workers. Unlike TFH, they are uniform- and badge-wearing agents.

Figure 4.2 Sit-In by Flower Villagers to Prevent Demolition
Photo Credit: Zhu Xiaoyang.

Their nature is like *chengguan* in the cities, who can enforce the bylaws of various agencies from industry and commerce bureaus to environmental protection to food safety. The ambiguous scope of their functions and the contractual nature of their employment often result in extralegal and unprofessional behavior.

> To force villagers to move out of the new village, the government looted our shops, beat up the shop owners, and stole expensive items. You tell me, who is this urbanization for (这到底是谁的城市化)?[21]

Looting of the shops by township government-led enforcers of bylaws became the straw that broke the camel's back. For years, villagers had endured the thuggish intimidation and bodily harm inflicted on certain individuals on the front lines; however, looting and property destruction—carried out by the government leader and uniform-wearing quasistate agents—amounted to a fundamental disrespect for the villagers' property rights and dignity.

The looting incident led the villagers to stage a protest, or mass incident (群体性事件), and with ensuing property damage it came close to a riot (骚乱). Enraged villagers set fire to the bulldozer, which came to symbolize "evil urbanization" (妖魔的城市化). The 300 riot battalion members deployed by the municipal government to put down protesters were met with brick-throwing angry villagers. The village authority also hired 50 thugs, or unidentified assailants, to beat villagers. The ensuing casualties led to 30 injuries, including an individual who permanently lost vision, and the detainment of eight villagers with three given jail sentences for disrupting the social order.[22]

"To loot" (抢掠) is to rob and plunder, depriving villagers of their possessions by violently taking things away from them. The flagrant nature of violence in looting is quite distinct from the humdrum, thuggish physical violence done to properties and individuals; furthermore, looting is an overt repressive act in contrast to thuggish acts like beatings in dark alleys, which tend to be covert in their physical manifestation. Mundane thuggish violence on a prolonged basis had not pushed the villagers to organize themselves into collective action until the looting incident.

The mass incident marked the beginning of the villagers' sustained resistance against the local authority. They tried petitioning to the provincial and central governments, all to no avail. The villagers supported five representatives to form a committee, intended to replace the village government as an alternative governing body. Among the committee of five were 79-year-old Lo and 62-year-old Liu, who led the villagers' resistance. The committee raised funds to provide public goods to the village: it built sewerage to prevent flooding, renovated dilapidated schools, and imposed fines on trucks that carried heavy loads. Fines were then spent on road repairs, petition expenses, and medical expenses for the injured villagers in the riot. Other services included organized garbage pickup by volunteers and fireworks displays for Lunar New Year celebrations. Aside from official matters, such as marriage and death certificates and hukou registration, which required the village authority's official stamps, the five-member representative committee had taken over other aspects of village governance.[23]

The committee came about because the village authority was widely perceived to have lost credibility and legitimacy among the villagers after the looting. This crisis of political legitimacy was compounded by the village government's chronic fiscal deficits that incapacitated its provision of basic public goods and services, such as garbage removal and road repairs. Mention of the village authority conjured up an image of "a corrupt, fiscally starved, inept, and morally bankrupt local government with leaders who pay scant attention to the villagers' welfare."[24] Village elections were nothing but skullduggery; village cadre positions were bought (买官卖官),[25] and the incumbents attempted to bribe the villagers to vote for them in the previous election.[26]

The relationship between the village authority and local gangsters (黑社会) lay somewhere between clientelistic and captured per my field observation. It was clientelistic because the local authority permitted gangsters to run gambling illegally in makeshift half-demolished houses; the gangsters were also allowed to collect protection fees (保护费) from street vendors at the vibrant village night market. In return, the village authority could call upon the gangsters to intimidate villagers using their muscle power when it needed to implement everyday policies.[27] The ties between the local authority and gangsters also approximated capture. As the Flower Village authority suffered significant deficits in fiscal capacity and moral legitimacy, they had to rely on outsourced violence simply to perform day-to-day functions, ranging from collecting birth control fines to grabbing land and demolishing homes. This gave rise to the strong bargaining power of the gangsters, who could in turn dictate their terms to the village authority.

The head of the gangster ring was a local villager, but the roughnecks hired to beat villagers usually were from other nearby villages, not Flower Village. In the closely networked rural society, using physical violence against local villagers would be considerably more challenging because of the repercussions aimed at the perpetrators' families and reputations.[28] Sociologist David Cunningham has observed a similar use of outsider-insiders by the Ku Klux Klan in their acts of violence during the U.S. Civil Rights era.[29]

With official recognition the old folks' association (老年协会) provided the villagers with a legitimate platform to gather, coalesce, and discuss village affairs. A new village guest hall (新客堂) provided the physical space for villagers to meet and celebrate special occasions; however, the association, or guest hall, might not have been the mobilizing structure—in social movement terms—for the collective resistance (Lu and Tao 2017). The real conversation about village affairs and organizing resistance, as I had observed, took place in private homes. I had the opportunity to sit in on some of the meetings as an observer. Meaningful in-depth conversations about Flower Village's political future were held over tea, meals, and knitting and embroidery gatherings among elderly women. And the delicious and renowned Yunnan rice noodle (云南米线) was a constant draw and staple to sustain the author during field research.

Recruitment of villagers for the resistance was enabled by the preexisting networks in the village. Some joined while others did not, based on their occupations, family backgrounds, and personalities, giving rise to a unique set of incentives and constraints for each family. One of the activists was forced to quit the resistance—and his job—because he held a government position. He later ran a small dry-cleaning store in the new village. Like elsewhere in China, teachers and those who work for the government or depend on the state for a means of living are generally reluctant to be involved in resistance. When the government attempts to pressure the community, they are also usually among the first to be targeted. This practice is central to the strategy known as punishment by implication, examined in detail in Chapter 5 (see section 5.4.1). By no means unique to China, the strategy of imposing pressure on dependents of the state has emerged in research on electoral coercion in Russia and Eastern Europe. The most vulnerable among the targeted are typically teachers and civil servants (Mares and Young 2019).

Often, nonviolent coercive strategy takes place alongside violent repression with no logical sequential pattern because much depends on pressure points available to the local authority. Although outsourcing violence yields greater efficiency, it is also riskier in the event of serious casualties. MTM takes time because negotiations and persuasion may become protracted, but it is significantly less costly in the likelihood of inviting backlash or organized resistance as the case studies in Chapter 6 will illustrate.

The activists in Flower Village were, by and large, former peasants, retirees, and small business-owners whose incomes were not dependent on the state; so, the local authorities were left without that leverage. The committee of five that led the resistance were villagers aged 55 and older, not particularly well educated and without previous experience in organizing civil resistance.[30] Nevertheless, I had come to admire their tenacity, righteousness, bravery, and social adroitness. I genuinely admired these people for putting into practice the knowledge that took those of us in the Ivory Tower years to master.

This case speaks to the utility of TFH and the theoretical foundation of everyday repression in several ways. Comparing the longstanding thuggish violence villagers have endured with the specific event that became the last straw is instructive. Thuggish violence had been hackneyed, citizen responses largely muted. What pushed the villagers over the edge was the looting of their shops; more importantly, this was carried out by government-led village enforcers of bylaws. Illegitimate violence perpetrated by the quasistate security agent and endorsed by the government leader—instead of everyday repression—drove people's wrath to participate in the mass incident and sustained the resistance over time.

Outsourcing repression to TFH, however, is not without cost. The village authority hired thugs to administer policies and execute actions for which they lacked the capacity or could not legitimately execute. Outsourced violence might be an expedient strategy to augment coercive capacity, but it resulted in usurpation of state autonomy when the thugs they hired grew too powerful. The village authority had to engage in a patron-client relationship with the thugs, consequently ceding some of its power. In exchange for borrowed force in implementing challenging everyday policies, the village authority allowed the gangsters to collect protection fees and run illegal gambling dens.

4.2.3 Massive Demolition and Violent Land Grabs in Zhengzhou in the Mid-2010s

I conducted field research in Zhengzhou, Henan's provincial capital, during the summer of 2014. Under the mayoral leadership of Wu Tianjun (吴天君), another ambitious political leader like Kunming's Qiu He, urbanization in Zhengzhou was put in fast gear with colossal demolition and relocation efforts. By no means was this a phenomenon exclusive to one or two localities in the city. I visited a total of nine villages within Zhengzhou's first, second, and third ring roads as well as the outermost national expressways—and none was spared the top-down frantic demolition and construction.[31]

Wu, a Henan native, accumulated remarkable "political achievements" when Xinxiang, a city north of Zhengzhou, was transformed into a "modern city" under his leadership. He brought the same political priorities to Zhengzhou when he was promoted to mayor. Nicknamed *yizhimei* (一指没), he had a reputation for destroying a village once he pointed his finger at it (Y. Shi 2020). During the 12th Five-Year Plan (2011-2015), he extended demolition plans to 627 villages—a rate of approximately 100 villages a year—which affected 17.5 million residents (iFeng News 2017). Although rural villages populated the city's outer edges, villages-in-the-city, home to many migrant workers, occupied the city center. This period has been described as the era of the Demolition Movement (拆迁运动) in Zhengzhou. Under Wu's leadership in the first half of 2010s, rapid economic growth in Zhengzhou was driven by massive construction activities; however, land-related social conflicts also reached a record high during his tenure with the lives of many families disrupted and destroyed and some lives lost in the process of demolition. When he fell from grace in 2016 because of corruption charges closely tied to his dealings with real estate developers, Zhengzhou residents hoisted banners and celebrated with fireworks (iFeng News 2017)!

4.2.3.1 Demolition Revolution (拆迁革命) in Sunzi Village
In the summer of 2014, I walked around Sunzi Village,[32] a *chengzhongcun* located to the north of Zhengzhou's Third Ring Road. Like most other villages-in-the-city, Sunzi was bustling with street vendors selling tasty barbecued meat on skewers, counterfeit Gucci, and other inexpensive consumer goods; yet Sunzi was also different from other villages-in-the-city I had visited. Many banners were tied to utility poles, displayed across the streets in the village. The banners

that came in two colors—red and white—were usually displayed as a set, though they articulated competing messages between the villagers and the authorities.

Sunzi Village was home to 800 households with 1,200 local residents and around 60,000 migrant workers. In the 1990s, Sunzi underwent unified village planning that replaced farmhouses with two-story brick shop houses. One family owned a unit, four units made up a block, and eight units made up a group. Zhengzhou's economy took off in the 2000s, attracting many migrant workers from rural villages in Henan and other provinces. Sunzi residents decided to demolish the existing two-story shop houses and replaced them with new seven-story blocks. Some migrant workers took up manufacturing jobs at Foxconn and other factories in Zhengzhou, while others made a living with microenterprising activities.

Not unlike the case in Flower Village, some Sunzi families emptied their savings and others borrowed money from banks and relatives to invest in new housing because they saw lucrative rental income potential. Each family usually occupied one or two lower floors and rented out the rest to migrant workers. Rental income was indeed handsome, averaging about an annual 150,000 RMB per family. During my visit in 2014, one fifth of the families had yet to repay their housing loans, and half of them had yet to recoup their investments.

As I had observed, the villagers were generally not highly educated; many had been farmers some two decades earlier. Despite the less-than-sanitary living conditions and ungentrified spaces in the village-in-the-city, residents there led an affluent lifestyle not dissimilar to those in the Zhengzhou city center. Most families were microentrepreneurs and landlords. Their relatively leisurely lifestyle had allowed my conversations with them to take place in their homes, shop fronts, and tea shops.

The villagers had held longstanding grievances against the village authority, leading to a lack of trust between the parties. They spoke about the village authority's use of thugs to threaten the personal safety of individuals who refused to vacate and profiting from the illegal sale of collective-owned land.[33] Before the proposed demolition took place, the village authority called for a mass meeting (群众大会), an assembly that had not been held for eight years, to purportedly seek villagers' approval for the demolition project. Up to 90 percent of them voted against it.[34] Despite the overwhelming disapproval, the authority launched an intense propaganda campaign aimed at changing people's minds. It put out posters and red banners declaring the project's benefits all over the village. Some of the red banners read:

"Renovation of the village is a people's project."

"Village renovation does not only stimulate the economy; it also enriches the people!"

"Ensure smooth implementation of the demolition project in order to protect villagers' legitimate rights!"

Evidently, the last slogan was intended to put the cart before the horse.

In an act of defiant retaliation, the villagers launched their own campaign. Couched in Maoist revolutionary language, the villagers invoked the words of Chairman Mao and Comrade Deng Xiaoping to support their demolition revolution (拆迁革命). Walking around the village, I spotted poles supporting the national flag erected by families and intended to signal their loyalty to the CCP and the country. Bearing the hallmarks of "rightful resistance" (O'Brien and Li 2006), the villagers countered the government's propaganda with their own banners, proclaiming:

"Chairman Mao, we love you!"

"Our great country needs you, our dear Chairman Mao!"

Both sides engaged in a zealous banner war (see Figure 4.3). Apparently intimidated by the villagers during the day, the red team of village cadres carried out their furtive actions of tying red banners to utility poles only in the middle of the night. On the following days, the white team of villagers retaliated by placing their white banners adjacent to the red ones with contrary messages, the banners of both teams littering the streets of Sunzi Village.

Although the white team's objective was to unite all the villagers, including the renter-migrant workers, the red team aimed at dividing those who had signed the demolition agreement and those who had not. The migrant workers became a crucial bargaining chip to win over in the propaganda war because their departure would impose substantial financial losses for the villagers and convince more to agree to demolition. The red team's propaganda tactic resembles the united front strategy of isolating the enemy by coalescing the vast majority and bringing them to the side of revolution, a central feature of Mao's Mass Line politics, further examined in Chapter 5 (see section 5.3.2). Mass mobilization via a banner war was not the only strategy deployed by the local authority. Given the rather effective counteracting strategy of the white team, the local authority decided it had to use violence to intimidate villagers into compliance.

On September 19, 2012, the village Party secretary marched in with a village patrol (巡防队员) wearing red armbands. Village patrollers do not wear uniforms because they are not part of the formal coercive force, but they are considered quasistate security agents often asked to assist the police in maintaining order. Following closely behind was a group of muscular and fierce-looking men wearing dark green camouflage military outfits (迷彩服); they ripped down all

Figure 4.3 Red vs. White Banner War in Sunzi Village, Zhengzhou
Photo credit: Radio Free Asia.

the white banners as they marched into the village. They were evidently part of the village leader's team intending to "create trouble."

The anger of the villagers over the destruction of their banners led to clashes with the village patrollers and thugs in camouflage, resulting in scores of injuries. Among the injured were two elderly female villagers aged 65 and 78, who required hospitalization. In Chinese society, any physical harm to the elderly—weak and defenseless—is considered disrespectful of traditions and is highly scorned.

Village patrols used no physical force themselves, but they were the accomplices who watched as the thugs used illegal force against villagers. A village patroller grabbed the cellphone of a villager trying to photograph the incident. More importantly, the village leader was also on the scene throughout the process. The entire incident from the beginning to the end was vividly captured by the CCTV cameras installed by village shop owners,[35] but when the villagers demanded to know who was responsible for injuring the elderly women, the village leader scapegoated a member of the village patrol.

This case provides several important lessons about everyday repression and the benefits and costs of outsourcing violence. First, as was the case elsewhere in China, banal violence committed by TFH was not uncommon in Sunzi Village, yet everyday thuggish violence had not caused the villagers to revolt against the authority until the violent clashes occurred between the village leader-led thugs and villagers. Second, thugs in camouflage had allowed the village authority to deny any direct responsibility. Even though the clashes were captured on video, the elusive nature of TFH had enabled plausible deniability and evasion of accountability. Third, undisciplined violence exercised by TFH, above and beyond what was necessary to complete the task, made them a liability for the local authority that hired them. The injuries of the elderly women generated widespread sympathy and cost the local authority its reputation.

Fourth, and most importantly, the official endorsement of illegitimate thuggish violence with the village leader-led team of thugs dealt the most severe blow to state authority. Given the village authority's long-standing poor governance record and tarnished reputation to begin with, injuries to the elderly gave rise to the emotions of anger and moral indignation, aptly captured by the phrase "the people's war" (民之殇), which hardened the villagers' resolve to fight on.[36] When I visited Sunzi Village in 2014, some two years after the bloody incident, the villagers still had only disdain for the local authority and were unwilling to budge on relocation. On each anniversary of the incident, the villagers gathered and marched to the village office to demand an official apology.[37] This pattern of officially endorsed illegitimate violence played out again in the village of Lunar, described next.

4.2.3.2 The People vs. District Government in Lunar Village
On March 5, 2014, close to a thousand elderly citizens from Lunar staged a sit-in to block the major roads to the village, the largest *chengzhongcun* in Zhengzhou.[38] They hoisted banners declaring their strong resistance to demolition. The largest of its kind in Zhengzhou, Lunar was home to 15,000 local villagers and ten times more migrant workers—150,000. Much like in Sunzi, migrant workers, who were renting residential and business spaces, constituted the single largest source of income for the local villagers.

Having 60 to 80-year-olds occupy the frontline in a protest to protect the demonstrators behind them, is not an uncommon strategy. What differentiated this case from that of Sunzi was the mastermind behind the demolition—the district government—rather than the village authority. The district government that oversees townships is two levels above the village authority in the administrative hierarchy. Village cadres, in fact, sided with the villagers but were coerced by the district government to comply with demolition orders. The villagers who held government positions, such as teachers and civil servants, were also forced to sign relocation papers.[39] Having witnessed and heard what happened in neighboring villages, Lunar villagers knew the government's promise of resettled housing had to be highly uncertain.[40] In an act of defiance, villagers put up posters challenging the legality of the demolition project and scolding the government: "Don't you dare cheat the people!" (see Figure 4.4).

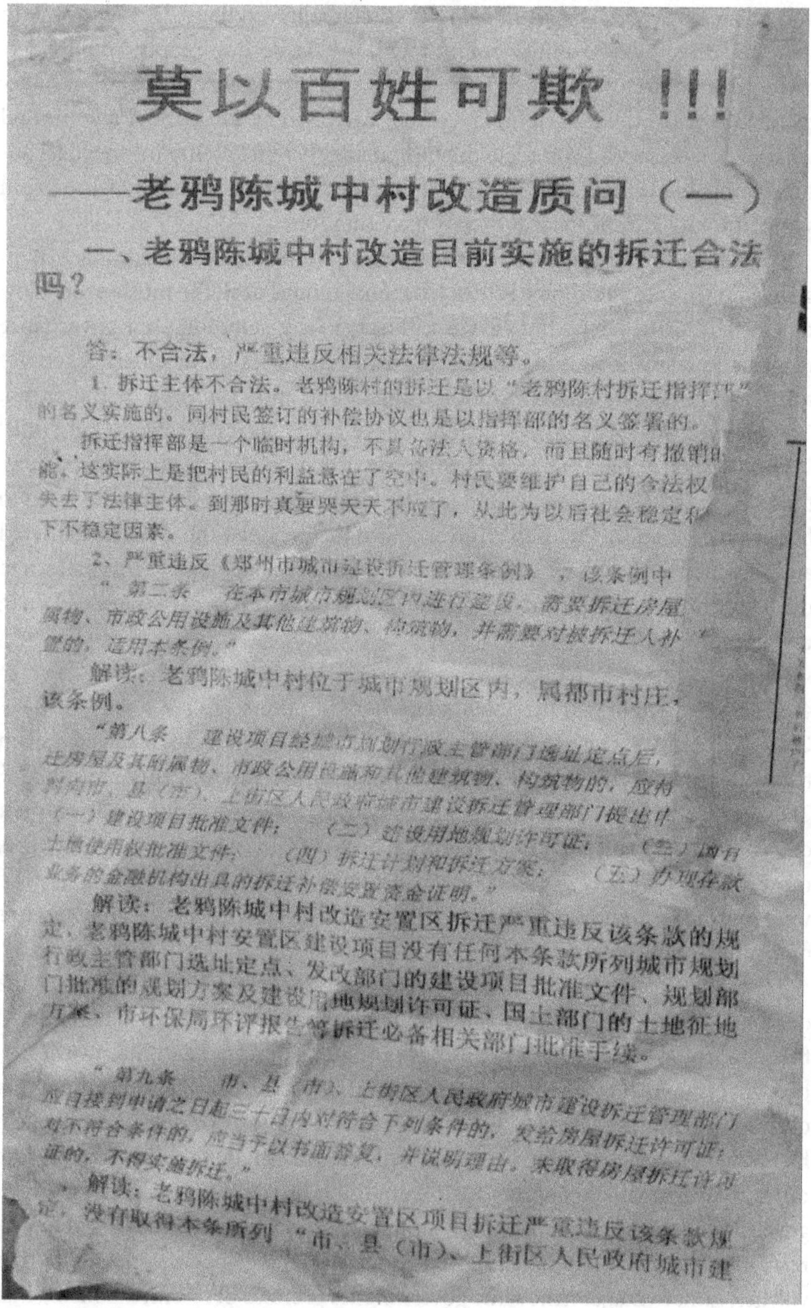

Figure 4.4 Villagers' Poster Titled, "Don't You Dare Cheat the People!!!
(莫以百姓可欺)" in Lunar Village, Zhengzhou

Photo credit: Author.

The villagers were actually more enraged by the district government's attempt to cut off their most significant income source—rental income—by chasing away migrant workers with the use of thugs and gangsters to harass them when they returned to the village late at night. One villager stated:

> We rely on rental income to survive. If the authority failed to compensate us properly, it's like cutting off our lifeline (命根子)! Naturally, we will be forced to revolt.[41]

This is evidently another case of "villagers forced by the officials to revolt" (官逼民反), a lesson in governance well rehearsed in Chinese history. In the name of demolition work, the district authority created a roadblock that impeded some villagers from holding a funeral procession. That angered some families. On March 5, 2014, according to an eyewitness account, a district Party secretary led a gang of wooden club-bearing thugs into the village as bulldozers drove in to tear down buildings—without the villagers' consent (wickedonna2 2014). With the elderly on the front line acting as "shields," villagers collectively prevented the bulldozers from driving in. Many climbed on top of the vehicles and smashed the glass windows. Nearly a thousand villagers joined the act of resistance by blocking the streets and damaging a bulldozer as a symbol of their defiance (Radio Free Asia 2014). The mass incident that ensued included clashes between both sides with some villagers being badly beaten by the thugs.

An incident of social unrest of this scale taking place in a provincial capital was far from commonplace. Most land-related resistance involved up to hundreds of protestors in the city outskirts or rural areas, yet Lunar Village is not typical of most demolition cases. With 150,000 migrant workers, it is Zhengzhou's largest *chengzhongcun* by far. This demolition project was apparently so important to the city's urbanization that the district government decided to become directly involved. When an authority two administrative levels above what they ordinarily encountered imposed a top-down order, the villagers faced headwinds in their struggle for justice.

Regular thuggish violence might be humdrum, but violence directly commanded by a district Party secretary was far from it; instead, it was an affront to the people's dignity. When a district leader swooped in, he and the bulldozers ready to take down homes could not be mistaken for representing anything but the state. Illegitimate violence led by a formal government leader, in addition to the enormity of financial assets at risk, was more than sufficient to push the elderly to risk their lives by placing themselves on the front line. Much like in Flower Village and elsewhere, the act of destroying bulldozers had become a potent symbol of the people's struggle against the state's encroachment on their property rights—all in the name of the supposed urbanization-led development!

The use of outsourced thuggish violence to force demolition was not restricted to Sunzi or Lunar Village by any means. The neighboring Lao village had suffered a similar fate. When Lao villagers were in negotiations with the local authority regarding an impending demolition plan in 2011, the village Party secretary and leader brought in a team of 300 unidentified safety helmeted gangsters armed with wooden clubs to attack villagers' homes in the middle of the night (Radio Free Asia 2011).[42] During my field research, I observed similar violent forced demolitions in Ran, Zhai, Zhu, and Xin districts in Zhengzhou municipality.[43]

Placed within the broader theoretical framework, outsourcing violence maybe an efficient and expedient strategy for taking down homes swiftly, but the severe casualties came with a price for Wu Tianjun, the mastermind behind Zhengzhou's urbanization campaign and the municipality's former Party secretary. That price was his job. The pretense for plausible deniability and evasion of accountability offered by TFH works so long as the violence is banal and mundane—hence the term "everyday repression." In addition, when TFH are exclusively deployed, tracing the principal who hires the violent agents is difficult. On the contrary, when government officials lead a gang of thugs to beat citizens, their copresence negates one of the key benefits of outsourcing violence, that is, to shrug off responsibility.

4.3 Intercepting Petitioners and Black Jails

TFH are widely engaged by local governments to intercept (截访) petitioners traveling to lodge complaints with the central authority in Beijing.[44] China's petition (上访) system allows citizens to seek redress from the central authorities for the corruption and misconduct of local officials. Although the central government intends for the system to serve as a gauge of local misconduct, paradoxically it also sets targets to ensure that the number of petitions does not spin out of control. The system punishes local officials, jeopardizing their career prospects, when they fail to maintain social stability, which the central government measures in part by the number of petitions registered. This encourages local officials to prevent disgruntled citizens from lodging complaints in Beijing (Lianjiang Li, Liu, and O'Brien 2012; Liao and Tsai 2019).

A village Party secretary in Henan Province explained to me:

Petitions are a headache for grassroots governments. Some villagers are not only stubborn but also impossible to please. You give them an inch; they want a yard from you. They think, "Babies who cry out loud get the mother's milk [会哭的婴儿有奶喝]!"[45]

"Babies who cry out loud get the mother's milk" is a popular adage in Chinese society that means the more noise one makes (闹), the more one is able to attract attention and sympathy from the authorities. When I asked the Party secretary whether the village authority had intercepted petitioners, he told me:

> Of course, we had to intercept petitioners. It will deal a big blow to our work performance if we let the disgruntled lodge petitions in Beijing. I have intercepted petitioners myself, by traveling to Beijing or ambushing them at the train station. But it is easier when we hire some Beijing-based security companies to do it for us now.

The use of TFH to intercept petitioners demonstrates the benefits and costs of outsourcing violence. Although local governments could send their own officials to do the job, doing so is not cost-efficient, given transport and lodging expenses. Thus, they often outsource the dirty jobs to private security companies that hire gangsters. Privately operated "black jails," in the form of secluded private residences, guesthouses, and basement apartments, allow the state to distance itself from such illegitimate actions. The makeshift nature of these facilities and the muzzling of abused victims make accountability tracing onerous (Amnesty International 2012); however, undisciplined and excessive violence can also be an issue given widespread reports of rape and death of petitioners while in custody.[46]

A male petitioner I interviewed in Beijing recounted:

> I was held captive in an underground room in a guesthouse for an extended period. I was routinely tortured with cigarette burns and was forced to write confessions about falsely accusing local government officials of wrongdoing.[47]

A female petitioner in Beijing told me:

> I was stripped naked and held captive in a windowless room with no light for 30 days. I was delivered one meal per day. The thugs kicked me in my stomach and poured cold water over me.[48]

The proliferation of black jails in the 2000s was a response to the rising number of petitioners flooding into Beijing following the abolition of the custody and repatriation centers in 2003 that authorities used to hold petitioners. Hence, black jails operated by TFH provide a means of augmenting local state coercive capacity to enable it to deal with growing numbers of discontented citizens. The fluctuating demand for private interceptors, that is, TFH, surges during politically sensitive periods, such as when the two sessions of the National People's Congress and the Chinese People's Political Consultative Conference meet, but ebbs at other times, justifying the preference for on-demand nonstate agents.

4.4 Conclusion

In this chapter, detailed case-study evidence shed light on the nuances of the empirical findings in Chapter 3. Quantitative evidence in the previous chapter supports the argument that TFH is a lower-cost repressive measure: when exclusively deployed, it minimizes the likelihood of collective resistance and violent backlash. As violent agents, they offer the benefit of plausible deniability to the principal-local authority if the nature of violence remains low-intensity and pedestrian, if their actions produce no serious casualties or large-scale confrontations, and if no overt government complicity is involved.

The case studies in this chapter are used to interpret the complex implications when one or more of these conditions is relaxed, for example, when outsourced violence resulted in deaths, such as in the 2005 Shanghai French Concession case; or led to large-scale confrontations, such as in the 2011 Kunming Dian Lake village case and in Zhengzhou throughout the 2010s; or was explicitly endorsed by government leaders, such as in Flower Village, Kunming or in Sunzi Village, Zhengzhou. Under these exceptional circumstances, TFH deployed undisciplined violence in excess of what was necessary to get the job done, and their illegitimate violence became a liability to the hiring authority. Worse still, when government officials appeared alongside these illegitimate agents in the events and were seen to endorse the use of illegal and illegitimate violence against local villagers or residents, the pretense for plausible deniability and accountability evasion evaporated. Official reprimand of government leaders happens infrequently in China, but occurrence of violent cases like these on a frequent basis will subject them to investigation and removal from office; such was the fates of the former Party Secretary Qiu He in Kunming and former Mayor Wu Tianjun in Zhengzhou.

In addition, the case of Flower Village, Kunming, illustrates the detrimental consequence for governance when the relationship between the local government and TFH transformed into one of patron-client from that of principal-agent. In other words, when TFH grow so powerful that the hiring authority can no longer control their behaviour but must cede a certain degree of power to them, the power of the hiring authority is at risk for usurpation. In that case, outsourcing violence escalates risk for the biting of the hands that once did the feeding.

These cases, involving large-scale protests or sustained resistance, are exceptional—rather than ordinary—a point that should be underscored. In other words, the case studies here do not represent a random sample of TFH at work.[49] Taken together, palpable benefits as well as the costs of engaging TFH are apparent. Over time the use of outsourced violence has declined, but the nonviolent strategies taking its place and rising to increased prominence is the subject of Chapters 5 and 6.

5

Networks of State Infrastructural Power

Brokerage, State Penetration, and Mobilization

> Some don't know they are brokering because they think of their activity as gossip, sociability, information-gathering, favor-giving, or mutual aid. (McAdam, Tarrow, and Tilly 2001)

In the 19th century the Qing dynasty extended its reach into rural society and conducted its administration through a system of dual brokerage. Prasenjit Duara has shown that the entrepreneurial brokers constituted the first type—the state-appointed agents who charged a fee to collect taxes on behalf of the state that appointed them. Collection of tax revenues was critical for the survival of the Qing dynasty because it was increasingly strained by internal rebellion and foreign invasion (Duara 1988, 42–57). These state-appointed brokers won prominence with the breakdown of the neighborhood surveillance *baojia* system. Once they assumed the tasks of urging tax payments, maintaining population registers, and reporting crimes and disputes, they also gained opportunities to abuse their power at the expense of rural citizens.

Abuse of power by entrepreneurial brokers eventually led to the emergence of the second type of brokerage, comprising the protective brokers who belonged to self-help associations that voluntarily organized communities to meet tax obligations. The intention was to safeguard community interests by bypassing predatory state-appointed brokers. Despite a lack of complete effectiveness in brokering between state and society, local communities considered the protective brokers to have legitimate authority, unlike the fee-collecting entrepreneurial brokers (Duara 1988, 42–57).

In this chapter I distinguish the types of brokers in contemporary China— political, social, and economic—according to the sources of their brokerage, their respective functions, and the nature and degree of legitimacy they command among the communities. Although political brokers, such as village and residents' committees, have received much attention in the existing literature (Read 2012; Tomba 2014), social and economic brokers have not. Political brokers derive their power from their state or quasistate status, and social brokers

Outsourcing Repression. Lynette H. Ong, Oxford University Press. © Oxford University Press 2022.
DOI: 10.1093/oso/9780197628768.003.0005

gain trust and command legitimacy because of the social capital they possess. The scope for economic brokerage stems from information asymmetry between state and society, which they help to bridge. Despite their position as nonstate agents, the Party–state can mobilize social brokers to further its ends.

Taken together, all these brokers are a part of the networks of infrastructural power that enable the state to govern more effectively, implement challenging policies, and resolve conflicts via proxy. Brokers who legitimate government actions help to lower the cost of repression. In this chapter I draw on field interview data, quantitative media-reported cases, and content analysis of government regulations to support these arguments.

China shows both continuity and discontinuity over time in the patterns of brokerage connecting the state and society. To varying degree, brokers help augment state power to penetrate society, mobilize, and govern more effectively. In the weak state of the late Qing period, the political brokers whom Duara called "entrepreneurial brokers" were appointed to collect taxes from the rural peasantry. Their predatory behavior led to self-organized social brokers (protective brokers) whose purpose was to conduct tax collection in order to ward off the political brokers. In the Maoist-era strong party building resulted in an army of brigade (village) cadres in rural society; serving as political brokers, they were an extension of the formal commune (township) governments. At the same time, the Maoist state was able to mobilize social brokers, namely volunteers and "activists" (积极分子), to work on state projects and participate in various political campaigns.

During the reform era political brokers have assumed greater agency, looking out for their own interests more than their counterparts in the Maoist period because of greater rent-seeking opportunities. Social brokers have risen in prominence since the early 2010s with the state's overwhelming emphasis on drawing on all societal forces (全方面社会力量) to maintain social stability. The growing gulf between state and society in an era when social stability is a high political priority led to the emergence of economic brokers, who can bring the two parties to negotiations and preclude social conflicts. Notably, brokers are largely nonviolent agents; violence is not a tool they use on a regular basis. Thus, TFH and brokers are conceptually distinct and by and large mutually exclusive.

5.1 Brokerage

Social science literature differentiates among different types of brokerage.[1] Political brokers can be party officials, individuals with party connections (Thachil 2014), or organizational brokers who represent their clients' collective interests outside political parties.[2] They facilitate clientelistic exchanges between political parties and voters (Auyero 2001; Stokes et al. 2013). They also identify clients' needs, distribute goods, and help monitor voter behavior. Political brokers tend to balance their rent-seeking interests with partisan or organizational interests (Stokes et al. 2013). Some citizens are forced to rely on political brokers in their role as gatekeepers for access to scarce resources, which provide them with considerable power or opportunities to accumulate power (Stovel and Shaw 2012, 147).

Economic brokers emerge when two transactional parties suffer from information asymmetry or do not know the fair price to offer or accept for a transaction. They are private individuals who have access to political insiders and who have gained the trust of both the state and society. The economic broker mediates across gaps in information and reduces the friction of economic transactions. Rewarded financially if a deal is successfully sealed (Stovel and Shaw 2012, 147), economic brokers are like market makers, who appear in transactions with asymmetry that needs to be bridged. For a price, brokers absorb the friction (Stovel and Shaw 2012, 147).[3]

Social brokers derive their power from their standing in the community, allowing them to cast influence over the constituency. They use their positions in elite social structures that maintain relations with different cleavages within the community to facilitate negotiations between rival factions. Their capacity to mobilize resources to bring about particular outcomes is another source of their power (Gould 1989).

In the context of contemporary China, social brokers can be leaders in three types of social networks. The first is formal civil society, or nongovernmental organizations (NGOs), such as labor unions and women's organizations. NGOs that are officially registered are under the tight control of the state and function largely as the Party-state's mass organizations (Mertha 2008; Teets 2014). Some of these registered NGOs have branches in local communities with leaders as standing members of the local village or urban residential governing structure. The second type is unofficial civil society, comprising unregistered groups not sanctioned by the state—often because they refuse to be regulated or prefer to remain autonomous and separate from the state (Gallagher 2004, 420). Examples include underground labor organizations (Fu 2018) as well as lineage and temple associations in rural areas (Tsai 2007).[4] Leaders from both registered and unregistered groups can become powerful social brokers by virtue of their positions in the organizations over which they preside and the members they are able to mobilize. They have received much deserved attention in the existing literature (Berman 1997; Mattingly 2019).

Instead, I emphasize the third type of social brokers, who have received little attention but command considerable power in the community. These are individuals who lead no registered or unregistered organizations in the community, yet they possess considerable social capital because of their longstanding devoted service to the community, often on a voluntary basis. Their selfless devotion and volunteerism make them part of the local elite social structure, providing them with access to various social networks despite their nonleadership positions. Hence, they can use their social capital to mobilize the masses, facilitate negotiations, and resolve community conflicts. They can be viewed of as the social nexus of power.[5]

Social capital amassed by social and—to a lesser extent—political brokers is premised on communal trust, which fosters interpersonal trust among community members. As opposed to civic trust, which is cultivated by citizens' associations that promote stable democracy,[6] communal trust is interpersonal trust shared among neighbors, villagers, schoolmates, coworkers, hometowners, and kinship group members (W. Tang 2016, 66). As an authoritarian society with Confucian traditions and a socialist legacy that once promoted communal work and living, China has been an outlier in cross-country studies that show a positive association between social capital and the robustness of democracy.[7] What distinguishes China from other countries is that its high interpersonal trust captures the communal trust that promotes regime legitimacy—rather than the civic trust typically found in Western democracies that pits the civil society against the state (Newton 1999; Newton and Norris 2000). Brokers, particularly social brokers, are in turn the key nodes of communal trust in Chinese society.

How does brokerage change the dynamics of the state–society relationship? Brokers help to connect the state with society by drawing on their political status, social capital, or economic power. They can represent the interests of the state, society, or both, and they can also look out for their own interests. This chapter takes the concept of brokerage one step further to illuminate how they augment the state's capacity to mobilize and control society.

5.2 Brokers in Chinese Society

In a comparative study of the effects of brokerage on poor citizens' access to public services, the numerous and fragmented roadside brokers in India who haggle with citizens are found to be more democratically accountable than the state-centered and hierarchical brokers in Indonesia (Berenschot 2019). In another study, higher competition among brokers and less social hierarchy have improved poor clients' access to public services in the Indian states of Gujarat and Bihar (Berenschot and Bagchi 2019). Do the brokers in China bear greater resemblance to those in India or Indonesia? As I will illustrate in this section, brokers in Chinese society have unique characteristics of their own according

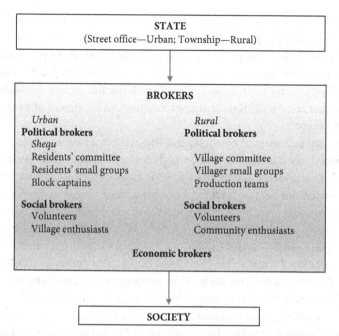

Figure 5.1 Brokered State-Society Relationship in China

to their role. By and large, however, they are more likely to act on behalf of the state—rather than for the society.

Figure 5.1 maps the contour of the brokered state-society relationship in China. Street-level offices (街道办事处) and township governments (乡镇政府) are the lowest level of grassroots government. Between the state and society lies a layer of brokers who help to connect them. Brokers can be categorized as political brokers, social brokers, and economic brokers according to the source of their brokerage, their functions, and the degree of trust and legitimacy they command in society. Together, they help the state to penetrate and better govern society.

5.2.1 Political Brokers

Political brokers, who derive their brokerage power from state appointment, are perceived as grassroots state agents or quasistate agents. I call them political brokers because of their agency: they can act on behalf of the state or society or look out for their own interests.[8] Granted, in comparison to other broker types, they are more likely to represent the state's interests and perform state functions of information collection, surveillance, and repression. Their repressive functions have been illustrated in the quantitative data and case study evidence in Chapters 3 and 4. Because their power stems from the state, their reception by citizens by nature differs from that of social brokers, who command social capital in the communities.

5.2.1.1 *Shequ*, Residents' Committees, Residents' Small Groups, and Block Captains

In the post-1949 Maoist era, the work unit (单位) became the basic unit of social control in urban China. Because urban residents worked for state-owned enterprises, the *danwei* system and work compounds became the key node of state-society interactions and through which the Party-state extended its control over urban society. Created in 1954, residents' committees (RCs; 居民委员会) report to street-level offices (街道办事处), the lowest level of urban government.

Despite a lack of status at a formal level of government, RC leaders serve as the state's designated liaisons, working closely with both state officials and citizens, hence their political brokerage role. Since the 2000s RCs have been increasingly merged into "communities" or *shequ* (社区; *CCTV News* 2000), which consist of a few thousand urban households, led by a nominally elected director and several vice directors.[9] In Southern China urban communities that were transformed from villages have more pluralistic governance structures, but the RCs still largely serve the interests of the state rather than residents (B. Tang 2015; S. W. Wong, Tang, and Liu 2019). Neighborhood institutions that act as transmission belts between the state and society are by no means unique to China.[10] Nevertheless, China stands out because the state still maintains tight control over these institutions, whereas other countries have allowed for more voluntary participation and grassroots initiatives (Whyte and Parish 1984).

Shequ and RCs are officially nonstate grassroots mass organizations, and residents' small groups (居民小组) and block captains (门楼长) constitute the foot soldiers of the state's expansive machinery. Together with the RCs, block captains oversee the basic functions of collecting information and surveillance. On some occasions they are also responsible for administering tedious and at times unpopular policies, such as household registration, population control, and low-income welfare.[11] They are urban political brokers because of the agency they possess. For instance, in the provision of low-income welfare or *dibao* (低保), they can provide assistance to needy residents or help the state maintain social stability by actively identifying residents who may turn into troublemakers even though they do not meet welfare criteria (Pan 2020).

Some RCs also serve a policing function. Recent research has documented the role of the RCs in grid management (网格化管理) as a bottom-up mechanism for local governments to monitor potential causes of social unrest (B.

Tang 2019). My own field research in Chengdu suggests that grid management has largely been outsourced to third parties—with the RCs playing a supporting role in connecting the third party and local residents.[12] The penetration and functions of *shequ* vary considerably among cities.[13] In the ethnic minority region of Xinjiang, *shequ* is not only a provider of social welfare, but it also extends heavy-handed controls over the policing of local residents—sometimes with dubious effectiveness (Tynen 2019). In a rapidly modernizing China, the supply of grassroots political brokers who are paid minuscule for their time-consuming and tedious work should not be taken for granted.

A *shequ* leader in Chengdu told me:[14]

> Nowadays it is not easy to find people to fill the job of *jumin xiaozuzhang* or *menlouzhang* (resident's small group leaders or block captains) because it does not pay an official salary, other than a 100–200 RMB year-end bonus. Registering people, filling out forms, collecting information, and keeping track of the movement of people in the community make for a tedious job. Thus, those willing to do it tend to be older, in their 60s or 70s and not involved in any money-making economic activities.

5.2.1.2 Village Committees, Villagers' Small Groups, and Production Team Leaders

During the revolutionary period the Party recruited poor peasants and those at the margins of the society to become Party cadres. When the commune system was established in the early 1950s, brigade (village) leaders became the nexus between the state and rural society (J. Wang 2017); however, the foundation of the intermediating roles was distinctively different from that of the gentry. Grassroots Party leaders in Maoist China who came from poor class backgrounds owed their social status to the Party and were judged on the basis of their political loyalty. In comparison, the gentry's status was not conferred upon by the state, and their own public contributions were the yardstick for performance (Lifeng Li 2014, 225).

The CCP constructed "the brigade (village) as the basic unit" of taxation and mobilization (C. Liu 2007, 98). Much like urban communities and neighborhood committees, its role in connecting the state and the peasantry remains crucial.[15] During the Maoist period rural cadres served two functions: extracting rural surplus and mobilizing the peasants for economic construction.[16] In brokerage terms, brigade leaders in Mao's times were political brokers who had some—but not a great deal of—agency. They were brokers, not state agents, because brigades were not a formal level of government. Major government decisions were made at the commune (township)-level.

Decollectivization did not remove the political brokerage role of the rural cadres, but with increased autonomy it made the cadre-peasant relationship more clientelist (Oi 1989).[17] Rural tax reform in the mid-1990s deprived village cadres of resources to which they were previously entitled; thereafter they were driven by self-interest (Kung, Cai, and Sun 2009). The central government ended the extraction aimed at rural society after the abolition of the agricultural tax in 2013. Since the 2000s, however, another form of exploitation began with the fervent development of land requisition. As the indispensable political broker between the state and farmers, village cadres enjoy some agency in requisitions of collectively owned land (Chen, 2015; Deng, O'Brien, and Zhang, 2020). At the same time, land acquisitions have been a major cause of corruption among rural cadres as well as a leading source of rural unrest because some of them try to personally profit from land transactions. This was the case in Wukan village, where protests erupted against predatory government behavior in illegal land transactions (CECC 2017). Corrupt land deals demonstrate the agency of political brokers because they can pursue their own self-interests at the expense of the state and society. As I demonstrated with the case studies in Chapter 4, village officials had so much personal stake in urbanization projects that they were willing to lead a gang of thugs to conduct illegal demolition. Since 2019, as part of Xi's campaign to root out corruption at the grassroots, village committees have been integrated into the Party with possible implication for their role as state agents.[18]

5.2.2 Social Brokers

The power of social brokers stems from the social capital they possess in the community, drawn from years of relationships, or *guanxi* (关系), they have cultivated with members and the attendant emotional ties or *ganqing* (感情). Unlike political brokers, who inherit their power from the state, social brokers earn the trust of the community by being long-term residents, volunteering themselves enthusiastically to help members in times of difficulties and for weddings, funerals, and other auspicious and inauspicious occasions (红白喜事). The earned trust bestows upon them a degree of social legitimacy among the citizenry. In many respects, they represent the activists in the civil "acquaintance society" (熟人社会).

Guanxi consists of instrumental and emotional dimensions as anthropological literature has informed.[19] Equipped with *guanxi*, social brokers fulfill their objectives through emotional mobilization, either by firing up people's enthusiasm, trapping them with guilt, or coercing them with peer pressure and psychological stress in order to achieve certain instrumental objectives. Undergirding these strategies are thick emotional ties, or *ganqing*, which they share with community members. In other words, *guanxi*, *ganqing*, and emotional mobilization are the essential tools and mechanisms through which social brokers exercise their power.

The power of social brokers takes on a narrower definition than Duara's "cultural nexus of power." To Duara, the nexus includes both hierarchical organizations, such as religious and merchant associations, and networks of informal relations, such as kinship and lineage ties (1988, 5). Per my conceptualization, brokers are individuals rather than institutions or organizations. Social brokers are individuals who are part of social networks rather than specific lineage or religious groups. Social brokers whom the state mobilizes can—but need not— be the heads of lineage temples or kinship groups.[20] Holding positions of power in those informal institutions would certainly help to mobilize their members, yet having access to the informal ties or *guanxi* is often sufficient to mobilize members of the networks via emotional mobilization.

5.2.2.1 Volunteers and Village or Community Enthusiasts

The foot soldiers of *shequ*, residents' committees, and village committees are largely volunteers or community enthusiasts. They are likely to be Party members; if no Party affiliation, they are likely to be retired cadres or former state-owned enterprise workers. Party membership or previous affiliation with state units serves as signals for their "political correctness," if not loyalty to the Party, which is necessary for the state to entrust them with mobilization work.

When I asked what makes a good volunteer, a *shequ* leader in Chengdu pinpointed the following personal traits:[21]

> The individual should command social prestige or respect (威望) among community members; and being a long-term resident in the community would definitely help. One's political correctness indicated by Party membership or former affiliation with Party or state-related organizations is critical. The other desirable traits, namely leadership ability, persuasiveness, and enthusiasm, are cultivatable.

He added, "however, an individual with no demonstrable record of Party loyalty would not be trusted with the position of resident small group leader."

This differentiates a political broker from a social broker. A resident small group leader (居民小组长) who is a political broker must possess a demonstrable record of Party loyalty, whereas a volunteer to whom the state entrusts the task of mass mobilization need not have Party membership. In other words, the threshold for "redness" demonstration is lower for social brokers, distinguishing them from the Party's rank and file (Koss 2018).

As with political brokers, finding young and economically active candidates to become social brokers can be challenging. If not driven by economic incentives, social brokers must have other motivations. Some community enthusiasts are motivated by a genuine sense of serving the people, if not serving the Party.

"We have enthusiastic retirees in their 60s and early 70s who are always looking for opportunities to contribute to the community. Instead of sitting at home, they would rather go out to interact with community members. Being a volunteer gives one a say or right to speak (话语权), and with that, social status (社会地位) in the community could be acquired," said the *shequ* leader in Chengdu.[22]

He added, "Financial incentives matter little for them; but these intangible benefits of social status could be attractive for retirees who used to be decision makers in their *danwei*. After retirement, they want to continue to feel they are still useful (有用), and hence opportunities to volunteer give them a sense of achievement (成就感)."

5.2.2.2 The Chaoyang Masses (朝阳群众)

The forgoing profile of volunteers befits the red armband-wearing Chaoyang Masses, who see the opportunities to serve as a genuine badge of honor.[23] Albeit less ideologically charged, they are close cousins of the activists in the Mao-era, who were willing to devote themselves to the Party (Perry 2002b). They exemplify the social brokers who help the state to maintain surveillance of their local communities by drawing on their social capital and familiarity with local residents. Long-term residents of the communities, they can easily discern outsiders or intruders. Brokering between the state and society, they provide the state—particularly the police—with valuable information about local communities, without which it would be costly for the state to acquire. Chaoyang volunteers receive financial rewards for clues provided to the police,[24] but they are fundamentally motivated by a desire to serve the community and a sense of responsibility in maintaining neighborhood security (L. Zhang 2017).

5.2.3 Economic Brokers

Economic brokers are private individuals who reduce information asymmetry by absorbing friction in transactions for a price. Imagine a situation where the government and a citizen fail to reach an agreement on a demolition. This creates opportunities for a for-profit broker to act as an intermediary. Economic brokers are individuals who have inside information and who can gain the trust of both the government and citizens. Social capital or *guanxi* pertinent to the functioning of social brokers may be useful but not essential in this context because economic brokers can gain trust by other means like demonstrating their past track records in facilitating similar transactions. An economic broker is not party to the transactions. When citizen Zhang tries to bribe a government official to issue his driver's license, he is not a broker; but if Zhang goes through a third party, Li, who gets what he wants by bribing an official and extracts a fee out of it, Li then becomes an economic broker. Duara's entrepreneurial brokers, who functioned like tax farmers taking a cut of taxes collected from peasants, are an example of economic brokers.

In Chapter 6 I draw on my field research in Shanghai to cover the so-called *huangniu*, or economic brokers, in housing demolition. *Huangniu* is a pejorative term to describe middlemen in China in general. In the current context, they identify households wanting to bargain for more compensation and match them with demolition officers willing to be bribed to provide the disgruntled with additional compensation. *Huangniu* take a cut from the increased payment given upon successful completion of the transaction. Other examples of economic brokers in contemporary Chinese society include lawyers and former court officials who try to secure better court outcomes by helping the appellants bribe sitting judges (Ling Li 2018), as well as professional petitioners (职业上访专业户) who help aggrieved households lodge petitions and secure favorable outcomes (Tian 2010).

5.3 Brokered State–Society Relationship

5.3.1 How Brokers Connect State and Society

Figure 5.2 shows how the three types of brokers connect state and society in various ways. Political brokers are appointed by the state, and their power comes from state authority. Acting as transmission belts to relay the state's directives to society, they are known as state or quasistate agents in the existing literature (Read 2012; J. Wang 2012). Social brokers derive their power from the social capital they possess in the community or the *guanxi* they have with community members. This confers them with trust from community members and legitimacy independent of the state; however, in China, the Party-state can mobilize social brokers to work on its behalf either through ideology, community spirit, or material incentives. Economic brokers are nonstate agents who arise from opportunities to profit from reducing friction in transactions between the state and society. The state gains by working with economic brokers who can seal an agreement with citizens, precluding them from taking their grievances to the streets.

Together, they form the state's networks of infrastructural power. To varying degrees, trust and legitimacy are crucial to the functioning of all three broker

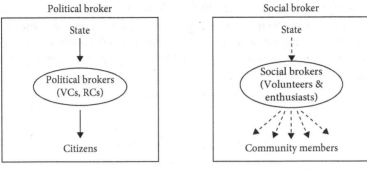

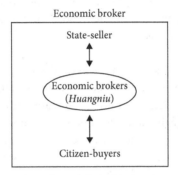

Figure 5.2 Schematic Representation of Brokerages

types. Political brokers need trust and legitimacy the least because their state or quasistate status allows them to enforce by fiat if necessary. Economic brokers require a degree sufficient to attract both parties to want to work with them, but ultimately financial payoffs are the motivators of the parties. Trust is indispensable to social brokers because a lack of trust can lead relationships or *guanxi* to break down and social capital to melt away, leaving them without brokerage power and value to the state. In terms of brokerage strategy, as indicated in Figure 5.2, political brokers impose from the top down, social brokers mobilize the community, and economic brokers facilitate bargaining.

Political, social, and economic brokers are analytically distinct categories; however, in reality, overlap cannot be ruled out. A neighborhood committee member who is a political broker may have lived in the residential neighborhood for decades, enjoying social legitimacy, and thus could be considered a social broker. An economic broker cannot be a political broker by default because the former must have a nonstate identity to be trusted by citizens to bargain with the state on their behalf. A social broker can become an economic broker, but because the two brokerage types are based on different premises—the former conducts mass mobilization for the state's pursuits, and the latter is motivated by profits—it is unlikely that the same individuals will wear two brokerage hats at the same time.

In the next section I delve deeper into specific functions of the brokers.

5.3.2   Functions of Brokers

What are the functions of brokers? What roles do they play in MTM? How do they help the state control society? The discussion here pertains to their functions in housing demolition and community renovation projects, but some of it also applies to their everyday tasks.

5.3.2.1   Intimate and Personal Information Collection

A basic function of brokers is to collect information on the villagers or residents affected by demolition. They begin by enumerating residents who have a local *hukou*—a household registration document—which may not be a straightforward process, particularly in the cities. Some may reside in the area, but others may not because they have married and left or attend school elsewhere; furthermore, marrying into families, daughters-in-law who may or may not have their *hukou* included can often complicate this process.

The enumeration performed here, however, far surpasses making citizens legible (Scott 1998) or counting numbers of heads (数人头) in the community. It also pertains to acquiring personal and intimate information about families, in terms of their employment, finances, relationships, and personalities, all of which are potential entry points into negotiations or nodes on which the state can apply coercive pressure.[25] As informed by my interviewees, relevant employment information includes the following: who works for state-owned enterprises, who run their own private firms but rely on state contracts, and who is unemployed or looking for employment. Financial situations, such as who is more generous or penny-pinching in the family and who faces financial difficulties, are relevant considerations, too.[26] The case studies in Chapter 6 will illustrate that knowing a family member's financial conditions reveals the upper and lower bounds of what they are likely to accept, which is critical information in negotiations of compensation packages. State employees or those reliant on the government as a revenue source are most likely to be targeted by the state to agree to relocation as the case studies in Kunming and Zhengzhou in Chapter 4 have demonstrated.

Relationship information is arguably a family's most intimate data—and requires significant investment to obtain—but can also prove to be the most vital for the state. Who does or does not get along with whom in the family? Do the father and son have a good relationship? Are the husband and wife in a rocky marriage? What are the sources of conflicts in the family? And what are the existing family feuds?[27] These data about intrafamily relations are useful for the state in addressing disagreements among family members on relocation decisions that each family unit must make. Feuds create chasms into which the state can enter via brokers to lure members to the state's side—and alienate those who are against it. Case studies in Chapter 6 will illustrate how this process works.

Family members' personality traits could also serve important functions. Is the husband or wife the decision-maker in the family? Who is more pliable or stubborn? Who among the family members is more easily moved by emotions and relationships (重感情)? Who is more faithful or loyal to friends and who is more likely to return a favor (讲义气)?[28] These traits provide clues as to how and on whom the state can apply emotional mobilization, how psychological coercion will be received, and the extent to which it will successfully yield outcomes favorable to the state.

Collection of this nuanced information constitutes the basic building blocks of an often long and arduous process of negotiations preceding demolition. It is most aptly described as shrewdly finding out what cards your opponent holds in a game of poker (摸清底牌)! Thus, brokers or information collectors must be individuals who are deeply embedded within the local community and who can penetrate the families to gain intimate details known only to close relatives or family friends.

All three types of brokers can collect basic information, but considerable division of labor exists among them. Political brokers, such as block leaders, production team leaders, and residential or village committee members, are deployed first to collect the most basic data about families' employment and financial situations. More intimate information pertaining to relationships and personalities must be collected by social brokers if political brokers have insufficiently penetrated the community. Economic brokers would have to invest significantly to gain the trust needed for a family to provide such personal data, leaving them generally ill-suited to such tasks. Social brokers, therefore, have a distinct advantage over the other two types in this function.

5.3.2.2 Mobilizing Vehicle for the State

The two key mechanisms through which MTM is carried out are the invocation of ideology and emotional mobilization, both of which have varied in their intensity throughout periods of Chinese history since 1949.

Ideology as Motivational Force

During the Maoist period mass campaigns fundamentally involved ideology, whether to fire people's enthusiasm to exceed Great Britain or surpass the United States in the Great Leap Forward or to root out all enemies of the masses during the Land Reform. When ideology was invoked to mobilize the masses, political and social brokers played their part in addition to or by drawing on propaganda, slogans, "big character posters," and revolutionary songs. The galvanizing effect of ideology, however, significantly declined in the post-Mao era.

Emotional Mobilization

With clever invocation of ideology and morality, the Maoist state was able to mobilize the masses by performing emotion work or thought work (思想工作) on the people (Perry 2002b). The Party systematized emotion work as part of a conscious strategy of psychological engineering. Such thought work was conducted during "struggle meetings," rituals of "speaking bitterness" (诉苦), and small group meetings (Y. Chen 1986; Lifton 1956; Teiwes 1993) with shrewdly constructed themes of victimization, redemption, and emancipation (Y. Liu 2010, 330). The strategy of emotional mobilization had been applied to numerous campaigns, including the Land Reform of the early 1950s, the Anti-Rightist campaign, the Four Clean-Ups Movement, and the Cultural Revolution.[29]

Another related strategy is the Party's united front tactic, the purpose of which is to "isolate the enemy by winning the vast majority to the side of revolution" (Van Slyke 1967, 3). This strategy underscored Mao's adroitness in creating social cleavages to rally popular political involvement in his campaigns and to bolster the regime's popular legitimacy (Perry 2007, 10). In recent years, the CCP has also allegedly used the strategy to influence Chinese residing outside China (Joske 2020). The precondition to creating cleavages is to identify sources of tension and then intensify them so that the Party can exploit them to further its own agenda. During the Land Reform, class divisions and often arbitrary labels of "peasants" vs. "landlords" were created to allow the state to pit one group against the other. Those labelled "rich peasants," "landlords," and "antirevolutionaries" became the imagined common enemies of the "poor peasants" and targets of anger venting. Thus, the seeds of lasting social conflicts were sown.

In Chapter 6 I will illustrate that the mobilizational capacity of social brokers stems from their ability to draw on their social capital in the form of neighbourly relationships and to expend it as a currency in the local community. The network of ties allows them to deploy emotional mobilization, that is, to provoke feelings of guilt, sympathy, and camaraderie among community members. In contrast, political brokers, whose power comes from the state, are automatically perceived as siding with the government in conflict situations and thus less suitable or effective in conducting emotional mobilization. In both the Maoist and contemporary eras, political and social brokers would likely draw on different resources to carry out emotional mobilization (see Section 5.4).

5.3.2.3 Conflict Manufacturing, Mediation, and Resolution

Brokers are as capable of manufacturing conflicts between two parties as they are mediating them. George Simmel argues that brokerage is the "sociological significance of the third element" or "The Triad." The three elements are the impartial third party's capacity to mediate conflict and restore harmony; the third party who benefits from the two parties' ongoing conflict, sometimes by pitting one side against another; and the third party who "intentionally produces conflict in order to gain a dominating position" (Simmel 1950).

These seemingly contradictory characteristics of brokers are amply demonstrated in the case study of *zigaiwei* in Chapter 6. By setting up self-reform committees in communities slated for demolition, the government has essentially transformed the nature of conflict from what once occurred between the state and society (because negotiations were conducted by government officials) to what occurs between society and society. In the new arrangement, those who desire a demolition organize themselves to persuade others—with brokers leading and facilitating the process.

The government incentivizes the first group of the willing with material rewards. As it works out, the first group often accuses the second of putting their own interests ahead of the communities while the second alleges the first of committing the "tyranny of the majority," imposing their wishes on others.[30] With facilitation and assistance from brokers, the state can manufacture conflicts between groups that ultimately allow it to legitimately implement an unpopular policy in the name of "community interests" or "democratic interests." In Chapter 6 I will argue that brokers become indispensable in the process.

The converse is just as true; brokers also play an indispensable role in mediating conflicts, as Chapter 6 will demonstrate. They allow the state to penetrate familial units to resolve family feuds preventing the members from signing demolition agreements. Mediation is often a state-preferred means of conflict resolution because it bypasses formal institutions like the court and lowers the cost of dispute settlement; however, mediation outcomes may not always favor the citizens involved because they are realized on the basis of emotional coercion and the pressure imposed upon those citizens.

5.3.2.4 Legitimating Vehicle for State Actions

In urbanization projects, mass mobilization involves mobilizing a willing majority to coax, persuade, or coerce the minority until the entire community gives their consent to relocate. This is often promoted as a "democratic" practice because demolition begins only when the entire community has consented and the wishes of the masses are fully respected, yet behind-the-scenes arm-twisting and psychological pressure, though invisible, are substantively coercive. Unlike violent repression, which leaves physical injuries as evidence, these seemingly nonviolent strategies have arguably longer-lasting impact on the victims than brute violence does, even though the acts may not be perceived as repression.

These nonviolent strategies are, however, part of the harmonious demolition (和谐拆迁) campaign promoted by the central government to address the rise in violence associated with land grabs and housing demolitions in the 2010s. The case study on the self-reform renovation committee in Chapter 6 demonstrates the Chengdu government's efforts to improve its own image after a controversial self-immolation case. When brokers who possess social capital among community members conduct mass mobilization, they become legitimating vehicles for the government's policy, obviating the need to deploy violence, which in turn makes it a harmonious (or nonviolent) demolition. Economic brokers also contribute to the "harmonious" outcome; rather than legitimating state actions, they pacify economic grievances and forestall any unruly street protests that might arise.

5.3.2.5 Legitimate State Repression to Induce Compliance

Legitimation of state repression by social brokers induces compliance. This may appear oxymoronic because repression by its very nature implies coercion imposed against the will of the masses, yet by mobilizing social brokers, who enjoy trust derived from social capital, the state can carry out repressive acts—viewed legitimate—by the citizenry. This involves a two-step process: first, the state mobilizes the brokers to work for its interests; and second, the brokers mobilize the masses to comply with the state's directives drawing on their own social networks. This role befits social brokers more than other types of intermediaries. The legitimacy of political brokers is inherently nonsocial or noncivil in nature because of their state or quasistate status. The impressive Party-state's institutions, which have received much attention in the existing literature,[31] may be effective in carrying out bureaucratic functions of tax collection or fee imposition, but they do not exactly allow for legitimation of state repression. When consent has to be coercively enforced or extracted, often resulting in social contention or loss of state legitimacy, social brokers who can adroitly manipulate social relations offer a distinctive advantage over political brokers or party cadres.

5.4 Government Agents and Brokers in Demolitions: Distribution, Strategies, and Citizen Responses

A range of government agents and brokers are involved in demolition work (see Figure 5.3). Local governments, comprising county governments (县政府),

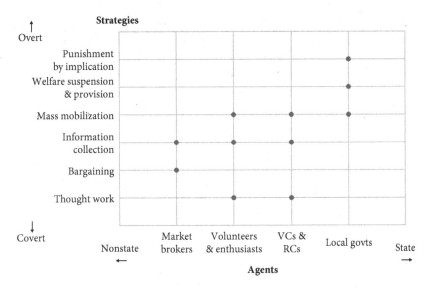

Figure 5.3 Agents vs. Strategies in Demolition

urban street offices (街道办事处), and rural township governments (乡镇政府), are involved in issuing instructions to government agencies and grassroots cadres. They have the power to impose punishment by implication and terminate or suspend jobs and social welfare to coerce citizens into desirable behavior. Village or residents' committee (VCs and RCs) members, who serve as the political brokers, are involved in mass mobilization, thought work, and information collection. Volunteers and community enthusiasts, or the social brokers, such as aunties' demolition teams,[32] similarly take part in mass mobilization, thought work, and information collection. Economic or market brokers are involved in bargaining and information collection.

Some differences in the functions of political brokers (VCs and RCs) and social brokers (volunteers and community enthusiasts) are notable even though they are more likely to complement rather than substitute for each other. Regarding information collection, VCs and RCs collect formal household and financial data, namely those enumerating the population; whereas volunteers and enthusiasts focus on more intimate data about family relationships and personality traits. When VCs and RCs carry out mass mobilization, they are likely to invoke the Party's ideology and the need to put the community's interests above oneself. In contrast, volunteers and other social brokers draw on their *guanxi* with community members and invoke *ganqing*—instead of ideology—making them more adept at emotional mobilization.

Moving down the Y-axis of Figure 5.3 shows that state strategies become less overt, more covert, and less explicitly coercive. Even though information collection and thought work (strategies at the lower end of the Y-axis) can contravene the wishes of citizens, they are often framed in a specific cultural context that makes them legitimate—hence acceptable—with a high likelihood of eliciting compliance. As we move from right to left on the X-axis, state agents are replaced by quasistate and nonstate agents. Moving toward the left, government agents and grassroots officials give way to volunteers and community enthusiasts, whose authority stems not from their formal power but from social capital accumulated over time, and to market brokers, who source their power from the ability to draw two parties closer. Drawing on a media-sourced demolition event dataset, I will test and discuss the results of the relationships between agents and strategies posited in Figure 5.3 in section 5.4.2 (results are reported in Tables 5.3 and 5.4).

5.4.1 State Strategies: Positive and Negative Inducements and Persuasion

State strategies can be divided into positive inducements (carrots), negative inducements (sticks), and persuasion through thought work.

5.4.1.1 Negative Inducements: *Lianzuo*, State Employment Termination, *Hukou*, Pensions, and Tax Audits

Lianzuo (连坐), a collective punishment system, has its origins in *zhulian* (株连), a similar mutual surveillance system, which first emerged in the Spring and Autumn Period (771-476 BCE) and the Warring States Period (475-221 BCE). The Qin Dynasty (221-208 BCE) adopted the *lianzuo* system and included family members, neighbors, and co-officials as targets who could be implicated in collective punishments.[33] If a family member learned of the intention of another member of the household to commit a major crime but failed to stop or report it, the responsibility fell on the entire family (Z. Liang 2002, 25). This was a system designed not only to punish major crimes but also to preempt their occurrence (Posner 1983; W. Zhang and Deng 2003). At the heart of collective punishment is the notion of collectivism that still permeates contemporary Chinese society and the official governance culture.[34] From the state's perspective, organizing society into collective units facilitates social control (Y. Huang 2006, 512). Collectivism emphasizes the group identities of the Chinese citizenry—extended family, kinship or clanship network, neighborhood, school, or university—which provide their members with recognition and mutual protection.

The 2004 Jiahe incident in Hunan illustrates the pernicious impact on society of punishment by implication. The Jiahe county government wanted to build a large-scale trade city (商贸城), expected to contribute taxes to the county's meager revenue base. Despite the project's commercial nature, the Jiahe government insisted on its public-interest dimension and put real estate developers in charge of the demolition project.

This grand trade city project involved 189 *mu* of land (31 acres) and affected the livelihood of 1,100 families. The county government mobilized more than 7,000 people and numerous government bureaucracies to assure that land requisitions occurred according to schedule. The government required *all* county officials to sign agreements related to land requisitions concerning their families and relatives. Failure to do so would result in the suspension of government positions. Government officials were also instructed to guarantee no petition, disruption, or foot-dragging; failure to comply could be met with job termination or transfer (Luo 2004).

Punishment by implication seriously tore apart the fabric of Jiahe society, resulting in acrimonious relationships among societal groups and among family members. It led to tensions between fathers and sons with adult children forging their parents' signatures to meet government deadlines. Husbands and wives were forced to file divorces in order not to implicate each other. Brothers became enemies (Luo 2004). The sheer number of people negatively affected in this project eventually caught the attention of the central government. A half-dozen county leaders were investigated and punished (C. Wang 2018b). Although the Jiahe Incident might be one of the most serious cases of its kind, smaller-scale incidents of punishment by implication still take place across China (see quantitative data in section 5.4.2).

Those dependent upon state employment, namely Party cadres, civil servants, and teachers, are usually the first to be targeted. Local governments may not threaten them directly with job termination, but the highly state-dependent nature of their main income sources gives the authorities leverage over them according to a Shanghai resident undergoing demolition.[35] They are usually among the first few families to part with their land or properties. If nail households have any family members holding government positions, they are likely to become targets as pressure points on their recalcitrant relatives according to the manager of a demolition company in Shanghai, who spoke with me.[36]

This goes to the heart of what Deng and O'Brien (2013) called "relational repression"; however, I emphasize that the practice is not just any type of relational coercion. It reflects the state's adeptness at singling out individuals over whom it can exert influence and maximize the pressure put on their relatives. This form of coercion is not entirely new from a comparative perspective. The literature on electoral coercion provides evidence of the regular use of negative inducements, such as suspensions of state pensions, by competitive authoritarian regimes to pressure civil servants into changing their voting behavior (Mares and Young 2019). Community Party secretaries in Chengdu told me that *hukou*, a residency status in China that provides qualification for local school admission, housing, and a range of other social welfare, is a crucial stick that local governments use against recalcitrant citizens.[37] To be clear, the social benefits that come with one's *hukou* status are carrots, but threats to withdraw the benefits turn them into sticks.

Another negative inducement regularly imposed on private firms is tax audits. The fact that the internationally renowned Chinese dissident Ai Weiwei has been subject to government tax audit (Jacobs 2012b) suggests the Party-state still has leverage over private entities that are supposedly independent of the state. If found guilty of tax evasion, private enterprises and private sector workers can be sentenced, a punishment at least as effective as termination of state employment. This was a common occurrence in an urban village in Guangzhou City, where I conducted field research in 2017. In Guangzhou, where many urban residents run their own businesses, tax audits are regularly used against citizens refusing to comply with demolition orders according to a villager who spoke with me.[38] Tax evasion—like skeletons in the closet—is pervasive in China: in order to stay profitable, almost every company must evade taxes (C. Zhang 2019). Thus, this strategy is particularly effective for punishing private firms.

5.4.1.2 Positive Inducements: Material Incentives and "Carrot-Shaped Sticks"

If a state can employ sticks to punish citizens, it is just as capable of offering carrots to induce desirable behavior, provided it has sufficient resources to do so. In contemporary Chinese society, where overt sticks are increasingly censured, local authorities often extend carrots to gain desirable behavior instead. Carrots can be, for instance, financial handouts to pacify the discontented, in what the sociologist Ching Kwan Lee calls "buying stability" (C. K. Lee and Zhang 2013).

Given the collectivist nature of Chinese society, this strategy is most effective if authorities offer carrots to a select group of people to mobilize them to influence the behavior of others. Essentially, this turns *lianzuo*, or punishment by implication, on its head. Instead of punishing residents for undesirable behavior, the state doles out sweet incentives to entice them to comply with state orders and holds up their exemplary behavior for others to emulate. An interviewee from a district government in Shanghai called this "reward by implication" ("连坐" 超点奖),[39] But it appears more like a "carrot-shaped stick" to me!

Demolition projects in a modern district of Shanghai require 90 percent consent from affected households before the project can move ahead. To swiftly gain households' consent, the district government rewarded all those who had signed the papers. When the consent rate rose by one percentage point, the existing signed parties would be rewarded with an additional 20,000 RMB in compensation, the section chief of a Shanghai housing management bureau informed me.[40] This impelled those who wanted to relocate to convince those who had yet to give their consent. In all likelihood, residents would persuade and exert psychological pressure on their relatives, coworkers, and neighbors. In this case, the enticement—instead of punishment—served as the motivating factor to convince others. Again, this has been touted by the local government as an innovative model to pursue urbanization while respecting the wishes of the people, purportedly a significant improvement over the previous punishment by implication strategy. This is, however, essentially the Maoist strategy of MTM, which has a crucial emotional dimension that I will illustrate in the following pages.

The use of carrots shows that in today's "harmonious society" (和谐社会), the Chinese state increasingly substitutes material rewards for penalties to pursue the same end of MTM. Another noteworthy aspect of reward by implication is the generally positive reception by citizens. Rejection of the policy means nonreward, which merely returns citizens to their original positions. Viewed in this light, it departs significantly from punishment by implication that results in job losses and community castigation in the event of noncompliance.

The suspension of state welfare, such as pensions and urban *hukou*, which is used as punishment to reprimand those who refuse to comply, can also be doled out as enticements (Chuang, 2014). The policy debate surrounding trading land for welfare (土地换社保) addresses the central livelihood question of the Chinese peasantry when confronted with a massive urbanization drive. After the local government's purchase of land from peasants, land is converted to state ownership and user rights are sold to private developers for extremely lucrative profits (S. Liu 2019). Offers of old-age pensions and urban *hukou* serve as enticements for peasants to give up their land. In addition, as Jennifer Pan (2020) has argued, urban low-income welfare subsidies (低保) are selectively disbursed to troublemakers in order to mute the public airing of their grievances.

5.4.1.3 Persuasion: Thought Work or Emotional Mobilization

Persuasion is another common strategy used to acquire citizen compliance. In Maoist terms, mobilizing the masses (群众动员) pertains to conducting thought work (思想工作) on the masses. In social movement parlance, thought work is the autocrat's use of emotional mobilization to acquire citizen compliance. This makes persuasion a tool of Chinese autocrats. To successfully persuade, the state must have the capacity to mobilize brokers, who can draw on their social capital to conduct emotional mobilization. I use case studies in Chapter 6 to examine the state's mobilization of brokers to that end.

5.4.2. Quantitative Data: Government Regulations and
Media-Sourced Data

This section presents and contrasts quantitative data on land taking and demolition collected from two separate sources. The first source comprises government regulations issued by central authorities and some of the municipalities where I have conducted field research, namely Shanghai, Chengdu, and Zhengzhou. Shanghai is a metropolitan coastal city; Chengdu, although a southwestern city, enjoys high income per capita; and Zhengzhou is an inland city with relatively lower income per capita. The variation among these municipalities offers some practical points of contrast. The second source includes land taking and demolition cases recorded in the media and by NGOs, reports filed by professional journalists, citizen journalists, and victims of property expropriations themselves. The media-sourced data is subject to potential biases discussed in Chapter 3 (section 3.3.1).

5.4.2.1 Content Analysis of Government Regulations
Table 5.1 summarizes the central and local government-issued regulations on land taking and demolition according to themes and subthemes.[41] Among the cities, Zhengzhou issued the fewest number of documents (32) to regulate land taking and demolition activities, and Shanghai issued the most (127). Issued by the central government as well as all three municipal governments, documents covering the maintenance of social stability have included proportionately greater attention to ex-post efforts than to preemptive ones; however, an increasing trend over time to adopt more preemptive measures was shown in Chapter 2. The central government placed the most emphasis on persuasion (59 percent), compared to sticks (punishment for unreasonable resistance; 41 percent), and carrots (positive incentives; 29 percent).[42] Persuasion is indicated by the use of key words in the regulations, urging officials to conduct thought work (思想工作) or "mass work" (群众工作). At the subnational level, however, all three municipalities appear to have emphasized the use of positive incentives and punishment over persuasion.

In terms of regional variation in temporal context, Figure 5.4 suggests the central government has placed more importance on persuasion since 2001, whereas the three municipalities have emphasized the use of rewards over punishments. Chengdu has placed a relatively stronger emphasis on persuasion than the other two municipalities.

Figure 5.5 indicates public hearings (听证会) have been the most common mode of citizen participation promoted by all governments since the 1980s; however, the central government has also emphasized the establishment of specific institutions to allow for citizen participation (自主改造 , 自主参与) and

Table 5.1 Central and Municipal Government-Issued Documents on Land Taking and Demolition: Themes and Subthemes

Category	Central Government	Shanghai	Chengdu	Zhengzhou
	No. (%)	No. (%)	No. (%)	No. (%)
*As a proportion of total documents issued by the city**				
Maintaining social stability	15 (33%)	20 (16%)	19 (31%)	9 (28%)
Means for promoting demolitions	17 (38%)	29 (23%)	30 (49%)	12 (38%)
Modes of citizen participation	17 (38%)	17 (13%)	16 (26%)	7 (22%)
Meeting citizens' demands	34 (76%)	49 (39%)	39 (64%)	17 (53%)
Total	45	127	61	32
*As a proportion of total documents in that category**				
Maintaining social stability				
Preemptive efforts	7 (47%)	10 (50%)	9 (47%)	6 (67%)
Expost efforts	12 (80%)	14 (70%)	17 (89%)	6 (67%)
Means for promoting demolitions				
Positive incentives	5 (29%)	24 (83%)	19 (63%)	9 (75%)
Punishment for unreasonable resistance	7 (41%)	10 (34%)	16 (53%)	8 (67%)
Persuasion	10 (59%)	3 (10%)	3 (10%)	0 (0%)
Modes of citizen participation				
Public hearing	13 (76%)	13 (76%)	12 (75%)	6 (86%)
Institutions for citizen participation	4 (24%)	0 (0%)	3 (19%)	1 (14%)
Majority consensus	1 (6%)	7 (41%)	9 (56%)	1 (14%)
Meeting citizens' demands				
Protect legal rights	33 (97%)	43 (88%)	38 (97%)	16 (94%)
Respond to grievances	11 (32%)	14 (29%)	14 (36%)	3 (18%)

*A document may contain several relevant keywords at the same time; hence the sub-categories add up to more than 100%.

Source: Author's analysis of data collected from *Beida Fabao*.

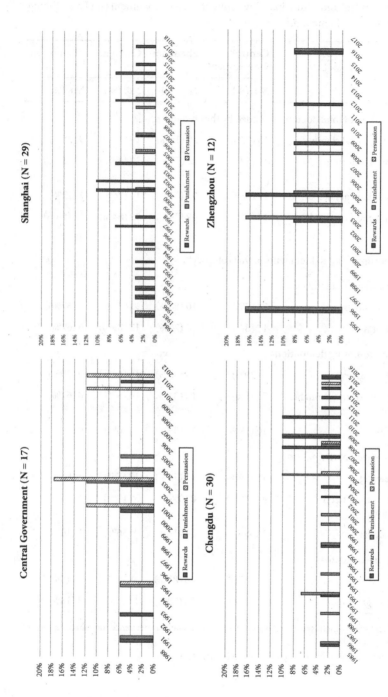

Figure 5.4 Modes of Promoting Land Taking and Demolition in Government-Issued Documents (as proportions of total documents in the category)

Source: Author's analysis of content in government regulations.

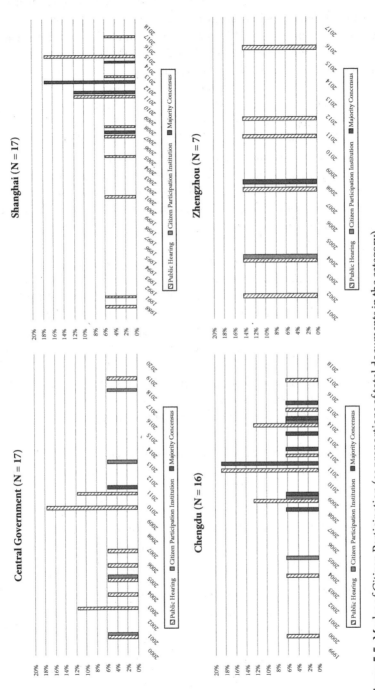

Figure 5.5 Modes of Citizen Participation (as proportions of total documents in the category)

Source: Author's analysis of content in government regulations.

"majority consensus" (多数群众意见) since the early 2010s. This appears to have lagged behind regional trends: majority consensus has attracted the attention of local authorities in Shanghai and Chengdu since the mid-2000s, and citizen participation institutions have appeared in Chengdu since the late 2000s, suggesting these modes are local innovations used to address and overcome the practical challenges regional authorities encountered in their work. The case studies in Chapter 6 will illustrate that they can be effective in galvanizing popular support for local government projects, and once proven successful, they are endorsed and promoted by the central government and emulated elsewhere in the country.

Government regulations may indicate the way authorities intend activities to be conducted, a point to be underscored; however, they may not necessarily reflect the reality on the ground. Empirical data suggest Zhengzhou had a significantly higher number of violent incidents than the other cities in the 2010s, a fact indiscernible from government regulations.

5.4.2.2 Media-Sourced Data Analysis

To investigate the relationship between agents and strategies discussed earlier, I collected media-reported demolition and land expropriation cases that involved the use of nonviolent strategies. The data sources are the same as for the violence data in Chapter 3 (section 3.3.1), and the methodology is discussed in Appendix C. A case was coded as collective punishment or *lianzuo* (连坐), rewards (奖励), thought work (思想工作), or welfare suspension (停止发放补贴) when those specific Chinese terms, or their equivalents, were explicitly mentioned in the articles. The coding in Tables 5.2, 5.3, and 5.4 is guided by expectations of agents and their respective functions as laid out in Figure 5.3.

Table 5.2 Rural vs. Urban Distribution of Nonviolent Strategies

	Rural (no. of cases; %)	Urban (no. of cases; %)	Total (no. of cases)
Collective punishment (*lianzuo*)	25 (40%)	37 (60%)	62
Rewards	13 (62%)	8 (38%)	21
Thought work	18 (46%)	21 (54%)	39
Welfare suspension	6 (55%)	5 (45%)	11
Miscellaneous	11 (42%)	15 (58%)	26
Total	73 (46%)	86 (54%)	159

Note: Here I adopt the official definition of "rural" and "urban." The former denotes incidents that happened in villages (村) and rural townships (乡); the latter indicates events occurring in city districts (区), prefectures (市), counties (县), and urban townships (镇).

Source: Author's collection of media-sourced data.

Table 5.3 Heatmap Distribution of Nonviolent Strategies by Agent Types[a]

Strategy	Govt officials	Grass govt	Grass nongovt	Thugs	Real estate developers	Others	Total number of strategies
Collective punishment	76%	10%	8%	3%	0%	3%	62
Welfare suspension	55%	0%	45%	0%	0%	0%	11
Thought work	41%	31%	26%	0%	0%	3%	39
Financial rewards	29%	19%	14%	5%	33%	0%	21
Misc	36%	21%	11%	25%	4%	4%	28

Count 0 10 20 30 40

Agent

[a]Numbers and percentages for this table can be found in Table D.9 in Appendix D.
Source: Author's collection of media-sourced data.

Table 5.4 Cases of Citizens' Compliance or Resistance Depending on Agent Strategies (percentages in parentheses)

	Collective punishment	Welfare suspension	Thought work	Financial rewards	Misc	Total
Compliance[a]	7 (13%)	0 (0%)	30 (79%)	14 (70%)	1 (4%)	52 (36%)
Resistance[b]	47 (87%)	10 (100%)	8 (21%)	6 (30%)	23 (96%)	94 (64%)
Total	54	10	38	20	24	146

Pearson's Chi-squared test. X-squared = 70.648, df = 5, p-value = 7.511e-14
Source: Author's collection of media-sourced data.
[a] Compliance is registered when no resistance is observed.
[b] Resistance includes an aggregate of categories, namely protest, legal mobilization, refused to relocate, call the police, harm the agents, petition, and other, such as publicizing the event on social media.

Given the much higher citizen compliance rate in response to nonviolent strategies, these cases are likely to be significantly underreported. To state the obvious, only conflicts are newsworthy. Separately, for cultural reasons, strategies like mass mobilization (群众工作) and thought work (思想工作) are considered part of everyday governance in China. Because they are generally considered noncoercive, they are deemed unworthy of news coverage. Underreporting can occur because of social acceptance of the strategies—and the compliant outcomes they bring about. Bearing these caveats in mind, I found a total of 159 cases in the 10-year period from 2008 to 2018.[43]

Table 5.2 shows that *lianzuo*, the illegal coercive strategy of putting pressure on residents who are also civil servants and government agents, was more likely to occur in urban than in rural areas. This likely reflects the dependency of urban residents on state-related employment and, therefore, their higher likelihood of being subject to *lianzuo*.[44] Financial rewards were twice as likely to be used in rural than in urban areas. Thought work and welfare suspension appeared to be equally likely to happen in urban and rural areas.

Table 5.3 is a heatmap distribution of nonviolent strategies by agent type. Darker shades show a higher frequency of the strategy used. The percentages in the boxes indicate the proportion of the total count of the strategy used by agent type. Repressive agents are divided into categories similar to the ones in the violence data covered in Chapter 3 (section 3.3):[45] government officials (including those from municipal and county governments, and all government departments), grassroots government officials (including street office, township government officials, and Party officials), grassroots nongovernment officials (including village committee members, community or neighborhood office officials, and all other village officials), thugs, and real estate developers. The grassroots nongovernment officials are essentially political brokers in my conception. Interestingly, media articles do not generally mention volunteers, community enthusiasts, or social brokers as repressive agents because they are inherently seen as part of the society. This leads to nonreporting of the roles of social brokers in this media dataset.

Consistent with my expectations as laid out in Figure 5.3, collective punishment was most likely to be deployed by governments officials (76 percent), followed by grassroots government officials (10 percent) because they have the formal prerogative to terminate state employment. Welfare suspension was most likely to be carried out by government officials and grassroots nongovernment officials or political brokers. Financial rewards were mostly given by real estate developers (33 percent) and government officials (29 percent).

Thought work was mostly conducted by governments officials (41 percent) and grassroots government officials (31 percent) and implemented by grassroots nongovernment officials or political brokers (26 percent). Again, media reports do not generally report thought work carried out by volunteers or social brokers because of the cultural nature of their identities.

Table 5.4 summarizes citizens' compliance or resistance given the strategies. Resistance was registered when citizens carried out one of these actions: appeal to media or social media, protest, petition, legal mobilization, refusal to relocate, call to the police, damage to properties, self-harm, or harm agent. Conversely, compliance was coded when none of these resisting acts was reportedly carried out.

Overall, we should expect cases that involved thought work and those resulting in the outcome of compliance to be systematically underestimated. Given these provisos, Chi-squared test suggests citizen responses are not unrelated to agent strategies. Collective punishment was met with citizen resistance in almost 90 percent of the cases. Welfare suspension also encountered a very high rate of resistance. Thought work and financial reward were most likely to yield compliance, in 79 percent and 70 percent of the cases, respectively. Notably, collective punishment was met with high resistance, but thought work, which includes use of psychological coercion, was met with little resistance.[46]

5.5 Conclusion: Brokerage and Networks of Infrastructural Power

Brokers allow the state to govern, implement challenging policies, and resolve conflicts via proxy. They become an extension of the state, part of its networks of infrastructural power, or the tentacles that penetrate society and influence citizen behavior. Social brokers derive their brokerage power from their *guanxi* networks, in contrast to that of political brokers, who have their power bestowed upon by the state. Hence, emotional mobilization conducted by social brokers is not generally perceived as coercion. Their social capital legitimates the repressive acts, of which political brokers are capable to a limited extent. This in turn lowers the cost of repression for the state. Despite being in analytically distinct categories, political and social brokers can sometimes overlap in reality with the same individuals appointed by the state and commanding social capital.

These arguments are supported by media-sourced data on nonviolent strategies. Although state officials used official coercive strategies, such as punishment by implication and welfare suspension, to acquire compliance, brokers mobilized the masses through emotional mobilization. These broker-mediated strategies are significantly more likely to result in compliance than resistance encountered by state agent-centered coercive tactics.

Content analysis of government documents suggests increased emphasis on persuasion and rewards at the expense of punishment as modes of extracting compliance. Institutions of majority consensus have been increasingly promoted by the central and local governments as a mode of citizen participation; however, I will argue in Chapter 6 that this amounts to the strategy of MTM, often resulting in tyranny of the masses. Drawing on field interview data, I will delve into the thick descriptive context in Chapter 6 to illustrate how *guanxi* facilitates emotional mobilization by brokers and the deployment of persuasion as a control instrument. I will also demonstrate the circumstances under which persuasion is unsuccessful when certain conditions are not satisfied.

6

Brokers in Harmonious Demolition

Mass Mobilizers, Mediators, and *Huangniu*

The threat of death is the last weapon of the weak. This extreme option is taken only when one is faced with no other solution . . . Once
again, it has become too apparent ordinary people are absolutely
disadvantaged when they face the government. Who on earth killed
Tang Fuzhen? Is it really herself?[1]
— Editorial, *Southern Metropolitan Paper*, December 3, 2009

The self-immolation case of the Chengdu woman, Tang Fuzhen, a victim of
forced demolition, shook the country in 2009. Like many others who had decided to set themselves ablaze in defense of their properties, she did not receive
the justice she deserved. Tang's sensational case generated widespread public
sympathy and was believed to have contributed to the downfall of Chengdu
mayor Li Chuncheng (李春城). Li was known for his ambitious plan to develop
the southwestern Chinese city, which resulted in many landless peasants and numerous casualties. It led to the central government's reflection on the costs of
violent demolition (暴力拆迁 Johnson 2013) and prompted adaptation of strategies for dealing with recalcitrant citizens. The national discourse on harmonious demolition (和谐拆迁) that has gained increasing traction since the early
2010s resonates with this line of thinking (O'Brien & Deng 2015; Gui 2017).

Using case studies collected during field research in Chengdu and Shanghai
from the mid- to late-2010s, this chapter illustrates the roles of different brokers
in harmonious demolition—information collection, mass mobilization, legitimation, and conflict resolution—as discussed in Chapter 5. Although compliance may be secured without the use of violence in these cases, the strategies
deployed were not necessarily less coercive in practice, yet such is the essence of
harmonious demolition—in the official Chinese parlance.

I draw on the discourses on the Maoist Mass Line and MTM to introduce the
political and social brokers the case studies engage. This chapter will demonstrate
that since the 2010s, some local governments have been creative in devising innovative models to tackle the practical everyday challenges of housing demolition. The examples introduced here include *zigaiwei* and "simulated demolition"

Outsourcing Repression. Lynette H. Ong, Oxford University Press. © Oxford University Press 2022.
DOI: 10.1093/oso/9780197628768.003.0006

in Chengdu. At the same time, local governments are also breathing new life into tried and true conflict-resolution models, such as people's mediation, while providing space for market-based brokerage to blossom if it can help to minimize social discontent and maintain social stability. I introduce persuasion as an authoritarian tool, which alongside carrots and sticks is aimed at controlling the society. Unlike overt coercion, persuasion is carried out by social brokers, who serve as legitimating vehicles for state repression.

The case study evidence from nonviolent demolitions that took place in Shanghai and Chengdu over the course of the 2010s was collected during field visits over the period from 2014 to 2019. I revisited some of the sites more than once to gather and triangulate information. Geographical locations of the field sites and times of visits are indicated in Figure 1.2.

6.1 The Strategy of Mobilizing the Masses

Brokers are key to the CCP strategy of mobilizing the masses (MTM) (群众动员). To understand how brokers mobilize at the grassroots level, the philosophy behind the Mass Line and MTM is instructive.

6.1.1 The Mass Line (群众路线)

The Mass Line (群众路线) in Mao's theory of democracy fosters a close relationship between CCP leaders and the masses with the aim of resolving class conflicts and constructing a socialist China. This strategy aims to make democracy work in China within the boundaries of socialism. As a form of people's democratic leadership, the Mass Line promotes resolution of conflicting interests between classes (Mao 1957). Following the Mass Line means "all we do are for the masses. Let's all rely on the masses. We came from the masses and go with the masses" ("一切为了群众，一起依靠群众，从群众中来，到群众中去"). In practical terms, this implies that "party members should be good at consulting the masses in their work and under no circumstances should they alienate themselves from the masses."[2]

In 2013, Xi Jinping officially endorsed the Fengqiao Experience (*Global Times* 2013). The district of Fengqiao relied on MTM for its socialist education movement in the 1960s, resulting in no arrests and minimal violence, thus gaining Mao's approval (批示). The techniques were replicated elsewhere in the country, and the Fengqiao Experience was revived after the end of the Cultural Revolution to control the rise of young criminals. In the postreform era, it evolved to become a strategy of relying on the masses to maintain social order and public security. It called for mass mobilization to resolve social conflicts and disputes locally while they were still in their embryonic stage.[3] Its rising prominence in contemporary China, particularly under Xi's rule, signifies the revival of the Mass Line.

6.1.2 Mass Mobilization (群众动员)

Table 6.1 makes clear that the CCP has relied upon mass mobilization as a policy implementation strategy since the revolutionary times in the 1940s.[4] The Party had relied on it to implement the "down-to-the-countryside" campaign (Kelkar 1978), to engage in economic construction during the Great Leap Forward (1959-1961), and to eliminate the Party's enemies in the Land Reform campaign, the Anti-Rightist campaign, and the Cultural Revolution (Walder 2019). Despite its decline in the post-Mao period, mass mobilization has been given greater prominence since Xi came to power. Exemplified by the Fengqiao Experience, the wisdom of the masses (群众智慧) has been increasingly relied upon to fight crime, execute everyday policies, and maintain social order.

In the era of Deng Xiaoping, conscious efforts were made to move away from ideology and mass mobilization toward formal institutions. Mass mobilization

Table 6.1 Mass Mobilization as a Political Strategy

Period	Area of application	Intensity (compared to previous period)
Communist revolutionary era (1940s)	Rectification Campaign (整风运动); Down to the Countryside Campaign	High (increased)
Mao's early socialist construction (1949-1959)	Social reconstruction; decimate ideological enemies (Land reform, Anti-Rightist Campaign, Four Clean-Ups Movement)	High (same)
Mao's economic construction and revolution (1959-1979)	Economic construction (Great Leap Forward), factional infighting (Red Guard Movement, Cultural Revolution)	High (same)
Postreform era (1980-2012)	Campaign-style governance, e.g., People's War against SARS	Low (declined)
Xi Jinping era (2013-present)	Social control, crime fighting, maintain stability, policy implementation (*Saohei* campaign, anti-corruption campaign, anti-poverty campaign)	Medium (increased)

Source: Author's summary.

was mostly reserved for crime control and social management (Perry 2007). In the postreform era until Xi's rule, campaign-style governance was largely restricted to crisis management, such as during the Tiananmen and Falun Gong protests, and the SARS epidemic (Perry 2011, 31–32); yet during the Xi Jinping era, mass mobilization has been revamped as a political strategy to legitimize increased state control of society. The Mass Line frame of "coming from the masses and following the masses" (从群众中来 到群众中去) is used to justify the Party-state's reassertion of authority over society. Correspondingly, this has resulted in the rejuvenation of brokers' roles in grassroots politics, such as those of residents' committees, block captains, volunteers, and community enthusiasts. Because of the limited capacity of political brokers, social brokers—like the Chaoyang Masses—have been increasingly sought after to implement the Mass Line.

6.2 Persuasion as a State Control Strategy: *Guanxi* and Emotional Mobilization

In the vernacular of authoritarian politics, the strategy of MTM is best understood as persuasion. Often conducted through emotional mobilization, in addition to carrots and sticks, persuasion is another—albeit oft-neglected—instrument in the autocrat's toolkit. In this chapter I will show that in order to persuade, a broker needs social capital that provides access to his wider *guanxi* network beyond his immediate family unit, which includes the subjects to be persuaded. The *guanxi* network encompasses members of the residential community, work unit, and affiliated associations, such as an old boys' clubs or university alumni associations. The social ties among members of the network in turn give rise to trust, which facilitates repression by emotional mobilization. Table 6.2 lays out what the concept of MTM implies in different contexts—Chinese governance, social movement strategy, the mobilizing resource it draws on, the agent who carries it out, and autocrat's toolkit.

Table 6.2 Conceptual Rubric of Mobilizing the Masses

Context	Manifestation
Chinese governance	Mobilizing the masses
Social movement strategy	Emotional mobilization
Mobilizing resource	*Guanxi* (social network)
Agent	Brokers
Autocrat's toolkit	Persuasion (alongside carrots and sticks)

Persuasion most befits the role of a social broker, who is a long-term member of the community. He can, but need not, preside over any lineage, clanship, or unregistered civil society organizations. Leadership status in grassroots civil society organizations can help in mobilizing members of the community but is not an essential condition. Political brokers whose legitimacy comes from state authority can also conduct persuasion, but they are not usually as effective as social brokers. Some political brokers who have provided long-term service to the community are able to gain the trust of the members independent of their state or quasistate status. For instance, a residents' committee member who has been in the position for over two decades would know families in the neighborhood well despite being a state appointee. To effectively persuade, however, the broker should have his authority drawn from nonstate sources as the case studies in this chapter will illustrate.

Guanxi, either in the form of corrupt exchanges of gifts for favors or more generic reciprocal relationships, is essential to the way brokers function. By controlling brokers who have relevant guanxi networks, the state can use them not only to penetrate society but also to mobilize the masses. This sort of guanxi is premised upon reciprocity, made possible by decades of social ties forged in alleyways, neighborhoods, communities, or villages. Mass mobilization cannot be achieved without these social brokers because formal government officials, such as cadres from street offices or townships, have no access to either urban or rural societies the way volunteers and community enthusiasts do. Meanwhile, the guanxi networks provided by economic brokers are more akin to paying bribes to secure favorable treatment.

Guanxi and emotions are also intertwined in the Chinese context. Cultivated over time, guanxi serves the dual purposes of sentimentality and instrumentalism (Kipnis 2002). Literally meaning relationship, guanxi resembles Bourdieu's (1986) concept of social capital; that is, the resources linked to possession of a durable network of mutual recognition. But guanxi has an added dimension of reciprocal obligation, which could be repaid in material or nonmaterial terms, taking the form of gifts or favors (Kipnis 2002). Practices of guanxi production rely on strategic attempts to generate ganqing (human emotions) and manipulate obligations (Kipnis 2002). Social relations can be constructed without relying on ganqing, such as through legal contracts, yet without using institutional means like contracts—or when contracts become unenforceable—ganqing can be effective in shaping human obligations.

Emotional mobilization, a well-recognized means of mass mobilization in China, is widely discussed in the literature on the Cultural Revolution (Y. Liu 2010; Perry 2002b). Here, I take the concept of emotional mobilization one step further by connecting it with persuasion as an autocrat's tool. Enabled by brokers' *guanxi* networks, emotional mobilization takes place through persuasion, which is aimed at mobilizing the masses. It is best captured in the Confucian aphorism, "Use of reason to convince, use of virtue or morality to gain submission, and use of emotions to move" (以理服人，以德服人，以情动人).

An independent instrument of state control, persuasion exists in addition to the traditional carrots and sticks. By engaging brokers with social capital to persuade, the state can change citizens' perceptions of repression. When someone who commands civic legitimacy persuades a fellow citizen to take up a government's offer, doing so is not generally perceived as a repressive act even though it may be coercive in nature. The same does not hold true for the repressive acts of government agents, such as punishment by implication or welfare suspension, despite their nonviolent nature (see Chapter 5). Invoking *guanxi* and its attendant emotions changes the perception of what is or is not a repressive act. Accordingly, legitimation by brokers spares state repression the usual backlash of citizens' collective actions, such as protest, petition, or legal action. Persuasion thus lowers the cost of repression for the state.

As an instrument of state control, persuasion is not necessarily successful whenever it is applied. As noted above, motivating proxies or brokers capable of carrying out persuasion effectively has become increasingly difficult for the Party-state, which must progressively rely on more material incentives. In addition, as the case studies here will illustrate, once brokers lose trust and legitimacy among the citizenry, their work of persuasion will be thwarted.

6.3 Mobilizing the Masses in Housing Demolition

Tang Fuzhen's case sparked the development of new innovative models by the Chengdu municipal government in conducting demolition. Prior to the innovation, decision-making was centralized where district (区) governments set up demolition command headquarters to supervise street-level demolition offices (街道办事处拆迁办) and workers in the communities (社区). One of the innovative models is the "Jinjiang model" (锦江模式), named after a district in Chengdu. In its rhetoric the model echoes the Mass Line: the state respects the wishes of the masses, by giving them the autonomy to make decisions. In official terms, this form of harmonious demolition is a progression from violent demolition. Cases of violent demolition have fallen indeed, yet as this section will illustrate, it amounts to the state outsourcing the job of convincing the masses *to the masses*. That is to say, the state mobilizes selected community members to persuade the reluctant segments of the community. Evidence for this section is drawn from field interviews conducted in several districts in Chengdu from the mid to late 2010s.

6.3.1 Self-Governed Renovation Committee or
Zigaiwei (自治改造委员会/自改委)

The self-governed renovation committee, or *zigaiwei* (自改委), is a demolition model applied to shantytowns and old housing renovations in Chengdu. These old neighborhoods, populated by residents from multiple generations and complex family arrangements, often pose a challenge to government's demolition and relocation efforts. The *zigaiwei* model, an innovation to overcome the practical challenges of demolition projects, is part of the government's rhetoric of community self-governance (Deng 2017).

In principle the community has the autonomy to elect its own *zigaiwei* members,[5] but in practice they are usually appointed by the neighborhood committee (居委会) or the street-level office (街道办事处) because of the need to ensure the character of people who connect them with society.[6] Members of *zigaiwei* vary, but they usually include resident small-group leaders (居民小组长), sometimes block captains, and members of the community.

By and large, *zigaiwei* are filled and led by long-term residents who are well known and command social legitimacy. These backbone personnel (骨干分子) of the community also take on the positions of grid management (网格化管理) group leaders.[7] They are the most socially active community members—akin to activists (积极分子) during Maoist times—who bear the responsibility of mobilizing the society on behalf of the state. They are mostly retired cadres or retired workers from state-owned enterprises who volunteer their time to the communities.

The composition of *zigaiwei* is often contentious because of the considerable power it wields over demolition. The head of *zigaiwei* in Chengdu's D District, Mr. Li, who was in his 60s, told me:

> I was born in this village, grew up, and have lived here all my life. My mother used to be the village chief. More than three-quarters of the native villagers do not live here anymore; they live elsewhere because of work and family reasons. Most of the current residents are migrant workers. Local villagers know me very well. As one of the few local villagers still living here, when I was asked to do the job, I simply could not refuse. I am a retiree from a state-owned factory, who now collects a pension.[8]

By my definition, Mr. Li is a social broker who commands social capital in the community, given his long-time residency record and his mother's service to the people. On the composition of the committee, Li told me, "Each block has a representative on the *zigaiwei*, who is usually the existing block captain (门楼长).[9] Likely, *zigaiwei* is made up of political and social brokers, who are the individuals equipped with either formal authority or *guanxi* networks to conduct mass mobilization.

Not everyone agrees with the selection of committee members. A 70-year-old resident of Chengdu's N District, Mr. Zhang, informed me:

> There's nothing democratic (民主) about *zigaiwei*. It's all about who has the money, relationships, and power in the community. A poor resident like me will never be elected or asked to sit on the committee.[10]

Mr. Zhang is a nonbroker by my definition but a member of the masses the brokers attempt to mobilize. He does not hold any position of power or command much social capital in the community. A dissenting voice in his community's demolition project, he was a target whom *zigaiwei* had been trying to persuade.

6.3.1.1 The Case of Caojiaxiang (曹家巷) in Chengdu

The case of the renovation of Caojiaxiang offers a telling example of how the complexities of MTM play out. Caojiaxiang is an old community in the central business district, a few kilometers away from Chengdu's city center, Tianfu Square. Each housing unit was small, and conditions of the housing complexes were dilapidated. In the early 2010s, the municipal government declared the neighbourhood a slum (棚户区) slated for renovation.

Community demolition projects are collective undertakings in every sense. Every single household will be affected once the project is given the go-ahead even though not all community members may consent to it. A family who refuses to vacate the premises will hold up the entire project; therefore, the consent—or forced consent—of everyone in the community must be sought before a demolition project can be implemented. The project must be approved by not only all families in the community but also all members within each family. Relocation agreements require signatures of all names registered on the housing deeds. Conflicts from diverging interests may, therefore, appear at two levels: among families in the community and among members of a family. Thus, brokers' mobilizational capacities must extend not only to family units within the community but also to members within a family unit.

As in some other old communities, Caojiaxiang residents were an amalgamation of the families of retired workers at a local state-owned enterprise and families who purchased apartment units from state worker families when housing was commodified two decades ago. Households in Caojiaxiang numbered 2,885 with 14,000 residents; 94 percent of the households comprised former state-owned enterprise workers who received work unit-allocated housing during the 1950s, and the rest made their purchases in the 1980s (*Chengdu Daily* 2012; Deng 2017). Those willing to accept the terms of the demolition were usually the families with three generations crammed into a small unit, which created less than ideal living conditions. The families who refused to sign were those who had been living in the neighborhood for several generations or were unsatisfied with the government-offered resettled housing, or both (*Zhaowen Tianxia* 2012).

The district government set up a *zigaiwei* to spearhead the renovation project. The committee consisted of resident small groups, block captains, and members of families who were willing to relocate. Early birds—members of the *zigaiwei* signing on to the project early in the process—were given bonuses by the government. The material rewards motivated them to give consent as well as to organize themselves to mobilize other families to do the same. In contrast to Maoist days, ideology had lost most of its appeal in mobilizing the masses in the 2010s, especially in high-stakes demolition projects. What has taken the place of ideology is material incentives.

The *zigaiwei*'s first task was to collect information on all the households in Caojiaxiang. Beyond enumerating citizens, their responsibilities were to seek information on family living arrangements (What are the names on the deeds? Do registered household members live on the premises? Have the daughters married and moved from the community? Are daughters-in-law included on the deeds? Does the family have a son who will marry soon? Do parents live with their adult children?), members' employment (Where do they work? Do they rely on state employment that the government can use to exert pressure? Do they run their own companies? What is the nature of the business, and who are the customers?), and finances (Does the family lead a comfortable lifestyle? Are they in need of cash, for instance, for children's higher education, a son's imminent wedding, or business investment?).

This process of discovering the basic underlying conditions (摸底) of community members is the necessary precondition for any demolition project. These tasks are conducted by political brokers, namely residents' committee members, residents' small groups, and block captains. Acquisition of this basic information about families helps the government compile a compensation package likely to be accepted. For instance, if parents lived apart from their adult children, they were likely to take the payout and move in with their children and grandchildren. Similarly, when a family has a son planning to marry, they might need cash and more spacious living quarters that could accommodate additional family members. Conversely, if a family has a young adult child who will move out to attend university, they might prefer to remain in their existing residence. Block captains, who are political brokers living in the same apartment blocks as the residents, are best positioned to collect household data of this nature.

MTM began with the *zigaiwei* setting up a voluntary publicity team (义务宣传队), consisting of aunties' demolition teams (大妈拆迁队). They propagandized the benefits of the renovation project by congregating and creating a scene outside the residences of those who had not signed on. Armed with microphones and loudspeakers, the team began their broadcast as early as dawn for two hours daily for several months (*Chengdu Daily* 2012; Deng 2017). The intention was not only to propagandize but also to harass and put peer pressure on those who had not yet consented. By invoking the rhetoric of us vs. them, the intention was to create a gulf between those who had signed and those who had not.

As illustrated in the statements below, the clever use of propaganda and slogan politics was highly reminiscent of the Maoist-era mass mobilization strategy.

Members of the propaganda team declared (*Zhaowen Tianxia* 2012):

> If you refuse to move, it means you do not support the government *beigai* policy! (你不搬，就是不支持"北改"，政府的政策!) *Beigai* refers to the renovation project of the northern zone of the city.
> This is a project about people's livelihood. Nail households, don't even dream about getting rich! (民生工程，"钉子户"妄想富!)

This strategy of othering the families that had not consented was intended to ostracize them. In a close-knit community where families see, rub shoulders, mingle, and socialize with one another daily, ostracism incurs enormous social and psychological costs.

The pressure imposed on an ostracized family is self-evident here (*Zhaowen Tianxia* 2012):

> I haven't signed [the relocation agreement]. I dare not step out of my home because I'm afraid the masses will come "fix" me (收拾我). When I was out in the neighbourhood, I was berated for not supporting the masses simply because I have not put my signature on the document!

As the quotation above suggests, a thin boundary exists between the conception of persuasion and coercion in practical terms. When residents are harassed or berated into agreement, brokers can claim they successfully persuaded the recalcitrant. After all, it was nonviolent verbal communication that effectuated compliance, yet seen in a different light, it was not persuasion based on logic or merits of arguments; the subject of persuasion is sometimes given no choice but to give in to the demand.

The aunties[11] who harassed and ostracized holdouts are social brokers demonstrating their less than benevolent side. These social brokers are deeply embedded in the community: they have lived in Caojiaxiang for decades. If not immediate neighbors of the families on whom they put pressure, they gossip and mingle with the families on a regular basis. Motivated by material rewards and summoned by the local government to mobilize the masses, they wore down the recalcitrant community members by applying psychological pressure on them. The very nature of their brokerage roles, which drew on their *guanxi* networks in the community, made the pressure successful. If they had been aunties recruited from the street, unknown to the families, whatever performative acts they might have staged would have been ignored and the pressure they applied would have gained no traction. Precisely because they were part of the big family of Caojiaxiang, they could exercise the brokerage clout of dividing the community and marginalizing those who were not on their side. Social brokers do not act alone; the state marshals them by motivating them with the carrots of early-bird bonuses and subsequently condones whatever strategies they have devised to mobilize the masses and extract agreements from the rest of the community.

During the mobilization process, the families who had not yet signed resorted to staying away from Caojiaxiang to avoid interactions with the community members. Some lived with their relatives, while others rented their shops out to avoid being confronted by residents in the neighborhood. "I have been labeled a sinner (罪人) for failing to take to heart the interests of other people," a resident told me.

6.3.1.2 Reminiscent of Mass Line Politics

Social labeling is very much reminiscent of the Maoist Mass Line politics. The labeling of rural citizens during the Land Reform of the 1950s based on class and wealth—often using arbitrary criteria—in effect created conflicts in society by pitting one group against another. Similarly, the designation of supporters vs. nonsupporters of community relocation also had the effect of manufacturing conflicts and made one group the enemy of the other in Caojiaxiang.

Mobilizing a segment of the masses to deal with other segments (以群众收拾群众) was another central feature of Mass Line politics. It reflects Mao's adroit exploitation of *people* as a resource and a legitimizing vehicle to achieve political objectives. This speaks to the scope condition of persuasion as an autocrat's tool. When is persuasion deployed vis-à-vis carrots and sticks? As I have previously argued, MTM is the strategy of choice when financial resources (carrots) are in short supply or when the autocrat wishes to legitimate his actions, both of which were true in the Maoist years, or when overt coercion and punishment (sticks) do not work effectively. In the present context, persuasion is deployed because using violence was too costly and the government could legitimize the coerced compliance using the rhetoric of harmonious demolition. Since the Tang Fuzhen incident, the Chengdu authorities have come under increased scrutiny for the way they conduct housing demolitions, which makes violence a risky and costly strategy. To be sure, the government instead used sweeteners to entice and marshal one group to get them to mobilize the rest, rendering it a legitimate people's project (民生工程) that respects the wishes of the masses (尊重群众意见).

6.3.1.3 National Breakthrough in Demolition Governance: Outsourcing Repression

Zigaiwei has been portrayed as a national breakthrough in demolition govern- ance that draws on the endless wisdom of the masses.[12] Endorsed by the Party, a Central Party School professor praised *zigaiwei* as a "great embodiment of dem- ocratic spirit" (民主精神非常好的体现) that is worthy of emulation by the rest of the country (Deng 2017; *Zhaowen Tianxia* 2012). Indeed, local governments from all over China have organized study tours to Chengdu to learn its "self- governed" demolition model.[13]

Seen in a different light, allowing the masses to make decisions on their own community transformation is an astute government strategy of shifting the responsibility of consensus-gathering and mass-rallying to the commu- nity directly. Consequently, the strategy puts the onus on the willing families and social brokers to coax, persuade, and convince the unwilling. Any pressure placed on the reluctant and obstinate is, therefore, instigated by the willing and enthusiastic—from one community group to another—leaving the state out of the tussle. The blame and conflicts that ensue will then be directed at members of the community—instead of the government. This ingenious state strategy of MTM effectively amounts to outsourcing repression to society while reaping the benefits of successful implementation. Thus, this strategy lowers the cost of repression.

The case of Caojiaxiang also illustrates how the dynamics of blame shifting played out. A resident harassed by the *zigaiwei* lodged a complaint with the dis- trict leader in charge of the demolition project. The district chief told the resident:

> The government condemns any extreme tactics (过激手段) deployed by any- body to get people to relocate. Any consent should be voluntary. Because this is a resident-spearheaded project, it is essentially up to the residents themselves to sort things out. (*Zhaowen Tianxia* 2012)

In essence, the government gained legitimacy by portraying itself as the savior by criticizing those who resorted to extreme tactics. Arguably, this went beyond the strategy of MTM; the government condemned the masses when it crossed the boundary, for the purpose of pleasing the other aggrieved masses. In the process, the government ensured no petition was filed and no protest was staged due to demolition. This is the quintessential model of harmonious demolition (和谐拆 迁), extolled by the central government and deemed worthy of emulation by the rest of the country.

Not all demolition cases involving *zigaiwei*, however, were successful. During my field research in Chengdu, I encountered at least two instances of stalled projects.

6.3.1.4 Failed *Zigaiwei* Case 1

To the extent that *zigaiwei* serves as a legitimating vehicle to mobilize the masses, it can be successful only if its legitimacy remains intact in the eyes of the masses. A case in Chengdu's J District failed because it violated this principle. Some community members accused *zigaiwei* members of nepotism by falsifying documents to inflate the compensation they and their relatives could receive. The *zigaiwei* was also accused of being a puppet of the street-level office and in collusion with the grassroots government to cheat the community. The quotation below came from my interviewee, Mr. Zhang, who opposed the *zigaiwei* and belonged to the minority group that refused to sign on.

"*Zigaiwei* members do things for themselves. They have never spared a thought for the interests of the masses. They are only interested in their own profit; it is not about serving the masses. Do not trust the crooked people! I am a victim. They squeeze the interests of the masses dry, eat your flesh, and won't spit out the bones! It's all about who has the social connections," my aggrieved interviewee, Mr. Zhang, lamented.[14]

Then he asked me, "What are you doing here finding out about demolition? Are you not afraid of thugs (流氓) sent by the *zigaiwei*?"

As Mr. Zhang explained, alongside the "democratic" model of *zigaiwei*, thugs were occasionally deployed to intimidate and silence residents when they complained about local government behavior and refused to give consent.

Meanwhile, *zigaiwei* members castigated people like Mr. Zhang for being selfish and greedy, dragging their feet in order to bargain for more, and sabotaging the interests of the majority.[15] One of them griped:

> The renovation project is a great opportunity for all of us. We have been waiting for this day to come when we can move out of dilapidated housing in a dirty and unsafe environment. But there is a group of people who are just avaricious (贪婪), who always haggle for more by dragging their feet. (*Tianya BBS* 2015b)

This case failed because the integrity of the *zigaiwei*, which was supposed to be autonomous and driven by the masses for the masses, was in tatters—as seen through the eyes of residents like Mr. Zhang. Once the legitimacy of brokers was lost, mass work, or persuasion, was no longer functionable. Tellingly, this underscores the notion that MTM as a political strategy is premised upon trust in social networks, through which persuasion is conducted. In the absence of relative trust and as far as absolute trust is never realistically attainable, people cannot be mobilized by emotions. (In the end, violence was used to intimidate the minority to give consent.)

This case illustrates an agency problem with respect to *zigaiwei*. The brokers or agents bring net benefits to the grassroots authority (principal) only if they are trusted by the masses to conduct mobilization. Brokers who used explicitly coercive tactics are no different from the tattooed TFH local governments engage elsewhere to extract community's compliance. Thus, the *zigaiwei* has been reduced to merely a façade to meet the Chengdu municipal authority's instruction to carry out harmonious demolition. When the project received consent from the entire community, the grassroots authority could endorse and promote it as a case of "democratic governance."

6.3.1.5 Failed *Zigaiwei* Case 2

This demolition project covered a large area in Chengdu's central business district. Citizens affected included long-term residents who were allocated housing by their former state-owned *danwei*, and others purchased residences from the secondary market and made investments in apartment renovations. Business owners also ran retail shops in the area, and many refused to vacate because of the premier location or the government's unattractive compensation package or both. The project also involved demolition of a renowned hotel in Chengdu with a noteworthy history of hosting revolutionary political leaders. Some residents lamented that demolishing the hotel would thwart cultural preservation, especially in this garden city that has long prided itself on its unique cultural heritage. Thus, various interest groups emerged among those affected by the demolition plans, broadly divided into residential families, businesspeople, and advocates for cultural preservation, according to my interviewee, a manager of the city's construction management corporation.[16]

This was a complex project that involved different groups of community members with diverging interests; some with material stakes, others with more obscure demands. These disparate interest groups did not come together as a unified community over which *zigaiwei* could exert their influence, drawing on their social capital to conduct mass work.[17] In other words, the basic thrust of MTM—a practice of persuasion through emotional mobilization—could not be exercised in this case. The aunties' demolition team armed with microphones and mobile loudspeakers that wielded tremendous power in Caojiaxiang could hardly hold sway with business owners and cultural preservation defenders whom they hardly knew.

6.3.2 Simulated Demolition

Simulated demolition (模拟拆迁), another model that has been applied in Chengdu and elsewhere in China, is also based on the rhetoric of self-governing demolition. In this type, the consent of the families is sought, compensation negotiated, and agreements signed *before* demolition work begins. The model is applied *prior to* the local government's issue of the official demolition approval. For a project to receive the green light, a minimum of 90 percent of families must agree.

In addition, financial incentives are offered to the early birds who give their consent. In a Chengdu community, the first to consent within 60 days is offered a 60,000 RMB (9,000 USD) bonus, and those who agree in the next 30 days are awarded with 20,000 RMB (3,000 USD) bonus. These material incentives become one of the drivers that compel some families to cajole the other families in the community to agree to the relocation.[18] To attain the 90 percent requirement, persuasion through emotional mobilization is conducted on the families who have yet to consent, much like the case with *zigaiwei*. The project will be aborted if the threshold is not met (X. Li, Zhang, and Zhang 2005; Yufeng Zhang 2014).

Obtaining the consent of 90 percent of the households is therefore a task left to the community itself. The onus largely falls on the families who want the project to proceed to organize and mobilize those who have not yet agreed, but RC officials and social brokers are also involved in conducting mass mobilization (Yufeng Zhang 2014).

This has two implications for the nature of conflicts. First, in the traditional state-led model, demolition conflicts occurred between the state and society; the local government wanted demolition to happen, but residents refused. Recalcitrant residents may then engage in foot-dragging tactics to delay the project in order to bargain for more compensation, or they may simply refuse to vacate. Second, now that the government has divorced or at least distanced itself from the process, the nature of conflicts has been transformed into that between one segment of the community and another—a society-society conflict.

Accordingly, this model has significantly reduced the cost of demolitions for the state, which no longer needs to acquire compliance directly. Driven by inherent self-interest, the willing masses now self-organize to persuade the unwilling masses; furthermore, the reduction in petitions, or popular protests, as a result of this new model contributes to social stability, another net gain for the state. By cleverly transforming the nature of conflicts, the state has effectively outsourced the dual responsibilities of compliance acquisition and conflict resolution to society. Societal compliance is acquired at a much lower *cost* to the state. Unsurprisingly, simulated demolition, much like *zigaiwei*, is promulgated as an innovative democratic model that empowers the people, yet the democratic element may in fact be a manifestation of the tyranny of the majority where the wishes of the larger willing masses are imposed on the unwilling.

6.4 Mediation: Conflict Prevention and Resolution

6.4.1 People's Mediation (人民调解)

Mediation has strong historical roots in imperial China.[19] In contemporary China, citizens are more likely to turn to people's mediation in rural than in urban areas. Urban society today is less a "society of acquaintances" (熟人社会) because of migration and changes in urban lifestyles. As the society and nature of conflicts became more complex during the reform era, mediators also became less able to penetrate their communities, their capacity to mediate declining over time.[20] Despite these trends, the Party-state still sees people's mediation as the "first line of defense" (第一防线) in conflict resolution.

Two major types of conflicts are associated with land expropriation and housing demolitions. One occurs between the government and families (state-society conflicts); the other, among family members (society-society conflicts). The first arises because of disagreements over compensation, corruption, illegal or forced evictions, or procedural irregularities, such as lack of consultation before demolition. The second arises from disputes over family wills, inherited properties, or lack of consensus among family members. During demolition, fathers and sons, husbands and wives, brothers and sisters, can become enemies when diverging material differences drive conflicts, sometimes exposing deep-seated family tensions. The intrafamily conflicts that result in a lack of consensus among family members can impede reaching an agreement between the family and the state. Mediation of the second type of conflict requires mediators to have the trust of family members to come among them and bridge their differences.

6.4.2 Mediation in Preemptive Conflict Resolution

The Chinese mediation system places strong emphasis on preemptive conflict resolution or "nipping conflicts in the bud" (化解纠纷苗头).[21] It is also meant to discourage the aggrieved from taking the government to court, lodging a petition, or staging a mass protest—all of which are considered threats to social stability.[22] Preventive conflict resolution, of which mediation is a core essential, is an indispensable element of stability maintenance (维稳). Formal conflict resolution institutions, such as the court, are considered means of last resort.[23]

People's mediation amasses political and social brokers who harness their political authority and social capital, respectively, to resolve conflicts. According to my interviewees, mediation is a task that VCs or RCs (political brokers) cannot conduct on their own; they must coopt community members who have social prestige and maintain close ties with the subjects—the social brokers.[24] Elderly folks with demonstrable records of serving the Party or state-owned units are more likely to be coopted because of the respect and reverence they command in the community. They need not preside over any lineage or clanship group, but leadership positions in informal organizations would certainly help.[25]

6.4.3 Mediation Case Study

This case study illustrates how intervention by mediators can resolve intractable disputes often rooted in broken family relationships. The human and emotional aspects of mediation are helpful in resolving conflicts; however, resolution may simply mean the state is able to eliminate a thorn in its side. It does not necessarily bring about a just outcome for the aggrieved, and yet in a tightly controlled authoritarian system in which the court is not independent of the state and popular contention does not yield desirable results, mediation may be a preferred channel for aggrieved citizens after all.

6.4.3.1 Case Study: Family with Deceased Father had Diverging Views on Settling Ancestral Property

A Shanghai family had five members. After the father's death two decades earlier, the mother lived in the family residence with her adult son and his family. Her two adult daughters and their families resided elsewhere. The old family home was the property in dispute. Although the son wanted to sell it and move his family elsewhere, the daughters disagreed on the grounds that they would not get a fair share of the compensation in addition to having to pay extra monthly financial support for their mother. The daughters viewed their brother, the only son in the family, as dominating family decisions and properties, and they refused to give in on this last family asset left behind by their father. Suffice it to say, the siblings' relations were less than amicable.[26]

Before mediation was carried out, the mediators first probed their neighbors about the temperaments of the individuals, their financial situations, and possible constraints. Then, the mediators spoke to each family member at great length to understand their perspectives on the dispute. Unsurprisingly, gaps emerged in their respective understanding of the situation at stake: the son saw it as the opportunity of a lifetime to upgrade his family's living quarters to a larger space, but the daughters perceived it as the last chance for them to safeguard the property left behind by their doting father.

Through repeated discussions with the family, the mediators were finally able to convince all of them to sign the agreement. Emotional mobilization through appeals to their emotional sensibilities have played a role. The following statements made by the mediators provide evidence of their attempts to mobilize the sisters by evoking family relations (*ganqing*) and filial piety:[27]

> Think about your elderly mother and your brother's children, who have to put up with such a cramped space! How can you ignore the welfare of your brother and his children? Don't you want your mother to live more comfortably in her remaining years?

> Do you think your father would have been happy with your insistence on not selling the property if he were alive today?

In addition, the mediators reminded the family members that the state could always apply to the court for a legal forced eviction order, in which case they would be compelled to comply even when the offer was not in their favor.[28] Mediation was able to bring this case to a resolution, which arguably brought a superior outcome for all parties. The state reduced the cost of demolition by not resorting to forced eviction, and the family was able to come to an agreement without resorting to a legal recourse, yet what appears to be an amicable resolution may mask the forced consent of some family members or simply a manufactured consensus imposed by the mediators or the state. When state-backed mediators knock on a family's door and offer to bring the parties together on a case that implicates the government, families are deeply cognizant of the lack of viable options.

"When you turn down an offer by the government, you are pretty much on your own," my interviewee told me.[29] She refused to elaborate, but her response was suggestive of either a legal option or institutional censures, such as suspension of government subsidies or everyday inconveniences that state agents can create.

6.4.4 Persuasion and the Grammar of Human Compassion

The official rhetoric of people's mediation invokes the grammar of human compassion (人文关怀), the attentiveness, patience, and sincerity (细心, 耐心, 诚心) of mediators and their ability to put themselves in the shoes of the disputing parties (从当事人的角度思考问题). The traditional Chinese adage that best expresses this official approach is "to move the people with compassion and to inform them with reason" (动之以情、晓之以理).

In practice, compassionate emotions can be a double-edged sword: they could mean special considerations given to the weak and destitute but at the same time, leverage used to persuade citizens to comply. Behind the façade of a seemingly moral and compassionate state could be nothing more than mobilization strategies via emotional coercion and moral blackmail (McConnell 1981). One's refusal to comply, either because of irreconcilable personal differences or diverging material interests, would be labeled betrayals of traditional morals or insensitivity to other people's conditions, carrying with it the risk of community castigation and even the state's reprisal.

Such is the political strategy of persuasion, which exists alongside carrots and sticks as a tool in the autocrat's toolkit. It is a standalone category, drawing on social capital and emotional mobilization to extract compliance. It is also distinct from sticks, which are manifested in overt and covert physical violence, collective punishment, or welfare suspension. Thus, in its utility as an autocrat's tool, persuasion does not take on its conventional meaning: to convince by logic or arguments. After all, the function of all the autocrat's tools is to extract compliance one way or another, whether by using money to buy cooperation from the citizenry, beating them to cause them to nod their heads, or emotionally coaxing or psychologically coercing them.

6.5 *Huangniu*: Professional Profit-Seeking Brokers

The political and social brokers discussed in this chapter thus far are grassroots intermediaries who connect the state and society, but they often act on behalf of the state's interests. Conceptually, they are closer to Duara's notion of state-appointed entrepreneurial brokers than protective brokers because the latter were independent intermediaries who tried to protect villagers' interests.

In this section I will discuss the case of professional demolition brokers (专业拆迁中介), who are a type of economic brokers.[30] Their *raison d'être* is to seek profits by bringing the state and aggrieved citizens to an agreement. Unlike social brokers, they need not necessarily rely on social capital or be long-time residents; however, they must build trust with both the government demolition office and community members whose homes are slated for demolition to effectively carry out the brokerage function.

Huangniu (黄牛), literally meaning cattle, is a profit-seeking broker hired by disgruntled citizens to bargain with the state. It is generally a pejorative term to describe middlemen who provide highly sought-after services at above-market prices.[31] Negotiations over demolition and relocation may become protracted without brokers' intervention. Economic brokers collude with insiders (demolition officials), who provide them with insider information and access to scarce goods, such as resettled housing allocations. These profit-seeking brokers represent the commodification of state–society bargaining by matching demands from discontented citizens with supplies of special favours by corrupt state officials. In so doing, a commercial and often illegal deal is clinched. The deal

involves a state official's allocation of compensation over and above that man-
dated by official policy, or what other citizens—in a similar condition but who do
not engage a *huangniu*—are entitled to. *Huangniu* are more likely to be found in
major cities where ample money can be made in housing demolition and refurbishment projects.

6.5.1 Nature of Bargaining

"Bargaining is essentially a mind game between the government and residents,"
declared my resident-informant in Shanghai who had negotiated with the government on three previous occasions.[32]

The process of bargaining begins with the demolition office sending an officer to knock on doors to appraise and probe families' situations often with the
help of an RC member. Cash-poor families are more inclined to accept monetary
compensation than housing units, whereas those with unmarried sons will likely
demand extra units to accommodate future needs. This information helps the
government determine the psychological floors (心理底线) of compensation
below which families would refuse to accept, hence their bargaining strength vis-
à-vis the families.

"The astute will hold his cards close to his chest so as to keep the other party
guessing," my informant told me,[33] adding, "If you reveal your base limit too
soon, you are likely to lose out on the gravy!"

By that, he meant the family was likely to receive only the minimum compensation officially specified while being passed over in terms of premiums the government was willing to pay to induce an agreement. "The simple-minded (老实
人) are usually the first ones to give consent [to vacate their properties], and they
are most likely to lose out."[34]

Veteran negotiators are astutely aware of the space between official policy
stipulations and the actual compensation for which residents can bargain with
the state. This grey zone gives government officials the latitude to provide carrots
to induce compliance when necessary.[35] Demolition officers employ various psychological tactics to coax residents into agreement. They may offer a bonus to
the first batch of families who give consent, but the bonus is meager compared to
what they will receive if they persevere to the end.[36]

6.5.2 *Huangniu's* Profile, Credentials, and Functions

Huangniu are usually people in their late 40s, 50s, or 60s with considerable life
experience. Adept at human relationships and skilled at negotiations, they are

not necessarily residents of the particular communities in question; but they are likely to have experienced demolitions first-hand, exposing them to the intricacies of the regulations and procedures involved.

The unique advantage of *huangniu* lies in their connections with insiders or government demolition officials. Insider connections give them exclusive knowledge of the upper and lower bounds of compensation feasible and acceptable to the government. Armed with this information advantage, they can negotiate with the families and forge agreements between the two parties.

Huangniu must have credentials to gain the trust of citizen-clients. On this point, my informants spoke of the credible brokers they know setting up makeshift offices adjacent to the government demolition office, bolstering their credibility and sending a strong signal to potential clients that their operation has received the blessing of government officials.

"A *huangniu* has said to me, 'Do you think I can run an operation here if I don't have good connections with the officials in charge?' and 'I am capable of providing any assistance you need on demolition matters,'" recounted my interviewee.[37]

Word-of-mouth recommendations and those from close social circles also served to establish a *huangniu*'s credentials. "Engaging a *huangniu* is like knowing someone in the demolition office," said my interviewee, Mr. Deng.[38] He then added, "It was only after we relocated that I realized my old classmate knew someone in the demolition office. If only I had known earlier, it would have been as good as engaging a *huangniu*."

By "knowing someone" (认识熟人), Mr. Deng meant having what Mayfair Yang or Doug Guthrie refer to as *guanxi* with the people who have the power to make decisions.[39] *Guanxi*, which is the exchange of gifts for favors, can be a substitute for legal institutional economic relations that make corruption work. (Note that the term *guanxi* takes on a slightly different meaning here from the context of social brokers. *Guanxi* in this case implies active solicitation of favors by way of gifting, whereas it denotes social networks in the previous context.)[40] In this mediated transaction, the economic brokers play a crucial function in establishing trust with each party. This helps to reduce information asymmetry between them and expedite the two parties to reach a (corrupt) agreement.

The role of the brokers is distinctively useful in corrupt exchanges as they help to lower the cost of distrust between parties. "Residents do not know whether the officers could be bribed. And officers do not know which families are willing to pay for their extra service," said my interviewee, an internal auditor for the Shanghai municipal government who has audited numerous demolition projects.[41] "Once a *huangniu* has gained the trust of both parties, he helps to assure each party that the other one will put his words into actions," he elaborated.

Why do some residents engage a *huangniu* while others do not? Although working with a *huangniu* could bring extra payouts, it also involves cost and risk. The resident will have to share with the *huangniu* any extra compensation awarded. To the extent that disgruntled residents feel those are their legitimate entitlements, they refuse to work with a *huangniu*, who would take half of their shares. These citizens tend to see state-society bargaining as a matter of principle rather than an opportunistic material pursuit. It is also risky because the illegal nature of transactions could potentially subject all parties to criminal prosecution, particularly under Xi's anticorruption environment.

A *huangniu*'s function goes beyond bringing the two sides together. The brokers provide an entire suite of services that completes the transactions, including counterfeit marriage, divorce, or birth certificates that could inflate the compensation.[42] Any extra payout the brokers help secure is split 50-50 between them and the clients. The brokers' gains are then shared with the officers who help seal the deals.[43]

Moreover, because each party to the corrupt transaction—the officers, the families, and the *huangniu*—receives a cut, no one has an incentive to become a whistle-blower. The only marginal loser is the government, which must pay the family more than what it initially budgeted, but because only selected families work with *huangniu*, the extra budget is a relatively small proportion of the total. These extra funds typically come from the reserves the government would have set aside as carrots to induce compliance.[44] In addition, the government benefits from completing the project on time. Thus, the government has little incentive to crack down on these (illegal) activities. In fact, demolition officers are paid a low base salary but are rewarded ample bonuses for securing relocation consent. In the Shanghai district where I conducted field research, an officer could be awarded a bonus as much as 2,000 RMB (about 300 USD) for every family who consented.[45]

6.5.3 *Huangniu* Case Study: Mechanisms that Make Economic Brokerage Succeed or Fail

In 2012, in Jiangsu's Xuzhou municipality, a *huangniu* surnamed Liu acted in collusion with his uncle, Xing, an officer in the demolition office, to help his family and clients secure higher compensation. To achieve that, Liu forged deeds, business licenses, and tax registration certificates for his clients. The other ploy the duo pulled off was the hackneyed trick of classifying a residential space as a commercial space (住改非), qualifying for additional compensation. This procedure necessitates the production of a business license and tax registration that can be forged only through collusion with government insiders.

The forgery of documents requires several parties—inside and outside government institutions—to act in cahoots. Typically, a *huangniu*, who is an outsider, produces some counterfeit documents, which are passed on to one or several officer(s) working in the demolition office. In addition, cooperation from a government auditor in charge of document certification is required to complete the transaction.[46] Without at least three parties—in three different positions—acting in tandem, deals that involve bogus papers will be difficult to complete.

Numerous reported cases involved the forgery of marriage and birth certificates by *huangniu*. An oft-heard saying in communities undergoing demolition is the following: "Although married couples don't live together, divorced couples do. Even though grandpas don't know their grandkids, the pavilion has more than nine registered family members under the same roof" (*Sohu News* 2007).

The cynicism is meant to ridicule the sham family arrangements prevalent among neighborhoods slated for demolition, a reflection of residents' frantic attempts to bargain for more. With the assistance of brokers, unmarried individuals are "wedded" to strangers from inland provinces who also bring with them "offspring" from previous marriages. Married couples file for "divorces" to increase their entitlements as singles. Wives transfer their parents' household registration to Shanghai from elsewhere to raise "the number of family members needing to be settled" (应安置人口), a criterion used to determine the size of compensation.

These practices are so widespread that residents have given them nicknames. Faking marriage certificates for singles is dubbed "first marriages" (头婚), and forging birth certificates is better known as "towheads" (拖头). Marriage or divorce rates are commonly two or three times higher in communities undergoing demolition than elsewhere in the city.[47]

However, the case in Xuzhou was eventually exposed, resulting in legal prosecution of Liu, Xing, and their accomplices. It broke down at two points. First, the trust between Liu, the *huangniu*, and Xing, his uncle at the demolition office, was eroded when the latter asked for more payment than they had initially agreed upon. Second, when Liu attempted to recruit Zhang as a new client, he took an initial payment of 100,000 RMB (15,000 USD) from Zhang for producing a counterfeit certificate. Unhappy with this arrangement, Zhang's wife demanded money back from Liu, but Liu had already passed on the bulk of the initial payment to Xing, his contact at the demolition office. Zhang's wife eventually wrote a complaint letter that landed both Liu and Xing in legal trouble (*Xinhua Net* 2012).

In other incidents, *huangniu* simply failed to gain the trust from citizen-clients. Citizens who distrust the local government saw the broker as someone sent by the authorities to extract more *from* them rather than acting independently to seek better deals *for* them. On one hand, *huangniu* need to establish sufficient credentials that they have *guanxi* in the demolition office. On the other hand, they must be able to maintain certain degree of autonomy from the local authorities. Such a fine balancing act can be inherently tricky (*Tianya BBS* 2013).

Essentially, *huangniu* offer services to disgruntled citizens who wish to bargain with the authoritarian state, where proper channels of citizen participation and conflict resolutions are blocked. The privileged and well-connected receive more favorable treatment compared to the underprivileged. Paying a *huangniu* with insider connections can help to overcome the shortcomings of being an outsider or under-privileged. In the absence of *huangniu*-facilitated bargaining, many disgruntled citizens may become involved in protracted standoffs, take their grievances to the streets, or take the government to court. In other words, even though the transactions are illegal, they help to meet the state's overriding priority in maintaining social stability. This is particularly relevant in an urban context where educated and media-savvy residents have become disenchanted from the government's push to demolish neighborhoods and relocate residents, often hastily, and without satisfactory compensation.

Distribution of state goods based on willingness to bribe will inevitably give rise to discord and resentment among family members, neighbors, and friends. Any community undergoing demolition often suffers significant diminution in social capital as the social fabric that binds members together is torn apart by competing material interests.

One of my informants did not engage a *huangniu*, but his elder brother who did was unsurprisingly awarded two extra apartment units, creating a rift between the brothers. One said, "When two families with similar conditions are given different compensation, we cannot help but question government policies and raise the issue of fairness."[48]

As for the other interviewee who engaged a *huangniu*, he refused to let his brother come on board:

> I couldn't share all the information with my brother even though he had asked me about it. The pie is only that big; a larger piece for him means a smaller piece for my family. We all need to make plan for ourselves.[49]

Although members of this family remain on speaking terms, the trust among them has likely been eroded by the protection of self-interests, which was exacerbated by the state's discriminatory compensation.

What are the potential agency problems in economic brokerage? From both the perspectives of citizen-clients and government officials, brokers who fail to gain the trust of either party cannot effectively mediate the transactions. Worse still, the absence of the broker's credibility may invite suspicion and lead to reporting, which puts all parties at risk of criminal prosecution. Like other brokers, the legitimacy of economic brokers holds the key to the brokerage function in bringing the parties to an agreement.

Violence is visibly absent in the Shanghai locales where *huangniu* were at work, especially upper middle-income neighborhoods where the use of violence could incur high costs because the educated and sophisticated residents are likely to press the higher authority for responsibility. If the consent of these residents could be expediently extracted through outsourced violent intimidation, the local authority would not have devoted energies to working with economic brokers, given the inherently protracted nature of negotiation.

Corrupt brokers thrive in an opaque environment, where rules for eligibility assessment are ambiguous and government agents in charge of projects enjoy enormous power. In Shanghai, prior to 2011, housing demolition was a nontransparent process where the government disclosed little information with respect to the criteria of assessment or each family's spatial area and household size. The opacity provided government agents with enormous power to allocate more resources to favored families while offering little recourse for grievance redress for others. The implementation of "sunshine demolition" (阳光拆迁), which makes public some relevant information, has helped to varying degrees in reducing the scope for "rent-seeking" (Z. X. L. Chen and Cui 2009),[50] but by no means has it eliminated brokerage altogether.[51]

6.6 Conclusion

The engagement of brokers with social capital legitimates the conduct of state repression by changing citizen's perception of repressive acts. Verbal persuasion—although it might be coercive in nature—is not generally seen as state repression, but the same cannot be said about violent crackdown or even nonviolent punishment by implication or welfare suspension. Persuasion, therefore, lowers the cost of repression by significantly reducing the likelihood of citizen resistance or backlash.

Delegating authority to brokers is also subject to agency problems. Their brokerage function is effective insofar as they have the trust of the masses, and they will act in the interest of the delegating authority. When brokers prioritize individualistic pursuits and personal gains, the vehicle for mass mobilization will be reduced to nothing but a façade. In those cases, the delegating authority engages thuggish violence alongside MTM as a smokescreen to coerce citizens into compliance.

Persuasion exists as an independent state-control instrument, supplementing and substituting for the conventional tools of carrots and sticks. In an era where violent coercion in demolition is increasingly taboo for local governments, mass mobilization and economic brokerage have become more attractive. Put differently, among the three social-control strategies—rewards (carrots), violence (sticks), and persuasion—when violence becomes more costly, persuasion and rewards have greater appeal to the state. Mass mobilization in the postreform era is a combination of persuasion and reward strategies: by using selective rewards, the state marshals members of society, usually including social brokers, to mobilize and persuade the rest of the masses.

By relying on the masses, mass mobilization bypasses institutions, such as the bureaucracy, the court, and the police in policy implementation and conflict resolution. In effect, it removes the institutional procedures, and predisposes policy implementation to ideological distortion, manipulation, or abuse of power by those in charge. In the long run, mass mobilization has negative implications for political development and the rule of law.

The Mass Line may seem befitting of what Tocqueville (1835) wrote in *Democracy in America*: "The moral dominion of the majority is based on the idea that there is more enlightenment and wisdom in many men combined than in one man alone." Relying on the moral superiority of the masses, however, has an equal danger of producing a tyranny of the majority, one of democracy's greatest perils. This danger is grave when the boundaries of the masses—the majorities vs. minorities or us vs. enemies—are artificially manufactured, such as in the case in the Maoist political campaigns. In contemporary China, these cleavages remain fluid.

7

Comparative Context

South Korea and India

This chapter contextualizes the empirical findings on China with those of South Korea and India. I first examine the extent to which these countries meet the scope condition of proxy complicity that allows for outsourcing of repression to take place. Notably, proxy complicity is based on either witting or unwitting participation; the former is a function of state capacity to control proxies' behavior while the latter occurs when proxies normatively believe their doing the state's bidding contributes to the public good. Next, I scrutinize evidence to determine whether these states have effectively engaged violent and nonviolent nonstate agents to implement quotidian policies and analyze the implications for *everyday state power*. When a country, such as South Korea, has undergone a political transition from an authoritarian to a democratic state, I analyze the effect of regime change on the outsourcing of repression *within* the country case. I will demonstrate with the case of South Korea that authoritarianism is not a necessary condition for the arguments of outsourcing repression to hold, even though an autocratic state can certainly assert better control over its proxies. In this chapter I also draw on primary data collected during a field trip to India in 2015 and available secondary sources.

The comparative case studies are based on a most-similar and another most-dissimilar case. The logic for such a case selection in small-N studies is laid out in Seawright and Gerring (2008). I start with South Korea, which, because of a set of sociopolitical and cultural factors, presents the case study most similar to that of China. South Korea was an authoritarian state until 1987. Historically, its hierarchically organized familial and societal structures have been strongly influenced by Confucian ideology. These similar and commonly shared initial conditions suggest South Korea has a higher likelihood of meeting the scope condition of proxy complicity by unwittingly participating in state repression. The country's transition from authoritarian rule to a democracy in 1987 allows me to examine the effect of regime change on *everyday state power*. South Korea's period of high growth and rapid urbanization from the 1960s to the 1980s under Presidents Park and Chun most resembled the reform era in China.

The second case is India, which presents itself as the most-dissimilar case. Unlike China, India is a democracy with a heterogenous society, where the caste

Outsourcing Repression. Lynette H. Ong, Oxford University Press. © Oxford University Press 2022.
DOI: 10.1093/oso/9780197628768.003.0007

system plays an important role in organizing societal groupings and contentious politics, including land resistance movements. India has been described as having a political society characterized by a thick middle layer between state and society (Chatterjee 2004), so the state must rely on a range of intermediaries with strong brokerage power to penetrate and reach into society; similarly, society must do so as well in order to bargain with the state. Prima facie, this suggests the scope condition of proxy complicity with their witting participation is unlikely to be met because state–society intermediaries or brokers command a high degree of power over the state. Accordingly, when outsourcing control to nonstate agents, the Indian state does not dominate society the way the Chinese state does.

India remains a democracy throughout the period studied. In this chapter I will illustrate that democracy does not negate the state's desire to outsource violence or mobilization. A difference between India and China is that when the Indian state marshals proxies—whether violent agents or social brokers—it cannot maintain tight control over them. Accordingly, the state must forge patron–client ties with the intermediaries, which may involve ceding partial local sovereignty or allowing criminal businesses to proliferate.

7.1 South Korea

The case of South Korea is divided into two phases: the authoritarian era led by Rhee Syngman (1948–1960) and subsequently led by Park Chung Hee and Chun Doo Hwan (1961–1987) and the democratic era (post-1987). Like China, South Korea pursued a strategy of high-growth urbanization. Its urbanization rate grew most rapidly during the authoritarian era of Park and Chun. Starting at a low 28 percent in 1960, the urbanization rate climbed to 41 percent in 1970, to 57 percent in 1980, and to 65 percent in 1985, stabilizing at over 80 percent in 2000 (Joo 2019).

7.1.1 Authoritarian Era (1948–1987)

7.1.1.1 Relations Between the State and Criminal and Civil Society

In postindependence Korea, the Rhee regime coopted criminal groups, mostly youth gangs, to fight communist sympathizers and to suppress dissent. The youths were street gangsters, known as *chumok* ("fists"), *oggae* ("shoulders"), and *kondal* (hoodlums), who self-organized and ran protection rackets in their own territories (Mobrand 2016). Many of these groups emerged from preexisting associations of anticommunist youth who fled North Korea. The patronage of elite politicians, including Rhee himself, provided political recognition to these youth groups, which were mobilized by Rhee to target internal political enemies.[1] In return, the authorities gave them political protection to venture into legal businesses. The relations between Rhee's regime and the youth gangs bear considerable resemblance with the KMT's clientelist ties with the Green Gang, which the KMT mobilized to fight the communists during the Republican period in China.

Korea's Confucian tradition and the Japanese colonial experience paved the way for a strong state and a network-based informal civil society akin to *guanxi* in China. Japanese colonization transformed the Korean state from a relatively corrupt and weak state into a strong authoritarian regime with the capacity to penetrate and control society (Kohli 1994). During the colonial period, a system of neighborhood administration like the Chinese *baojia* system was established. Society was organized into small groups called *ban*, a village-level administrative unit, to control colonial subjects;[2] however, state–society relations diverged from those in China after achieving independence from Japan in 1945. The Korean state, unlike the CCP, did not establish institutions that allowed it to deeply penetrate society. The grassroots administrative *ban* system managed only a nominal existence after independence, resulting in a lack of mobilizational capacity by the state over the nonviolent grassroots society (Seo and Kim 2015); but this did not imply independent autonomy of society from the state because the regime remained repressive.[3]

Rhee's downfall after the 1960 April Revolution[4] and the subsequent emergence of the Park Chung Hee administration ushered in a new era during which economic development was prioritized. Economic growth led to expanding income and a better educated society, whose members increasingly demanded political accountability. This placed constraints on the government's explicit collaboration with gangsters, but it did not end their relationship. To shore up its legitimacy, Park's government conducted a series of campaigns to remove the highest-profile gangsters, leading to the demise of "street leaders" (Mobrand 2016); yet the government continued to engage criminals—in a covert manner— to implement economic policies in addition to dealing with political enemies.[5]

In the 1960s and early 1970s, when urbanization was in high gear, housing demolitions took place frequently. Police and district administrators often encountered citizen resistance in their relocation work. As in China, the government hired thugs to carry out coercive removal of residents. A prime example, the Korea Youth Reclamation Corporation, made up mostly of ex-convicts, was mobilized to clear existing residences. The strategy of outsourcing violence to thugs for urban development projects continued into the Chun Doo Hwan administration. During this period, most demolition companies hired street gangsters to use violent means against squatters and property owners in order to carry out their projects. This policy was justified on the grounds that criminal groups were being transformed into industrial warriors (Sunil Kim and Porteux 2019).

Although South Korea remained an authoritarian regime after the toppling of Rhee, the state's relationship with society gradually changed under the leadership of Park and Chun. In order to pursue economic development more effectively, the Korean state cooperated with certain segments of civil society.[6] Park's regime revitalized the *ban* system and incorporated it into the *bansanghoe* (BSH) system, an organizational network for population monitoring and co-opting dissent—much like residents' committees (居委会) in China and *Chonaikai* in Japan. The BSH was a monthly meeting of a *ban* (which consisted of 20 to 30 households) under the guidance of a ward office, the lowest administrative unit in Korea's bureaucratic structure.[7] By 1976, the BSH system became firmly established in all corners of Korean society (Seo and Kim 2015).

Collections of "exemplary BSH sessions" published by the government show that they usually opened with stories about the moral decay of urban life, which had to be overcome by communal morality.[8] BSH became a medium through which "the authoritarian state could create its image as a moral preacher and guardian" (Seo and Kim 2015, 78). Although no record indicates overt use of BSH for mass mobilization, as similar organizations did in China, they served the more subtle function of ideological persuasion, which helped foster political legitimacy and sustain the authoritarian regime.

7.1.1.2 Eliminating Shantytowns and Urbanization

After the Korean War ended in 1953, urban development efforts were concentrated on eliminating squatter settlements and shantytowns. As cities developed, the government relocated residents to the outskirts, mostly without any legal basis.[9] Often, relocation was not followed by the provision of effective resettlement—only forced removal and the "dumping" of families in a new location (J. Y. Lee 2000, 6). As of the mid-1960s, when Seoul became the country's center of economic growth, large-scale evictions took off. The city's famous squatter settlements were demolished for the construction of modern buildings. About 10 percent of Seoul residents were forced to move involuntarily from 1966 to 1972 (Soo-hyun Kim 2010). Existing settlements within five to 10 kilometers of the downtown core were forced to move to the city's outskirts, and around 40,000 low-income households were relocated to 20 new areas. Much like contemporary China, no record of large-scale organized protests exists; only isolated resistance was staged, despite the massive scale of relocations (Soo-hyun Kim 2010).

In the late 1960s, when President Park Chung Hee tried to secure his power and improve social harmony, the government initiated self-help development schemes to improve the living conditions of squatters in settlements but with only limited success.[10] During the period between 1973 and 1982, Seoul acknowledged practical tenure rights in the relocated squatter areas in a bid to win the political support of residents (Mobrand 2016). Ironically, this was the most repressive era in South Korea with the beginning of the authoritarian Yushin constitution in 1972, the Chun-led military coup, and the Gwangju massacre in 1980. Overall, Korea made impressive progress on urbanization during the authoritarian era. Between 1955 and 1981, a total of 69,844 households (327,194 residents) were removed from their residences (Mobrand 2016). The state achieved this with considerable use of outsourced violence, which came at a significant cost to squatters' rights; and their resistance, though frequent, was largely localized and muted—much like in contemporary China.

7.1.2 Democratized South Korea (1987–)

7.1.2.1 Demolition Service Companies with Violent Agents

South Korea's authoritarian era came to an end in 1987.[11] Democratization raised the cost for state collaboration with criminals and the use of outright violence against citizens. Facing greater pressure for political accountability, the democratized Korean state became more wary of brewing social grievances that might foment mobilization. Now that state legitimacy no longer depended solely on economic growth and maintaining security, the government needed to expand and protect democracy to justify its rule (Sunil Kim and Porteux 2019). Although this may have ended overt state-sponsored violence, covert state-condoned private violence continued to exist on a smaller scale. Privatized violence is not limited to demolition but also extends to other areas like labor repression, an area in which similar thuggish harassment and coercion have occurred as in China (Y. Lee 2019).

Democratic Korea saw the emergence of demolition service companies, the first one established in 1986 and comprising a group of hired thugs who intimidated evictees. The group grew to offer comprehensive services, including forced eviction, demolition, and guarding of construction sites. When a government agency initiated a development project, the agency would hire a demolition service company to carry out evictions in order to maintain an arm's-length relationship with the criminals. The Seoul metropolitan government outsourced the implementation of its housing redevelopment projects to demolition service companies to "prevent the image of public servants from being damaged by any 'accidents' that might occur" (Porteux and Kim 2016, 381). As a result, demolition service companies flourished and secured contracts with government agencies, public corporations, and private developers. *Chokjun*, the largest demolition service company, which had contracts for handling 60 percent of redevelopment projects in Seoul, was officially registered as a security service provider and a building structure demolition company (Porteux and Kim 2016).

In the late 1980s the government characterized redevelopment projects as civil affairs; consequently, all related disputes had to be settled between the developers and evictees (Porteux and Kim 2016, 381). The police adopted a position of nonintervention on disputes arising from redevelopment projects unless they were extremely violent. The demand for the services of demolition service companies grew as more private developers relied on these companies to perform forceful evictions and demolitions (Porteux and Kim 2016, 381). As a result public criticism of the violence committed by the street thugs who constituted demolition service companies intensified in the 1980s and 1990s.[12] Faced with increased international pressure, the Korean government had to raise the bar for employment qualifications and business licences for security businesses; however, DSC services were too comprehensive to be effectively regulated. Despite increasing lawsuits against these companies, most ended up with only minor criminal charges. Throughout the 2000s the private security industry continued to grow, and violence became ever more pervasive despite efforts by civil society to hold them accountable (Porteux and Kim 2016, 383).

Thus, the key feature of postauthoritarian Korea is that the provision of violence has become a professional for-profit service offered by private security companies; that is, demolition service companies that serve clients, ranging from government agencies to real estate developers. In the previous authoritarian era outsourcing violence existed as a contractual service carried out by gangsters who offered their muscle power to get jobs done. The condition in contemporary China approximates that in authoritarian, not democratic, Korea.

7.1.2.2 Housing Movements and Civil Society

The transition to democracy spurred the growth of new civil society organizations, including the rise of evictee organizations, boosting society's power vis-à-vis the state. In the lead up to the Olympics and the Asian Games in the 1980s, protests were based on the frame of *saengjonʼgwon* (the right to subsistence) with demands centered on government provision of relocation housing, such as public rental housing. With the rise of the democracy movement in the backdrop, even though each member of the political alliance (students, progressive intellectuals, trade unions, farmers, urban poor) had its own agenda, human rights became a "shared frame for collective actions" (Shin 2018, 362). Urban evictees adopted this framing, too, believing that a more democratic state would protect their subsistence rights (Shin 2018, 361–362).

In contrast to the muted resistance of the authoritarian era, violent forced evictions in Seoul in the 1980s were met with increasingly organized resistance. In 1987, the Seoul Council of Evictees, a citywide organization, was formed to provide resource support to individual protests. In response to pressure from civil society, in 1989 the government introduced a new policy offering cash or rental housing compensation for evictees. This state concession, supported by other social movements, came as a result of the evictees' grueling battles with the alliance of the state, developers, and landlords-cum-speculators (Shin 2018, 362). In the 1990s under this new scheme, the central focus of the housing movement changed from the right to subsistence to the right to housing. Housing was framed as a part of basic human and constitutional rights. The National Coalition for Housing Rights was established in 1990 as an umbrella organization for all housing-related social movements (Shin 2018, 362–363).

Civil society continued to grow more robust, taking on unique characteristics of its own after democratization. Democratic reforms that President Roh Tae-woo instituted in 1987 resurrected societal groups that were previously forced underground (Ra 2014). Although this gave rise to vibrant and raucous social movements, including labor, students, and evictee movements, these constituencies were not systematically included in the policy-making process (Koo 1993; Oh 2012). Democratization saw the emergence of a strong—and contentious—civil society and the continuation of a strong state. This took place in an absence of established institutions linking the state and society, which has limited the ability of civil society to shape formal political outcomes (Oh 2012); however, under the presidency of Kim Dae-jung from 1998 to 2003, the Korean government collaborated with civil society groups more actively and incorporated some of their leaders into the decision-making process (Sunil Kim and Porteux 2019).

Since 1987 the Korean state's control over neighborhood groups via the BSH system has also loosened, and residents' participation has become voluntary. Instead of a state channel for surveillance and political monitoring, the BSH has become a forum for the free and open discussion of ideas among residents and a platform of social activism regarding local concerns (Read 2012; Seo and Kim 2015). Given Korea's underlying cultural foundation of affective networks, the BSH remains relevant today.

7.1.2.3 Rapid Urbanization Came with Strident Discordance

Given the rise of civil society after 1987, the state's urbanization efforts were unsurprisingly met with strident discordance and social instability. Seoul became the epicenter of urban redevelopment during the 1980s, accelerated by the hosting of the 1986 Summer Asian Games and the 1988 Summer Olympic Games. From 1983, the government introduced the *Hapdong Jaegaebal* (Joint Redevelopment Program) to Seoul neighborhoods, implicating about

10 percent of the city's total population.[13] Unlike in the authoritarian era, however, the people were now allowed to have a voice and to make themselves heard through organized resistance.[14] Faced with harsh displacement and relocation conditions, squatter tenants in the joint development program organized an anti-eviction movement. Tenants' resistance became more strident by the late 1980s. The housing movement grew to become a systematic and sustained social movement that worked in conjunction with the larger democratization movement (Soo-hyun Kim 2010; La Grange and Jung 2004).

In sum, South Korea offers a useful case of contrast on state mobilization of third-party criminal groups for economic and political pursuits. The country's political transformation over the last century from hard authoritarianism to a liberal democracy altered the very nature of the relations between the state and violent groups as the summary in Table 7.1 makes clear. During the authoritarian

Table 7.1 The State's Relations with Criminal and Civil Society, and Everyday State Power in South Korea (1945-Present)

Periods	State's relations with criminal and civil society	Everyday state power
Early authoritarian era of Rhee (1948-1960):	Direct engagement of youth gangsters to deal with political enemies and leftist dissent and to conduct evictions The grassroots *ban* system became obsolete. State lacked roots to extend into society	Penetrated society to solicit participation of violent youths as agents Lacked nonviolent proxies to reach into civil society
Developmental authoritarianism of Park and Chun (1961-1987):	Cooptation of criminals, more covert than before, for urban redevelopment projects Grassroots BSH system established to monitor, collect, and transfer information and to bolster legitimacy	More covert and less overt violent strategies to extract societal acquiescence. Nonviolent proxies reestablished to penetrate society and indoctrinate and bolster state legitimacy
Democratization (post-1987):	Disappearance of overt state-sponsored violence; state-condoned violence conducted by private companies State and police siding with developers for latter's use of violence for urban development purposes Visible evictees' movements with framing around housing rights as human rights	Power diminishes but does not dissipate altogether. Societal compliance still attainable by condoning private violence. Greatest challenge to state power came from increased strength of organized civil society.

era, the scope condition of proxy complicity was largely met, enabling the strong state either to overtly engage criminal groups under Rhee's rule or to coopt street gangs under Park and Chun for development projects. Although the state no longer actively engages with criminals, in the post-1987 democratic era privately sponsored violence against evictee activists for the sake of urban development was condoned.

The Korean state's relationship with nonviolent civil society also changed over time. The government under Park revamped the *ban* system by turning it into the BSH, which rebuilt the state's infrastructural capacity over informal civil society. Although it never went as far as allowing the state to mobilize the masses like China, the BSH system played a role in ideological indoctrination and bolstering state legitimacy. Later, as Korea democratized, an increasingly contentious and raucous civil society developed, a manifestation of which is the evictee movement.

To put it in the context of *everyday state power*, the Korean state under Rhee's strong authoritarian rule was able to penetrate society to solicit the participation of youth gangsters to become violent proxies in order to enforce obedience on society; however, it lacked nonviolent proxies to reach into civil society when the grassroots *ban* system became obsolete. Under the autocratic rule of Presidents Park and Chun, violent agents had to deploy more covert and less overt strategies to extract compliance from society. Meanwhile, the grassroots BSH system had been reestablished, allowing the state to penetrate and conduct ideological indoctrination on society that bolstered its legitimacy, but in the postdemocratic era, *everyday state power* has diminished because the state has to maintain an arm's-length relationship with violent proxies in order to preserve its legitimacy. This does not, however, imply a complete dissipation of power. Through the condonation of private violence, the state is still able to acquire societal compliance on a range of issues, such as demolition and labor suppression; yet the great challenge to state power came from the increased strength of organized civil society, which acts as a check on state encroachment of citizens' rights.

The way in which the state's coercive patterns shifted after democratization in Korea offers some poignant lessons for China, should the regime relax its grip on society. Greater demand for political accountability is likely to forbid outright engagement of thugs or other violent groups, yet a state that remains fixated on economic performance will place revenue above the concerns of marginalized citizens. Under this circumstance, the state and the police are likely to condone privately sponsored violence against thorny resistance. The state may shy away from the direct engagement of TFH, but it could still be willing to turn a blind eye to illegitimate violence committed by private entities if it helps to achieve growth objectives. The experience of South Korea also suggests the professionalization of violent service providers is a likely trend in China. When criminal groups are swept away through government crackdowns on crime as is the case in Xi Jinping's *saohei* campaign, these violent agents may simply form legal private companies to continue offering their services under the guise of legitimacy. Table 7.1 presents a summary of the salient points of contrast with China.

7.2 Contemporary India

Because of the differences between China and India in terms of social make-up and state-society dynamics, India offers an interesting case for contrast.[15] Starting in 1991, India underwent a shift in state ideology from a generally social democratic outlook to a neoliberal doctrine that prioritized economic growth. Economic liberalization fostered competition among state governments for the attraction of foreign and domestic investment (Sinha 2005; Vadlamanti and Khan 2013). Inspired by the success of export-oriented industries in China, the Indian government passed the Special Economic Zone (SEZ) Act in 2005 to attract investment. In India, as in China, regional governments lure private investors by promising a range of incentives, including duty exemptions and tax deductions, and by invoking the power of eminent domain to requisition land.

Indian hierarchical society is informally organized according to the caste system.[16] Members within the social groupings of castes, subcastes, and religious communities are interdependent, serving to enhance the life opportunities of one another (Heitzman and Worden 1996). In Partha Chatterjee's (2004) term, India's political society is characterized by the interpenetration between state and society, or the sphere in which complex networks of political actors operate. Poor citizens living in urban slums and rural areas rely on these actors to pressure the bureaucracy on their behalf in order to gain access to essential public services. This leads to a blurred boundary between the state and society and the sharing of state sovereignty by local politicians with brokers who facilitate interactions between the two entities (Berenschot 2011).

What accentuates the usefulness of these brokers, in addition to the patronage networks of political parties, is a weak state beset by bureaucratic incapacity to meet the demands of the country's poor. According to Ward Berenschot's (2011) study of the state of Gujarat, court cases take long to settle, the police are corrupt, and the police and courts require bribes to register and settle cases. Thus, resorting to unofficial or alternative means of dispute resolution is easier; moreover, the decline of old civic institutions, such as the *Pol Panches* (neighborhood committees) and *Mahajans* (trade guilds), further opens up the space for a network of local political actors—local politicians, *goondas* (criminals), and local social elites—to serve as brokers between citizens and the state (Mehta 2013). These conditions suggest the scope condition of proxy complicity is unlikely to be met because the intermediaries wield power over the state. Put differently, the state often *has to* work with brokers and criminals to carry out everyday state pursuits.

7.2.1 Stalled Urbanization

Unlike many developing countries, India has not experienced exponential growth in urbanization. Its level of urbanization remains low, growing only modestly from 23.7 percent in 1981 to 27.8 percent in 2001, to 31.2 percent in 2011, and finally to 34 percent in 2019.[17] Behind these slow urbanization rates are frequently stalled plans by regional governments to build new towns and SEZs. Most of India's urbanization efforts can be characterized as a process of contestation between the government and organized opposition from farmers. Considerable regional variation exists, however, depending on the strength of organized civil society and the state's relationships with violent groups and nonviolent brokers who act as go-betweens. Such an outcome that departs fundamentally from China's reflects the robust and complex nature of Indian civil society.

Until the enactment of the Land Acquisition, Rehabilitation, and Resettlement Act (LARRA) in 2013, land acquisition in India was regulated by the colonial Land Acquisition Act of 1894. The colonial act provided the power of eminent domain to acquisition land for a specific public purpose, and regulated compensation to farmers at fair market value. What constituted public purpose was, however, often contentious; and fair market value compensation might never be actualized.[18] The LARRA 2013, which paid legal attention to rehabilitation and resettlement for the first time, contains provisions for a social impact assessment and consent requirements before a project takes off.[19] The SEZ Act of 2005 provides another avenue for land acquisition for zones that host industrial, residential, and commercial properties (Jenkins 2011; Levien 2011; Sud 2014b). Unlike China, where industrial zones are owned by the state, SEZs in India are owned and managed by private developers. Even though private corporations in India can purchase land directly from farmers under Indian law, they face high transaction costs in direct negotiations because hundreds or thousands of farmers may hold small parcels of land in a given area. In addition, multiple claims to land rights often give rise to disputed property titles in India. This further gives rise to the need for land brokers (Levien 2011).

7.2.2 *Goondas* and Violence

Violence has become an effective means of getting things done in India because the official courts take a long time to resolve disputes and because businesses and

citizens cannot enforce contracts, collect debts, or access everyday state services. Its premise is much like in the case of TFH, in which violence or the threat
of violence offers the most expedient means of solving a problem. *Goondas*, or
gangsters, use violence to establish authority within neighborhoods and are capable of resolving disputes, intimidating rivals, and raising campaign funds for
local politicians (Berenschot 2011); yet their considerable local influence is not
based on intimidation alone—it also rests on their capacity to get things done
and shape citizen behavior, including their voting patterns.[20] *Goondas* forge
clientelist relations with local politicians whereby in return for their violent services, politicians protect their illegal businesses from police interference.

As the economy developed over time, *goondas* evolved to become full-
fledged criminal organizations. During the 1970s Mumbai experienced housing
shortages as rural migrants moved to the city in search of better lives. This created golden opportunities for *goondas* to become involved in land speculation
and property development. To accommodate the growing population, the local
government turned a blind eye to the proliferation of squatters on public lands.
Goondas built squatter settlements to provide housing to the migrants, making
them slumlords, and helped address the acute housing shortage problem (L.
Weinstein 2008). In addition, mafiosi also helped slum dwellers with access to
basic services, such as water and power connections and cooking gas, albeit illegally. Hence, the slumlords are also members of "water mafias" (Ranganathan
2014), functioning as informal sovereigns in parts of the cities (L. Weinstein
2008). *Goondas* also registered new slum dwellers to become voters and deliv-
ered "vote banks" to local politicians.

Although TFH contribute to plausible deniability in China, the utility of
goondas to local politicians lies in their capacity to execute tasks—including settling disputes, policing localities, and clearing squatters from land for infrastruc-
ture projects—which they themselves lack the capacity to carry out (Berenschot
2011). Thus, *goondas'* violence contributes to the augmentation of capacity,
bringing value to their existence; whereas in China a by-and-large strong state
uses hired violence to deny accountability. In India, the criminalization of politics, or patron–client relationships between politicians and criminals, reinforces
a vicious circle that further limits the capacity of the police, courts, and other
state bureaucracies in performing their respective functions (Berenschot 2011).

Violence is far more prevalent and politicized in contemporary India than in
China. *Goondas*, along with public employees and organizations, are often involved in communal violence before and during elections or movements of mass
mobilization designed to sway public opinion.[21] These "fire tenders" or "riot
specialists" in Paul Brass' (1997) terms manufacture communal violence as a
tinder to shape political outcomes in India, a phenomenon not seen in post-Mao
China. Because local politicians have to forge clientelist ties with the *goondas*,

they have no direct control over the violent agents' behavior—another important point of contrast with China.

7.2.3 Brokers and Informal Networks

Goondas deploy violence as an instrument to get things done, whereas brokers exploit interpersonal trust to bridge the gap between state and society. The demand for grassroots brokers arises similarly out of clientelist exchanges in a patronage democracy where voters rely on them to connect with and lobby state bureaucracies for public goods (Berenschot 2015). Brokers in India span the entire range from local municipal councillors (Berenschot 2010) to caste leaders to profit-seeking intermediaries who facilitate transactions between the government and citizens (Sud 2014a). Much like social brokers in China, those prominent in contemporary India are the ones who can sway public opinion by drawing on informal networks that they share with local communities. As in China informal networks that facilitate trust among members are an essential element of brokerage. In the absence of reliable enforcement mechanisms, trust constitutes an implicit guarantee for the fulfilment of obligations by both parties, which in India has been shown to be crucial in swaying votes[22] and lobbying politicians for access to public goods (Berenschot 2015) as well as intermediating land transactions (Levien 2015).

Given the complexities of land deals, land brokers called *dalals* are prevalent in India. They work on small plots of land concentrated in a district or part of a district. For larger plots, they work under land aggregators at the top of the land brokerage chain and put together small land holdings into a larger plot for commercial use (Sud 2014a). Much like the *huangniu* or economic brokers in China, land brokers in India help to overcome information asymmetry and trust deficits between urban buyers and farmers. Michael Levien shows that in rural Rajasthan, land buyers, who are usually urban outsiders, often find village life opaque. A local village *dalal* from the same caste group as the farmers can bridge the trust deficits between farmers and urban buyers (Levien 2015). As with the *guanxi* networks of social brokers in China, the social capital embedded in the caste system is what facilitates the brokerage functions.

However, the implications for social control diverge between China and India. The Indian state is constrained by local brokers as powerholders without whom state actors face tremendous challenges in requisitioning land or penetrating rural society in general. This dependency hampers the state's ability to regulate social behavior in a direct fashion, an inevitable outcome given the nature of its political society, or the broker-populated layer separating society from the state

(Chatterjee 2004); therefore, while brokers in China facilitate the state's control of society, brokers in India hinder it.

7.2.4 National and Regional Land Resistance Movements

In addition to a strong informal civil society, the strength of organized civil society in India is demonstrated in raucous land resistance movements; however, regional variations exist, conditioned by social cleavages, most notably the composition of caste groups in rural communities. Caste composition may facilitate or impede organized resistance against land grabs. In comparison with China, the lack of land reform in India gave rise to a heterogeneous pattern of landholding and its correlation with caste groups (Ong 2019b). Thus, any land movement faces the challenge of building solidarity across society, and successful movements must usually cut across caste to garner widespread support.

Despite the predominance of local resistance, a few larger-scale cross-regional movements emerged in India. The National Alliance of People's Movements, a platform comprising autonomous people's movements across the country opposing displacements from any cause, has also organized numerous national-level protests against the new land acquisition act and pressed the government to subject development projects to approval by local assemblies (Levien 2013). Ekta Parishad is another example of a mass movement that organizes nonviolent grassroots struggle and advocacy at the state and national levels (Carr-Harris 2005).[23] For example, it mobilized 100,000 farmers and activists in a march to Delhi in 2012 to put pressure on the national government to legislate land laws that protect poor farmers' rights;[24] however, the funding situation for NGOs has become challenging under the Modi government, which is known for its political conservatism and unfriendliness toward civil society, especially those engaged in "rights-based" advocacy work.[25]

In terms of _everyday state power_ in India, the state depends on _goondas_ to provide housing settlements for the influx of migrant workers from rural areas. _Goondas_ in turn become informal sovereigns or slumlords in those pockets of cities, providing basic public services to the residents. This hampers the state's ability to penetrate the slums prevalent across the cities to service the poor directly. Instead, local politicians must forge clientelist relations with _goondas_ for voter support. Similarly, the state lacks capacity to penetrate rural society and influence citizen behavior itself. State power is checked by the strong brokerage power of upper caste leaders, who act as intermediaries between state and society. Put differently, these proxies—_goondas_ and brokers—are so powerful that the state must concede certain authorities in exchange for their electoral support and capacity to facilitate bargaining with society; moreover, state power in India is further checked by a vibrant organized civil society.

India is an illuminating dissimilar case for comparison with China. Both countries have adopted the neoliberal doctrine of pursuing high growth through industrialization and urbanization, but India has been far less successful than China. The two countries have rather diverse state–society dynamics. The strength of Indian society, both in terms of informal caste groups and formal society vis-à-vis the state, has meant the latter cannot assert effective authority over the former. When the state relies on violent agents or civil brokers to mobilize society, it must forge patronage relationships with the intermediaries over whom they have little control; yet regional variations exist within this weak state–strong society national pattern. The strength of civil society does not give rise to uniformly successful land resistance movements across regions. The success of land resistance is often contingent on the movement's capacity to build broad-based support across different caste groups and other social groups, beyond those directly affected by land taking (Jenkins, Kennedy, and Mukhopadhyay 2014; Kennedy 2019, 14). Table 7.2 presents a summary of the salient points of contrast with China.

Table 7.2 The State's Relations with Criminal and Civil Society, and Everyday State Power in India (1967–Present)

State's relations with criminal and civil society	Everyday state power
Local politicians' reliance on the *goondas* to provide housing settlements for the poor	*Goondas* become slumlords or informal sovereigns because of state incapacity to penetrate slums in the cities.
Prevalence of slums in big cities ruled by mafia slumlords that the government cannot effectively demolish; limited urbanization growth rates	State power checked by clientelist relations with *goondas*, who provide public services to slum dwellers and deliver votes to local politicians
Goondas directly shape voting behavior of slum residents who depend on them for access to basic public services.	Patron-client relations between local politicians and local upper-caste leaders as brokers, who hamper the state's ability to penetrate society and regulate social behavior directly
Brokers with exclusive social networks, often including caste identities, help to mediate between state and society.	
Strong organized civil society but uneven strength of land resistance movements across regions	State power further checked by organized civil society

7.3 Conclusion

These comparative cases present a considerable degree of variation in the independent variables of state-criminal and state-societal broker relationships, which result in divergence in *everyday state power* between South Korea and India as well as within each case. These case studies suggest state attempts to recruit criminals as proxies do not end when a country transitions into a democracy. Violent criminalized demolitions are still being carried out in democratic South Korea, albeit less blatantly, with the state condoning violence ordered by private real estate companies. Violent land expropriations similarly take place in democratic India, providing further testimony to my argument that authoritarianism is not a scope condition.

The case closest to contemporary China in violent strategies is the high-growth authoritarian era in South Korea (1961-1987), during which the strong state's relations with criminals most closely approximates that of a principal-agent relationship. As in China, the South Korean state under Presidents Rhee, Park, and Chun was able to exert relatively tight control over the violent agents they engaged and through them carry out state policies and repress society. State-criminal relationships in India are better described as patron-client ties, in which the state lacks control over the mafias and the two parties collude to exchange favors (votes for access to citizens).

The case that stands the furthest apart from China in the engagement of grassroots brokers is India. As in China, India has a range of political, social, and economic brokers intermediating between state and society; however, in contrast to China, the brokers in India command strong brokerage power, their social capital within caste groups providing them with unimpeded access to in-group members, whom the state must engage. Thus, instead of marshaling brokers to shape citizen behavior as the Chinese state does, the brokers in India can represent the interests of societal groups to bargain with the state while drawing profits from the intermediating roles.

The robust organized civil society in India means farmers can organize land movements across regions that culminate in national-level resistance against land grabs. These contentious activities afford Indian farmers better legal protection than their Chinese counterparts, allowing them to seek institutional channels to resist expropriation and resolve disputes. Juxtaposing the raucous regional and nationwide land movements in India with the atomized and localized, albeit frequent, land protests in China underscores the way *everyday state power* impacts the state's ability to spearhead developmental projects by imposing its will on society and society's capacity to organize itself to rise up against the state's transgressions.

8

Conclusion

In this concluding chapter, I will briefly summarize the key findings of this book, demonstrate how outsourcing repression has been applied to a range of issue areas beyond urbanization, and discuss its relevance to other countries beyond China. Then, I will analyze the rationale of Xi Jinping's recent political campaign to sweep away criminals and draw implications for China's political future and regime durability. I conclude with thoughts on field research and data collection in Xi Jinping's China.

When I began conducting research for this book in 2011, China was a vastly different place in terms of the degree of state control of society. Over the course of the 2010s, the CCP has increasingly repressed its own citizens, becoming more belligerent and assertive in projecting its power to the world. Make no mistake, though—the *everyday state power* and the repressive strategies this book encapsulate are still very much in operation in China today.

In July 2020, authorities in Shandong province deployed the same violent tactics in forcing mass mergers of villages (合村并居) in order to free up farmland, leaving thousands of farmers homeless and without compensation (J. Tang 2020).

Over the last decade, political repression has also taken a new dimension in China. In the ethnic minority region of Xinjiang, where arbitrary mass detention, reeducation, involuntary collection of biometrics, and forced labor and marriages have occurred (Greitens, Lee, and Yazici 2020; Maizland 2020; Ramzy and Buckley 2019; M. Wang 2020), repression takes on a meaning different from what this book covers. To be sure, both dimensions of repression—outsourcing repression and the Orwellian-style social control in Xinjiang—coexist in China even though they vastly diverge. The blatant, brutal, and all-encompassing political crackdown in Xinjiang obviously produces impacts on society rather different from outsourcing repression. In June 2020, Beijing passed the National Security Law with the intent of reining in violent protests and containing "subversive activities" in Hong Kong. It has had chilling effects on freedom of expression, academic autonomy, and legal independence as well as far-reaching jurisdictional impacts that extend beyond Hong Kong's borders and residents.[1] Through the covert operations of United Front organizations, the Chinese government has been accused of influencing domestic politics in Western democracies, including New Zealand, Australia, Canada, and the United States (Hamilton and Ohlberg 2020).

Outsourcing Repression. Lynette H. Ong, Oxford University Press. © Oxford University Press 2022.
DOI: 10.1093/oso/9780197628768.003.0008

Despite the CCP's increasingly repressive policies, various public opinion polls conducted by the Asian Barometer Survey (ABS) and the Chinese General Social Survey show trust in the central government still runs high. Although trust in local governments lags—as it always has—recent studies suggest that the gap is narrowing (Steinhardt 2012; Wu, Li, and Song 2020).[2] Moreover, the COVID-19 pandemic has further boosted trust in all levels of government in China (Guang et al. 2020).

8.1 Main Findings

In this book I study how the state acquires power *through* society or via society itself. By outsourcing repression to nonstate actors, *everyday state power* to reach, penetrate, and enforce the state's will on society is strengthened. As state-society boundaries blur and push against society, *everyday state power* conjures up a powerful image of an octopus with many tentacles that ensnare its prey. State power stems from the ability of the state to make proxies complicit in its pursuits. These proxies are violent and nonviolent actors who can make the society acquiesce to state commands.

This book shows that outsourcing violence to thugs-for-hire (TFH) is an expedient strategy for carrying out actions in which the state lacks legitimacy or legality. These actions are an integral part of "everyday repression," a term I coined to denote banal and prosaic repressive acts in which low-grade violence is used to intimidate and gain from citizens. Its alternative is nonenforcement, arising from the inability to deploy formal state coercive agents to carry out illegal or illegitimate actions, lack of state capacity, or lack of political will. The elusive nature of nonstate agents allows for plausible deniability and the possibility of evading accountability. Thus, outsourcing violence allows the state to accomplish dishonorable and dirty work that it cannot otherwise do while minimizing the costs typically associated with violent repression. The state can draw on this benefit if it can effectively distance itself from the illegitimate violence committed and if the violence does not result in severe casualties that will provoke public outcry. Often, these conditions are met, given the inherently low-level violent nature of TFH.

My empirical findings also suggest that grassroots brokers—particularly social brokers, who draw on social capital with local communities—can carry out a range of state functions from information collection and surveillance to conducting "thought work." In social science parlance, thought work is the equivalent of emotional mobilization—the adroit exploitation of emotions to enforce compliance to state policies. Because brokers are embedded within local communities, the emotional mobilization they conduct is undergirded by social relations, or *guanxi*, lubricated by affective emotions, such as love, trust, and respect. The practice of *guanxi* is principled on reciprocity, which serves both utilitarian and sentimental purposes. Thus, this study introduces a new autocrat's tool—persuasion—in addition to the conventional carrots and sticks. It is central to the way the Chinese state gains consent to its power. As brokers with social capital serve as legitimating vehicles for state repression, persuasion induces compliance and minimizes dissent and backlash.

I theorize a counterintuitive form of repression; that is, by outsourcing acts of repression, the costs to the state are significantly lowered. Because the state's repressive power is part of its authority, I also invite readers to stretch their imagination on how outsourcing repression has recalibrated the traditional contours of state power. When the state is able to reach into society and mobilize the masses within for state pursuits, it credibly occupies new ground and territory that was previously out of reach. As a corollary, I argue state power has been augmented to include the dimensions of participation, acquiescence, and legitimation. While outsourcing violence to TFH contributes to gaining citizen participation and acquiescence, social brokers legitimate state repression and thus induce compliance and minimize resistance. The scope condition of proxy complicity undergirds the newly animated creature of the state, one that is largely capable of preserving its legitimacy despite quotidian and prevalent repression. This study includes constructed data and carefully assembled evidence from multiple sources to demonstrate the empirical validity of these theoretical arguments. More generally, my findings suggest that comparative politics scholars need to pay greater attention to the practical and theoretical implications of blurred state–society boundaries enabled by proxy complicity.

8.2 Application of Outsourcing Repression Beyond Urbanization

The Chinese state's outsourcing of repression extends well beyond urbanization projects. As outlined in Chapter 2, the outsourcing of violence has been reported in the collection of rural taxes and illegal fees before the mid-2000s, forced sterilization before the abolition of the one-child policy in the mid-2010s (Hardee-Cleaveland and Banister 1988), and in the handling of protests (*China Labour Watch* 2010), petitioners (as described in Chapter 4), and dissidents. They share the common characteristics of being illegitimate or illegal acts because the exactions were exorbitantly high, the imposition (of forced sterilization) was inhumane, or repressive acts were simply illegal. Given these intrinsic characteristics, outsourcing violence is politically expedient and less costly for the state, compared to deploying its formal coercive agents or the option of nonenforcement. Accordingly, TFH become part of the repertoire of routine repressive measures of local governments.

One of the most high-profile cases of outsourcing repression occurred when the actor Christian Bale tried to visit the blind dissident Chen Guangcheng in a Shandong village in 2011. Upon Bale's arrival, he was manhandled and punched by dozens of guards in olive-green, military-style overcoats, attracting significant international media attention (Steven Jiang 2015). The hiring of thugs to break up labor strikes was another incident that drew such attention. In 2010, a series of strikes at Honda plants spread throughout Guangdong province, where the strikers halted production and disrupted the supply chain of the auto parts industry. Over the course of several weeks, the movement gained the support of nearly 2,000 workers while receiving substantial attention from the Chinese and Hong Kong media. Then, the local authority finally intervened—about 200 thugs were sent to mount physical assaults on the workers. The local trade union, which acts as a mass organization of the CCP, reportedly gave the order for the thugs to attack (*China Labour Watch* 2010; Kolo 2010). Thugs are also commonly sent to repress labor in South Korea as I explain in the next section.

With respect to the strategy of mobilizing the masses, when Xi Jinping called for a "people's war" against the COVID-19（人民战"疫"新冠肺炎）, invoking the Maoist rhetoric of mass mobilization, he mobilized not only public officials, but also community volunteers and neighborhood committees. The latter group acted as grassroots enforcers responsible for quarantine controls, temperature taking, and the delivery of groceries and daily necessities to residents around the clock (Mozur 2020; Zhong and Mozur 2020). The national army of political and social brokers served effectively as the foot soldiers for the war against the virus, without whom the victory would not have been scored so speedily. This is strong testimonial evidence to the critical mobilizing functions of the grassroots brokers on an everyday as well as emergency basis.

Community residents did not necessarily view the human surveillance and privacy intrusion as coercive either. This is a journalist's account of her community volunteer quarantine handler in Beijing:

> She calls me in the morning to remind me to send her my temperature. She calls again if I forget to send the afternoon reading. She texts rose emojis, asking me to "please cooperate" with the rules. . . . I would also need to submit my temperature five times a day—every three hours from 9 a.m. to 9 p.m. . . . To the outside world, China's lockdowns and strict quarantine requirements are evidence of its vast state power and draconian tendencies. But on the ground, the implementation is often bureaucratic and bumbling, the measures more tedious and overbearing than intimidating. (Kuo 2020)

Notably, China's success in suppressing COVID-19 was achieved in the absence of organized civil society. Nongovernmental disaster relief and philanthropic organizations have been more heavily regulated and suffered more crackdowns since the passing of the Foreign NGO Law and the Charity Law in 2016-2017. Under Xi Jinping, the scope within which organized civil society can operate has shrunk significantly if not completely (Spires 2020). This points to a direct relationship between the state's strong mobilizational capacity and the shape of the organized civil society sector. The inhibition of civil society in China is as much a function of the state's capacity to mobilize grassroots brokers as it is a consequence of the state's regulation of its growth. After all, if the state has strong capability to mobilize brokers to carry out its endeavors, the functional utilities of the formal civil society sector are significantly diminished from the state's perspective.

8.3 Generalizability of Arguments Beyond China

To what extent can these arguments be applied to contexts outside China? I have underscored that the complicity of proxies or nonstate agents to whom the state outsources repression is a key scope condition. I use China as a case to study the implications of outsourcing repression, but authoritarianism is not a scope condition for the arguments I have advanced.

In the wake of the 9/11 attacks, the United States under George W. Bush similarly contracted private security companies to fight the war on terrorism, including hiring the notorious Blackwater to torture and extract confessions from Abu Ghraib prisoners (Avant 2005a; Chesterman and Lehnhart 2007; Leander 2005). Rather than deploy its own security forces, it is politically less costly for the United States to hire private contractors because doing so does not require the same level of political mobilization (Avant 2005b, 126); furthermore, "when private security personnel break laws, it is not clear how to hold them accountable" (Avant 2005b, 128). Thus, a democracy may also outsource violence for reasons of political expediency.

Chapter 7 has provided illustrations for the application of the arguments of outsourcing repression to South Korea during the authoritarian and democratic eras as well as in democratic India. When states maintain a tight leash over violent criminal groups, they can direct them to control society and implement quotidian state policies. Outsourcing violence was indeed politically expedient in carrying out swift evictions under the authoritarian rule of Presidents Rhee, Park, and Chun in South Korea, yet when states lose their upper hand to criminal groups, they must forge clientelist relations and exchange favors with them, risking "capture" and the ceding of part of their territorial sovereignty. In a democratic context, where the pressure for political accountability remains high, they become reluctant to engage with violent agents directly; instead, they mobilize violent nonstate actors through an arm's-length relationship. Thus, *everyday state power* has diminished as a result of increased scrutiny from the public, but it has not disappeared altogether.

The comparative cases of South Korea and India also illustrate the extent to which states can outsource nonviolent mobilization depending on whether the brokers can be made complicit to state actions. The heterogeneity of Indian society and strong in-group caste identities have meant that the state in India cannot penetrate society and mobilize caste leader-brokers the way the Chinese state can with its grassroots brokers. The brokers in India hold strong brokerage power because they are the essential middlemen with whom the state must deal in order to reach society and with whom society must engage to bargain with the state.

A democracy that allows for vibrant organized civil society organizations can serve as mobilizing structures for land and housing movements. South Korea's transition to a democracy makes clear the point that a robust civil society is important in constraining the encroachment of state power. Illegitimate evictions may still occur when the state condones private violence hired by demolition companies, but the capacity of the aggrieved to organize themselves for collective action can bring about more favorable outcomes compared with the past, especially when the movements connect themselves with larger nationwide ones.

The case of Russia is also instructive in illustrating that the state's capacity to rein in criminals is an important consideration for the condition of complicity. This is demonstrated through the change in government from Boris Yeltsin's weak leadership in the 1990s to Vladimir Putin's in the 2000s. In summary, after the collapse of communism in 1989, the weak Russian state became "captured" by powerful mafia groups; however, when the state gradually reasserted its dominance over society under Putin's leadership, criminal groups began to collaborate with the state accordingly. Under Putin, the Russian state has outsourced repression to violent nonstate agents for the purposes of voter mobilization and carrying out repression in domestic and foreign territories.

The Russian state's coercive capacity significantly declined with the transition from Soviet rule. Upon coming to power, President Yeltsin's government split the state's three main coercive institutions—the KGB, the Ministry of Defence, and the Ministry of Internal Affairs, perceived as threats to the new political regime—into more than a dozen separate ministries.[3] These agencies also suffered severe budget cuts and reductions in manpower amid economic crises in the 1990s. The criminal world became pervasive and penetrated all layers of society and the economy in the 1990s (Cheloukhine 2008, 370). Organized crime groups, which were directly tied to large banks, controlled at least 40 percent of the economy by 1997 (Hirschfeld 2015, 10). In the 1990s, criminal groups in Russia were noted for their rampant use of violence, which the police and other security agencies could not contain. As state institutions became too weak to provide law and order, citizens and businesses sought alternative suppliers.[4]

Businesses turned to "enforcement partners" provided by violent entrepreneurs for protection. Enforcement partnership involved "the skillful use of violence on a commercial basis . . . to provide security, contract enforcement, dispute settlement, informational support, and relations with the state bureaucracy, for clients" (Volkov 2002a, 41).[5]

In contrast to the anarchy of the 1990s, Putin reasserted state authority by introducing heavy-handed policies to rein in crime and violence. Under Putin public expenditures on national security and law enforcement, or the "power ministries," more than tripled between 2000 and 2007 (Taylor 2011, 54). In particular, the FSB—the successor of the KGB—became increasingly powerful with its formal powers expanded to include areas like border protection; and its personnel spread throughout the other power ministries (Taylor 2011, 68).[6]

The Russian state under Putin recaptured control of state functions performed by violent entrepreneurs in the 1990s and shrank the scale and prevalence of everyday criminal violence.[7] As the mafias' relative strength vis-à-vis the state declined under Putin's rule, the remaining criminal groups switched to working with—rather than against—the state.[8]

In 2012, the Cossacks—a paramilitary group associated with the Russian Orthodox Church—were enlisted to prevent members of the punk band Pussy Riot from performing protest songs (Sharafutdinova 2014; Solodovnik 2014, 78–79). Nashi, a nationalistic pro-Kremlin group made up of young people and football hooligans, was often mobilized by the Russian state to intimidate grassroots political opposition (Cheskin and March 2015, 264; Stephenson 2017, 422). Russian intelligence agencies have enlisted organized crime groups to directly carry out or aid in attacks against opposition in foreign territories, such as supporting Kurdish terrorists to destabilize Turkey (Galeotti 2018, 242), backing a paramilitary group behind the 2016 Montenegro coup (Galeotti 2018, 252), and recruiting gang members to fight alongside Russian Special Forces in the annexation of Crimea (Galeotti 2018, 243, 246; Rauta 2016, 95). These instances of outsourcing repression by the Russian state under Putin present stark contrasts to the weak transition state under Yeltsin that could not keep violent criminals under control. Instead of outsourcing violence, the state's power during the 1990s was usurped by the violent entrepreneurs. Thus, the Russian case demonstrates that the complicity of violent agents is largely a function of state strength vs. proxy strength. The implication is the effectiveness of the Chinese state in outsourcing violence is not a given and should not be taken for granted. As soon as the state loses its upper hand to criminals, violent agents can become liabilities.

8.4 Xi Jinping's Sweeping Black Campaign

The CCP launched a nationwide Sweeping Black or *saohei* campaign (扫黑除恶) aimed at rooting out corrupt grassroots officials who provide protection umbrellas (保护伞) to the mafias and criminal organizations in 2018. The campaign received so much attention that it was dubbed one of President Xi Jinping's signature campaigns to shore up the Party's legitimacy and resuscitate eroded public confidence.[9] The campaign was intended to work in tandem with Xi's infamous anticorruption campaign ongoing since 2012 to reduce endemic corruption plaguing the Party. The anticorruption campaign targets both high-ranking officials, known as "tigers," and lower-ranking officials, popularly depicted as "flies." Indeed, the Sweeping Black campaign was more focused on swatting the flies, but the campaign's scope extended deep into the local Party-government system (党政系统) that governs the society (Ong 2021; Greitens 2020; C. Wang 2018a).

Practically, the Sweeping Black campaign provided evidence for the Party's—and Xi's—stark recognition that criminals and mafias, who were growing stronger, could become potential challengers to the Party's power. As Xi himself put it, "It's about restructuring [the] grassroots political and legal systems, building the Party's own networks, and resolving grassroots political crisis" (Fazhi 2019). In other words, Xi foresaw a looming grassroots political crisis—into which the "evil forces" of criminals and mafias were deeply embedded (J. Liang 2018).

Sweeping Black singled out two types of organizations for elimination (Fazhi 2019). The first comprised "dark and evil forces" (恶势力); that is, smaller and less sophisticated criminal groups. These violent groups consist of more than three members but operate without a clear leadership and repeatedly use violence or the threat of violence to engage in illegal acts, bully citizens, and cause serious harm to society. TFH belong to this group. The second type was criminal organizations (黑社会性质组织), referring to structured and well-financed criminal groups that enjoy political protection to control certain territories. The first type occupies the lower echelon of a "black society," and the second represents the more sophisticated, structured, and well-funded mafia organizations; yet when left unchecked, the former TFH-like groups can eventually become the latter mafia-like organizations.

The distinctions between the two types are consistent with the definitions of criminal organizations and mafias used in the Chinese Criminal Law (Atkinson-Sheppard and Hayward 2019; Broadhurst 2012; Chin and Godson 2006; Xia 2006) and in criminology. On one hand, TFH are structurally and characteristically more proximate to the less sophisticated criminal groups. On the other hand, mafias are hierarchical criminal organizations with distinct codes of conduct and whose primary activities include protection racketing, dispute arbitration and resolution among criminals and brokering and enforcing illegal transactions (Gambetta 1993; Varese 2010). The campaign specifically targeted 12 criminal and mafia groups. Among those targeted are groups involved in land grabs, housing demolitions, and construction projects, suggesting their perceived threats to the legitimacy of grassroots governments.[10] In addition, the singling out of "village tyrants" (村霸) as a target also underscores the central government's recognition of criminals' infiltration into village politics.

How was the Sweeping Black campaign different from other similar campaigns? In contrast to the anticorruption campaign that targets Party members, both at the upper echelons (the tigers) and lower echelons (the flies) of power, the Sweeping Black campaign focused on society and the collusion between grassroots political elites and criminal organizations. It shared some notable similarity with the Strike Black or *dahei* campaign (打黑除恶) championed by the former Chongqing Party Secretary Bo Xilai: both were Maoist-style campaigns aimed at achieving their political goals by skirting the rule of law. It appears that Xi had emulated Bo's adroit popularity-boosting political strategy even though Bo was widely known to be Xi's political nemesis (Y. Zhou 2018). Xi's campaign was, however, far more comprehensive than Bo's *dahei* because Xi's focused on reinvigorating the Party's roots into society with "no blind corners left" (不留死角; Radio Free Asia 2018).

In addition to crime fighting, the Sweeping Black campaign was also said to have the unstated objective of confiscating illicit wealth to finance local fiscal shortfalls (J. Liang 2018) resulting from local governments' heavy debt burdens (Ong 2006, 2012b). Thus, a large number of private enterprises had been targeted, and their illicit wealth transferred to local government coffers once the firms were found to have criminal connections.[11] By the end of 2018, the campaign had swept away 100 mafia organizations (涉黑犯罪组织) and destroyed 1,129 criminal organizations (恶势力犯罪集团) in the first 10 provinces investigated. It had also frozen and confiscated 4.9 billion RMB worth of illegal assets, of which 2,896 cases involved protective umbrellas (*Xinhua Net* 2019a).

As with all Maoist-style campaigns, however, once hard targets are set, overzealous implementation by local officials ensues because they are punished if targets set by higher-ups are not met. But what constitutes criminal targets is often ambiguously and arbitrarily defined. The central authority was apparently cognizant of the arbitrariness of what constituted criminal targets across different locales, leading it to standardize and regulate. Some village authorities, for example, had included "left behind children" in their definitions of criminals. Because some adolescents, left behind by their parents who departed for the cities as migrant workers, became juvenile delinquents, their inclusion into the local campaign scope was a bureaucratic shortcut to meet the set target (J. Liang 2018). When efforts were concentrated on meeting targets, resources could be diverted from removing the corrupt grassroots government leaders or police officers providing protection umbrellas (保护伞) to criminals, that is, those who are at the very root of the crime-politics nexus (B. Chen 2018).

In the summer of 2019, I came across an electronic signboard at a foreign chain four-star hotel in Shanghai urging people to engage with the campaign in order to bring about a harmonious society (Figure 8.1). I found the signboard striking because sweeping away criminals seemed oddly incompatible with the ambience of a luxurious four-star hotel in downtown Shanghai.

Figure 8.1 Electronic Signboard Spotted at a Four-Star Hotel in Shanghai Promoting the Sweeping Black Campaign
Photo Credit: Author.

8.5 Implications for China's Political Future

How sustainable is outsourcing repression? What does it bode for regime durability and the political future of China?

In various conceptualizations of state vs. society, whether the state is viewed as vying for control as part of the melange of social organizations (Migdal 2001) or if it must resist against "cages of (societal) norms" to assert its authority (Acemoglu and Robinson 2019), outsourcing repression has fundamentally changed the dynamics between the Leviathan and its subjects. By permeating state–society boundaries, the state can marshal key nonstate agents to conduct repression or mobilization on its behalf. This effectively turns the cages of norms—that are supposed to restrain the state—upside down, *empowering* the Leviathan instead of constraining it. By taking control of the cages of norms, such as the social networks that bind members together, the state can turn them into instruments of control instead of serving as mobilizing structures that coalesce members and organize them into collective actions. Put differently, insofar as the state can continue outsourcing repression to nonstate agents and use social networks and their accompanying capital to its advantage, society will remain weak; and the likelihood of a narrow corridor of liberty emerging remains slim. I believe that the outsourcing of repression is a major reason that the CCP has stayed strong and durable despite its quotidian coercion of society that would otherwise risk backlash or social revolts.

For the first three decades after the Reform and Opening Up policy instituted in 1979, the CCP largely sustained its rule through performance legitimacy deriving from economic growth with the notable exception of the military crackdown on Tiananmen protesters in 1989. In the mix of autocrats' tools, carrots and sticks accounted for the largest proportions of instruments deployed during this period. However, this study suggests that, since 2011, a conscious and increasing shift to the deployment of persuasion has occurred as a strategy to mobilize society at both the central and local levels. As the relative importance of carrots declines over time, persuasion has taken on increased prominence. I have argued that outsourcing repression reduces the typical costs associated with repression, and this has contributed—to no small extent—to sustaining the regime's grip on power.

How do we then square cost-minimizing outsourcing of repression with the brutal and harsh crackdowns implemented in Xinjiang and Hong Kong under Xi Jinping's rule? My empirical evidence suggests both types of repression, even when they fundamentally diverge, coexist in the same timeframe. But an overall greater emphasis has been placed on sticks—blatantly wielded by state agents—in Xinjiang and elsewhere, such as through the mass arrests of labor activists and human rights lawyers for the crime of subversion of state power. Although a small proportion of the population in China (but substantially larger in Xinjiang) is severely repressed, the CCP continues outsourcing the repression of most of its citizenry. With censorship and other institutions of information control in place, the people on the receiving end of outsourced repression know little about those targeted by blatant and harsh repression like human rights advocates. The multiple equilibria of repression outcomes taking place within one country keep the regime strong and durable. It is a sophisticated authoritarian regime with calibrated strategies of outsourced repression aimed at most of the population on one hand and targeted brutal crackdowns on its most vocal critics and cleansing of those groups deemed ethnically incompatible on the other. Juggling so many balls requires skills and enormous concentration. Without brutal crackdowns and ethnic suppression, the regime could conceivably enjoy—on a prolonged basis—the fruits that outsourcing repression bears, which minimizes costs and—some may even say—love and loyalty. Blatant repression, however, makes the question of sustainability a lot less uncertain; yet that is the direction in which the regime is presently headed.

8.6 Future of Field Research in China

The tightening of political environment in China under Xi Jinping and the passing of the National Security Law for Hong Kong have profound implications for the future of China studies. They affect the safety of researchers and interview subjects, data availability and harvesting, and a possible turn toward secondary data of specific types. Imagining that these changing parameters will fundamentally shape the future of the field is not difficult.

The initial one-third of this research was conducted during the Hu-Wen era, and the other two-thirds, during Xi Jinping's reign. The degree of fieldwork challenge, escalated from low to high as this research progressed deeper into Xi's rule. On-the-ground ethnographic research not only became increasingly problematic over time, but it was also nearly impossible by the tail end. In the first half of the 2010s, this researcher was almost free to roam the streets of rural towns and ruins of half-demolished villages and walk into government offices, subject only to the everyday hassles of the Chinese bureaucracy. This was no longer the case beginning around 2016, a few years after Xi Jinping's ascendency to power.

The multifaceted impacts of the deteriorating political environment in China on academia has been a topic of discussion and will become more intensely so in the coming years (Greitens and Truex 2020; D. Wang and Liu 2021; Gueorguiev, Shao, and Crabtree 2017). The current authoritarian turn bears not only on the viability of ethnographic research, upon which this book has depended to a large extent, but also on the scope within which commercial and independent media can operate. Whether it was imposed by the authority top-down or on a voluntary basis, media censorship affects the quality and integrity of media-sourced event data, upon which I have drawn in this research along with a stream of upcoming works. In many respects, wrapping up this book project feels like ringing down the curtain on a bygone era—an era that many scholars, including myself, relished.

Appendix A: Content Analysis of Government Regulations

These are the steps involved in the content analysis of government regulations on land taking and housing demolition. First, I retrieved relevant government documents for the central governments and the three municipalities (Shanghai, Zhengzhou, and Chengdu) from *Beida Fabao* by using keyword searches. There were a total of 45 relevant documents issued by the central governments, 127 documents issued by the Shanghai municipality, 61 documents issued by the Chengdu municipality, and 32 documents issued by the Zhengzhou municipality.

Second, I analyzed the documents according to two metrics: whether they pertain to any relevant procedure, and relevant activity, respectively. The procedures were divided into preparation, implementation, and conflict resolution. For instance, a government document may specify rules for officials to observe when preparing for land taking, whereas another document may layout the procedures for implementation of policies, and resolution of conflicts. Examples of keywords for preparation are "调查"(investigate), "摸底"(fact-finding expedition), "登记"(register), etc. Examples of keywords for implementation are "评估" (assessment of housing values), "公示信息" (information publicization), "签订合同" (signing agreements), and "补偿安置合同" (compensation and resettlement agreement). Examples of keywords for conflict resolution include "调解" (mediation), "裁决" (arbitration), "司法途径" (legal options).

The types of relevant activities include maintaining social stability, promoting demolitions, allowing for citizen participation, and meeting citizens' demands. Maintenance of social stability is divided into preemptive and expost efforts, respectively. We group the promotions of demolitions and land taking into three categories: positive incentives, punishment for unreasonable resistance, and persuasion. The modes of citizen participation are grouped into public hearing, institutions for citizen participation, and majority consensus. Lastly, there are two ways of meeting citizens' demands: by protecting their legal rights, or responding to their grievances. The list of relevant keywords are stated in Table A.1 below.

Table A.1 Keywords used in Content Analysis of Government Regulations

Activities	Content	Keywords in Chinese	Details
Maintaining social stability	Preemptive efforts	确保秩序;确保安全;秩序;安全;群众的疏导,稳定,不满;稳定;紧急;重大;突发事件;防范;预案;社会稳定;严重不满;风险评估;风险;维护社会稳定;把拆迁矛盾及时、妥善地化解于萌芽状态;化解矛盾;拆迁矛盾	拆迁执行工作之前的前置预防措施,包括进行风险评估,制定风险预案,化解可能出现的矛盾等。
	Expost efforts	确保秩序;确保安全;秩序;安全;群众的疏导,稳定,不满;稳定;严重不满;重大;突发事件;信访;上访;来信;来访;息访;投诉;专人负责;依法认真调查处理;上访反映的问题;群众反映的问题;反映的问题;排忧解难;核实	针对拆迁执行工作后产生的,可能影响社会稳定的矛盾和纠纷,政府的相应处理措施。
Means for promoting demolitions	Positive incentives or carrots	补偿;补助;补贴;奖励;奖励;提前搬迁奖励;提前;积极搬迁;给予奖励	为鼓励被拆迁人提前搬迁或按时搬迁的激励措施,主要是金钱激励措施。
	Punishment for unreasonable resistance or sticks	不履行政裁决;不搬迁;未搬迁;拒绝搬迁;先于执行;履行义务;履行;不停止原决定的执行;不停止执行;依法作出的行政拆迁决定;维护正常的拆迁秩序;拆迁秩序;拆迁顺利执行;维护好现场治安秩序;治安秩序;行政强制拆迁;顺利执行;拆迁顺利执行;闹事;无理取闹;依法处理	对于无合理理由由拒绝搬迁,或拒绝按期搬迁的被拆迁人,政府相关部门出具的具有法律效力或法院出具的强制拆迁的决定以及处罚决定。
	Persuasion	调解;思想工作;思想;教育;群众工作;宣传教育;说服	对于无合理理由拒绝搬迁,或拒绝按期搬迁的被拆迁人,政府相关部门对其进行劝说、教育。这种手段既非物质激励,也非处罚措施,它是一种没有法律效力的措施,最常见的做法是"动之以情,晓之以理"。

	Keywords	Description
Modes of citizen participation		
Public hearing	征求意见；征求；问卷调查；民意测验；座谈；座谈走访；听证会；论证会；听证；论证	在拆迁或征收过程的各个环节中，特别是涉及到方案制定、做出决定时，如拆迁或征收决定、拆迁计划的做出或征收的做出等，通过听证会或征收意见的方式，将受拆迁影响主体的意见纳入为考虑。
Majority consensus	大多数征收人；群众；大多数住户；多数住户；多数；签约比例；同意拆迁；不同意拆迁；改造意愿；群众意愿；意愿；民意；尊重；以人为本	这一形式的参与主要出现在拆迁决定或征收决定做出这一环节，主要是指将计划将拆迁或征收区域内的大多数住户的意见，作为做出最终决定的决定性意见。比如，如果大多数住户同意拆迁，即使存在少数反对意见，拆迁决定也会做出。
Institutions to involve citizens' participation	鼓励群众；主动参与；自主性；积极性；群众监督作用；自治改造；自改委；居民民主选举；推选；住户代表；积极分子；自主改造；股份制改造；住户代表公开进行投票；自改同项目实施单位形成联动工作机制；联动工作机制	群众自发实施拆迁或土地征收行为的机构及其主要职责。这些机构并不完全是自发组织，但是构成成员为拆迁范围内的住户。一些地区将这种机构视作一种推进拆迁，减少拆迁过程中政府与被拆迁人矛盾的有效手段。
Protecting legal interests and rights	权利；法律救济权；合法利益；合法权益；维护；维护；足够时间理解拆迁改策；合法权益；搬家准备	在拆迁或征收过程中主动考虑，保护被拆迁人的利益和权利。可以是具体体现的规定，如，在强制拆迁中为被拆迁人留出足够的搬家时间；也可以是概括的原则，如，要求维护被拆迁人的合法权益。
Meeting citizens' demands		
Responding to grievances	拆迁信访；信访；上访；来信；来访；息诉；投诉；专人负责；群众反映的问题；依法认真调查处理；上访反映的问题；反映信访；调查处理；排忧解难；投诉；投诉电话；投诉中心；核实；投诉	回应被拆迁人或征收人反映的诉求。征收活动影响到的市民的诉求。因此，市民反映诉求的方式大多包括信访与电话投诉，设立投诉电话等，回应行为包括调查处理信访，还包括一些原则性的要求，如要求认真回应诉求，为群众认真排忧解难等。

APPENDIX B

List of Interviewees

Interview No.	Abbr. (MMYY–LO–PO)	Date	Admin Level	Province/Municipality	Country	Institution	Position/Occupation	Detail
1	1211BHAFG1-1	Dec 2011	District	Anhui	PRC	B District, Hefei City	Villager	Focus Group 1
2	1211BHAFG1-2	Dec 2011	District	Anhui	PRC	B District, Hefei City	Villager	Focus Group 1
3	1211BHAFG1-3	Dec 2011	District	Anhui	PRC	B District, Hefei City	Villager	Focus Group 1
4	1211BHAFG1-4	Dec 2011	District	Anhui	PRC	B District, Hefei City	Villager	Focus Group 1
5	1211BHAFG1-5	Dec 2011	District	Anhui	PRC	B District, Hefei City	Villager	Focus Group 1
6	1211BHAFG1-6	Dec 2011	District	Anhui	PRC	B District, Hefei City	Villager	Focus Group 1
7	1211YHAFG2-1	Dec 2011	Town	Anhui	PRC	Y Town, Hefei City	Villager	Focus Group 2
8	1211YHAFG2-2	Dec 2011	Town	Anhui	PRC	Y Town, Hefei City	Villager	Focus Group 2
9	1211YHAFG2-3	Dec 2011	Town	Anhui	PRC	Y Town, Hefei City	Villager	Focus Group 2
10	1211YHAFG2-4	Dec 2011	Town	Anhui	PRC	Y Town, Hefei City	Villager	Focus Group 2
11	1211YHAFG2-5	Dec 2011	Town	Anhui	PRC	Y Town, Hefei City	Villager	Focus Group 2
12	1211YHAFG3-1	Dec 2011	District	Anhui	PRC	Y District, Hefei City	Villager	Focus Group 3
13	1211YHAFG3-2	Dec 2011	District	Anhui	PRC	Y District, Hefei City	Villager	Focus Group 3
14	1211YHAFG3-3	Dec 2011	District	Anhui	PRC	Y District, Hefei City	Villager	Focus Group 3
15	1211YHAFG3-4	Dec 2011	District	Anhui	PRC	Y District, Hefei City	Villager	Focus Group 3
16	1211YHAFG3-5	Dec 2011	District	Anhui	PRC	Y District, Hefei City	Villager	Focus Group 3
17	1211QHAHH	Dec 2011	Village	Anhui	PRC	Q Village, Hefei City	*Huiqian* Household (those who return to original village location)	

Interview No.	Abbr. (MMYY-LO-PO)	Date	Admin Level	Province/ Municipality	Country	Institution	Position/Occupation	Detail
18	1211MHAHH	Dec 2011	County	Anhui	PRC	M County, Hefei City	*Huiqian* Household	
19	1211SHAHH	Dec 2011	Village	Anhui	PRC	S Village, Hefei City	*Huiqian* Household	
20	1211BHAOD	Dec 2011	District	Anhui	PRC	House Expropriation Office, the Bureau of Urban–Rural Development, B District, Hefei City	Office Director	
21	0812GKYVG-M70	Aug 2012	Village	Yunnan	PRC	F Village, G District, Kunming city	Villager	
22	0812GKYVG-F	Aug 2012	Village	Yunnan	PRC	F Village, G District, Kunming city	Villager	
23	0812GKYVG-M70	Aug 2012	Village	Yunnan	PRC	F Village, G District, Kunming city	Villager	
24	0812GKYVG-M60	Aug 2012	Village	Yunnan	PRC	F Village, G District, Kunming city	Villager	
25	0812GKYFG4-F50-1	Aug 2012	Village	Yunnan	PRC	F Village, G District, Kunming city	Villager	Focus Group 4
26	0812GKYFG4-F50-2	Aug 2012	Village	Yunnan	PRC	F Village, G District, Kunming city	Villager	Focus Group 4
27	0812GKYFG4-F50-3	Aug 2012	Village	Yunnan	PRC	F Village, G District, Kunming city	Villager	Focus Group 4
28	0812GKYFG4-F50-4	Aug 2012	Village	Yunnan	PRC	F Village, G District, Kunming city	Villager	Focus Group 4
29	0812GKYFG4-F50-5	Aug 2012	Village	Yunnan	PRC	F Village, G District, Kunming city	Villager	Focus Group 4
30	0812GKYVR-M40	Aug 2012	Village	Yunnan	PRC	F Village, G District, Kunming city	Village Representative	
31	0812GKYVG-F30	Aug 2012	Village	Yunnan	PRC	F Village, G District, Kunming city	Villager	
32	0812BKYVG-F	Aug 2012	Village	Yunnan	PRC	B Village, G District, Kunming city	Villager	
33	0812BKYVG-M	Aug 2012	Village	Yunnan	PRC	B Village, G District, Kunming city	Retired Police	
34	0812GKYRE	Aug 2012	Village	Yunnan	PRC	Rural Credit Cooperative, H Village, G District, Kunming City	RCC Employee	
35	0713QCSCC	Jul 2013	District	Sichuan	PRC	P Community, Chengdu City	CCP Committee Chair	
36	0713QCSRD	Jul 2013	District	Sichuan	PRC	K community, Chengdu City	Resident	
37	0713QCSRD	Jul 2013	District	Sichuan	PRC	K community, Chengdu City	Resident	
38	0614ZZHNH-M40	Jun 2014	Village	Henan	PRC	Z Village, G District, Zhengzhou City	Nail Household	
39	0614ZZHVG-M40	Jun 2014	Village	Henan	PRC	Z Village, G District, Zhengzhou City	Villager	
40	0614ZZHTD-M40	Jun 2014	Village	Henan	PRC	Z Village, G District, Zhengzhou City	Taxi Driver	
41	0614ZZHPS-M50	Jun 2014	Village	Henan	PRC	Z Village, G District, Zhengzhou City	Peasant	

#	Code	Date	Level	Province	Country	Location	Role	Focus Group
42	0614ZZHVR-M50	Jun 2014	Village	Henan	PRC	Z Village, G District, Zhengzhou City	Villager Representative	
43	0614DZHPS-F70	Jun 2014	Village	Henan	PRC	D Village, G District, Zhengzhou City	Peasant	
44	0614JZHPS-F60	Jun 2014	District	Henan	PRC	Y Community, J District, Zhengzhou City	Peasant	
45	0614JZHPS-M60	Jun 2014	District	Henan	PRC	Y Community, J District, Zhengzhou City	Peasant	
46	0614JZHPS-F50	Jun 2014	District	Henan	PRC	Y Community, J District, Zhengzhou City	Peasant	
47	0614XZHVG	Jun 2014	Village	Henan	PRC	X Village, M Township, J District, Zhengzhou City	Villager	
48	0614XZHPS-M40	Jun 2014	Village	Henan	PRC	X Village, M Township, J District, Zhengzhou City	Village Party Secretary	
49	0614LZHVG-M60	Jun 2014	Village	Henan	PRC	L Village, C Street Work Committee, H District, Zhengzhou City	Villager	
50	0614LZHVG-M70	Jun 2014	Village	Henan	PRC	L Village, C Street Work Committee, H District, Zhengzhou City	Villager	
51	0614LZHVG-F60	Jun 2014	Village	Henan	PRC	L Village, C Street Work Committee, H District, Zhengzhou City	Villager	
52	0614LZHFG5-1	Jun 2014	Village	Henan	PRC	L Village, C Street Work Committee, H District, Zhengzhou City	Villager	Focus Group 5
53	0614LZHFG5-2	Jun 2014	Village	Henan	PRC	L Village, C Street Work Committee, H District, Zhengzhou City	Villager	Focus Group 5
54	0614LZHFG5-3	Jun 2014	Village	Henan	PRC	L Village, C Street Work Committee, H District, Zhengzhou City	Villager	Focus Group 5
55	0614LZHFG5-4	Jun 2014	Village	Henan	PRC	L Village, C Street Work Committee, H District, Zhengzhou City	Villager	Focus Group 5
56	0614LZHFG5-5	Jun 2014	Village	Henan	PRC	L Village, C Street Work Committee, H District, Zhengzhou City	Villager	Focus Group 5
57	0614LZHFG6-1	Jun 2014	Village	Henan	PRC	L Village, C Street Work Committee, H District, Zhengzhou City	Villager	Focus Group 6

Interview No.	Abbr. (MMYY-LO-PO)	Date	Admin Level	Province/ Municipality	Country	Institution	Position/Occupation	Detail
58	0614LZHFG6-2	Jun 2014	Village	Henan	PRC	L Village, C Street Work Committee, H District, Zhengzhou City	Villager	Focus Group 6
59	0614LZHFG6-3	Jun 2014	Village	Henan	PRC	L Village, C Street Work Committee, H District, Zhengzhou City	Villager	Focus Group 6
60	0614LZHFG6-4	Jun 2014	Village	Henan	PRC	L Village, C Street Work Committee, H District, Zhengzhou City	Villager	Focus Group 6
61	0614LZHFG6-5	Jun 2014	Village	Henan	PRC	L Village, C Street Work Committee, H District, Zhengzhou City	Villager	Focus Group 6
62	0614LZHFG7-1	Jun 2014	Village	Henan	PRC	L Village, C Street Work Committee, H District, Zhengzhou City	Villager	Focus Group 7
63	0614LZHFG7-2	Jun 2014	Village	Henan	PRC	L Village, C Street Work Committee, H District, Zhengzhou City	Villager	Focus Group 7
64	0614LZHFG7-3	Jun 2014	Village	Henan	PRC	L Village, C Street Work Committee, H District, Zhengzhou City	Villager	Focus Group 7
65	0614LZHFG7-4	Jun 2014	Village	Henan	PRC	L Village, C Street Work Committee, H District, Zhengzhou City	Villager	Focus Group 7
66	0614LZHFG7-5	Jun 2014	Village	Henan	PRC	L Village, C Street Work Committee, H District, Zhengzhou City	Villager	Focus Group 7
67	0614SZHFG8-50-1	Jun 2014	Village	Henan	PRC	S Village, L Township, J District, Zhengzhou City	Villager	Focus Group 8
68	0614SZHFG8-50-2	Jun 2014	Village	Henan	PRC	S Village, L Township, J District, Zhengzhou City	Villager	Focus Group 8
69	0614SZHFG8-50-3	Jun 2014	Village	Henan	PRC	S Village, L Township, J District, Zhengzhou City	Villager	Focus Group 8
70	0614SZHFG8-60-1	Jun 2014	Village	Henan	PRC	S Village, L Township, J District, Zhengzhou City	Villager	Focus Group 8
71	0614SZHFG8-60-2	Jun 2014	Village	Henan	PRC	S Village, L Township, J District, Zhengzhou City	Villager	Focus Group 8

#	Code	Date	Level	Province	Country	Location	Role	Notes
72	0614SZHAW-M40	Jun 2014	Village	Henan	PRC	S Village, L Township, J District, Zhengzhou City	Auto Worker	
73	0614SZHRV-M60	Jun 2014	Village	Henan	PRC	S Village, L Township, J District, Zhengzhou City	Retired Villager	
74	0614SZHFG9-50-1	Jun 2014	Village	Henan	PRC	S Village, L Township, J District, Zhengzhou City	Villager	Focus Group 9
75	0614SZHFG9-50-2	Jun 2014	Village	Henan	PRC	S Village, L Township, J District, Zhengzhou City	Villager	Focus Group 9
76	0614SZHFG9-60-1	Jun 2014	Village	Henan	PRC	S Village, L Township, J District, Zhengzhou City	Villager	Focus Group 9
77	0614SZHFG9-60-2	Jun 2014	Village	Henan	PRC	S Village, L Township, J District, Zhengzhou City	Villager	Focus Group 9
78	0614SZHFG9-60-3	Jun 2014	Village	Henan	PRC	S Village, L Township, J District, Zhengzhou City	Villager	Focus Group 9
79	0614SZHBO-M50	Jun 2014	Village	Henan	PRC	S Village, L Township, J District, Zhengzhou City	Business Owner	
80	0614RZHPL-M50	Jun 2014	Village	Henan	PRC	R Village, T Street Work Committee, Z District, Zhengzhou City	Protest Leader	
81	0614RZHVG	Jun 2014	Village	Henan	PRC	R Village, Z District, Zhengzhou City	Villager	
82	0614RZHVG-F40	Jun 2014	Village	Henan	PRC	R Village, Z District, Zhengzhou City	Villager	
83	0714FBJVP-F	Jun 2014	Municipality	Beijing	PRC	F District, Beijing	Villager Petitioner	
84	0714FBJVP-F	Jun 2014	Municipality	Beijing	PRC	F District, Beijing	Villager Petitioner	
85	0714FBJVP-M	Jun 2014	Municipality	Beijing	PRC	F District, Beijing	Villager Petitioner	
86	0714FBJRW	Jun 2014	Municipality	Beijing	PRC	F District, Beijing	Railway Worker	
87	0714FBJRW	Jun 2014	Municipality	Beijing	PRC	F District, Beijing	Railway Worker	
88	0714FBJRW	Jun 2014	Municipality	Beijing	PRC	F District, Beijing	Railway Worker	
89	0714FBJPT-M	Jun 2014	Municipality	Beijing	PRC	F District, Beijing	Petitioner	
90	0714FBJPT-F40	Jun 2014	Municipality	Beijing	PRC	F District, Beijing	Petitioner	
91	0714FBJPT-M50	Jun 2014	Municipality	Beijing	PRC	F District, Beijing	Petitioner	

Interview No.	Abbr. (MMYY-LO-PO)	Date	Admin Level	Province/ Municipality	Country	Institution	Position/Occupation	Detail
92	0714FBJPT-F60	Jun 2014	Municipality	Beijing	PRC	F District, Beijing	Petitioner	
93	0614JCSRD-1	Jun 2014	District	Sichuan	PRC	J Community, J District, Chengdu City	Resident	
94	0614JCSRD-2	Jun 2014	District	Sichuan	PRC	J Community, J District, Chengdu City	Resident	
95	0614HCSRD	Jun 2014	District	Sichuan	PRC	H Community, J District, Chengdu City	Resident	
96	0614BCSRD	Jun 2014	District	Sichuan	PRC	B Community, J District, Chengdu City	Resident	
97	0614MCSRD	Jun 2014	Village	Sichuan	PRC	M Village, J District, Chengdu City	Resident	
98	0614RCSRD	Jun 2014	Village	Sichuan	PRC	R Village, L Town, L District, Chengdu City	Resident	
99	0614LCSRD	Jun 2014	District	Sichuan	PRC	T Community, L District, Chengdu City	Resident	
100	0614JCSPS-M20	Jun 2014	District	Sichuan	PRC	J District, Chengdu City	Peasant	
101	0614JCSNH-M50	Jun 2014	District	Sichuan	PRC	J District, Chengdu City	Nail Household	
102	0614JCSPS-F	Jun 2014	District	Sichuan	PRC	J District, Chengdu City	Peasant	
103	0614JCSPS-M	Jun 2014	District	Sichuan	PRC	J District, Chengdu City	Peasant	
104	0614JCSPS-M50	Jun 2014	District	Sichuan	PRC	J District, Chengdu City	Peasant	
105	0614SCSBO	Jun 2014	County	Sichuan	PRC	S County, J Township, Chengdu City	Business Owner	
106	0614SCSFG10-1	Jun 2014	County	Sichuan	PRC	S County, J Township, Chengdu City	Villager	Focus Group 10
107	0614SCSFG10-2	Jun 2014	County	Sichuan	PRC	S County, J Township, Chengdu City	Villager	Focus Group 10
108	0614SCSFG10-3	Jun 2014	County	Sichuan	PRC	S County, J Township, Chengdu City	Villager	Focus Group 10
109	0614SCSFG10-4	Jun 2014	County	Sichuan	PRC	S County, J Township, Chengdu City	Villager	Focus Group 10
110	0614SCSFG10-5	Jun 2014	County	Sichuan	PRC	S County, J Township, Chengdu City	Villager	Focus Group 10
111	0614SCSFG10-6	Jun 2014	County	Sichuan	PRC	S County, J Township, Chengdu City	Villager	Focus Group 10

#	Code	Date	Level	Province/State	Country	Location	Role
112	0614SCSFG10-7	Jun 2014	County	Sichuan	PRC	S County, J Township, Chengdu City	Villager	Focus Group 10
113	0614SCSFG10-8	Jun 2014	County	Sichuan	PRC	S County, J Township, Chengdu City	Villager	Focus Group 10
114	0614SCSFG10-9	Jun 2014	County	Sichuan	PRC	S County, J Township, Chengdu City	Villager	Focus Group 10
115	0614SCSFG10-10	Jun 2014	County	Sichuan	PRC	S County, J Township, Chengdu City	Villager	Focus Group 10
116	0614SCSPT-F60	Jun 2014	County	Sichuan	PRC	S County, J Township, Chengdu City	Petitioner
117	0614SCSPT-F40	Jun 2014	County	Sichuan	PRC	S County, J Township, Chengdu City	Petitioner
118	0614SCSOA-F40	Jun 2014	County	Sichuan	PRC	S County, J Township, Chengdu City	Petitioner, Online Activist
119	0614HCSVG-1	Jun 2014	Village	Sichuan	PRC	H Village, H Township, Chengdu City	Villager
120	0614HCSVG-2	Jun 2014	Village	Sichuan	PRC	H Village, H Township, Chengdu City	Villager
121	0614HCSVG-3	Jun 2014	Village	Sichuan	PRC	H Village, H Township, Chengdu City	Villager
122	0614HCSVG-4	Jun 2014	Village	Sichuan	PRC	H Village, H Township, Chengdu City	Villager
123	0614JCSRD-1	Jun 2014	District	Sichuan	PRC	D community, J District, Chengdu City	Resident
124	0614JCSRD-2	Jun 2014	District	Sichuan	PRC	D community, J District, Chengdu City	Resident
125	0614JCSRD-3	Jun 2014	District	Sichuan	PRC	D community, J District, Chengdu City	Resident
126	0614JCSRD-4	Jun 2014	District	Sichuan	PRC	D community, J District, Chengdu City	Resident
127	0614JCSVL-1	Jun 2014	District	Sichuan	PRC	*Chaiqian* Mobilization Assembly, D Community, J District, Chengdu City	Volunteer
128	0614JCSVL-2	Jun 2014	District	Sichuan	PRC	*Chaiqian* Mobilization Assembly, D Community, J District, Chengdu City	Volunteer
129	0614JCSFH	Jun 2014	District	Sichuan	PRC	J District, Chengdu City	*Huiqian* Household
130	0614JCSFH-F	Jun 2014	District	Sichuan	PRC	J District, Chengdu City	*Huiqian* Household
131	0614JCSRD	Jun 2014	District	Sichuan	PRC	J District, Chengdu City	Resident
132	0615PMMED	Jun 2015	District	Maharashtra	India	Economic and Political Weekly, P District, Mumbai	Editor
133	0715NDDFE	Jul 2015	District	Delhi	India	Business Standard, New Delhi	Former Editor
134	0715NDDPO	Jul 2015	District	Delhi	India	Ford Foundation, New Delhi	Program Officer
135	0715NDDPS	Jul 2015	District	Delhi	India	Council for Social Development, New Delhi	Professor

Interview No.	Abbr. (MMYY-LO-PO)	Date	Admin Level	Province/ Municipality	Country	Institution	Position/Occupation	Detail
136	0715NDDHA	Jul 2015	District	Delhi	India	New Delhi	Human Rights Activist	
137	0715NDDRA	Jul 2015	District	Delhi	India	The Delhi School of Economics, New Delhi	Research Associate	
138	0715NDDPL	Jul 2015	District	Delhi	India	Ekta Parishad, New Delhi	Party Leader, Activist	
139	0715NDDSA	Jul 2015	District	Delhi	India	Landesa Rural Development Institute, New Delhi	Senior Advisor	
140	0715NDDEB	Jul 2015	District	Delhi	India	Centre for Policy Research, New Delhi	Ex-Bureaucrat	
141	0715NDDMP	Jul 2015	District	Delhi	India	Indian National Congress, New Delhi	Member of Parliament	
142	0715NDDAE	Jul 2015	District	Delhi	India	Business Standard, New Delhi	Associate Editor	
143	0715NDDPM	Jul 2015	District	Delhi	India	The Communist Party of India, New Delhi	Party Member	
144	0715DGUSA	Jul 2015	Town	Uttar Pradesh	India	Shiv Nadar University, D Town, G District	Social Anthropologist	
145	0715NDDSO	Jul 2015	District	Delhi	India	Center for Advocacy and Research, Northeast Delhi	State Project Officer	
146	0715NDDOC	Jul 2015	District	Delhi	India	The Minister of Rural Development in the previous Congress government, New Delhi	Officer	
147	0715NDDAP	Jul 2015	District	Delhi	India	Institute of Economic Growth, New Delhi	Anthropologist	
148	0715QCSRC	Jul 2015	District	Sichuan	PRC	Q District, Chengdu City	Retired Cadre	
149	0715WCSDD	Jul 2015	District	Sichuan	PRC	L Community Residential Committee, Chengdu City	Deputy Director	
150	0715JCSCD	Jul 2015	District	Sichuan	PRC	T Community, T Township, Chengdu City	Community Director	
151	0715JCSCD-M30	Jul 2015	District	Sichuan	PRC	W Community, J District, Chengdu City	Community Director	

#	Code	Date	Level	Province	Country	Location	Role
152	0715JCSDD	Jul 2015	District	Sichuan	PRC	S Street Committee, J District, Chengdu City	Deputy Director
153	0715JCSRW-M70	Jul 2015	District	Sichuan	PRC	S Street Office, Chengdu City	Retired Worker
154	0715JCSGD	Jul 2015	District	Sichuan	PRC	Self-Development Committee (*zigaiwei*), S Street Office, Chengdu City	Group Director
155	0715DCSGD	Jul 2015	County	Sichuan	PRC	Self-Development Committee (*zigaiwei*), D County, Chengdu City	Group Director
156	0715JCSRD-M	Jul 2015	District	Sichuan	PRC	F Street Office, J District, Chengdu City	Resident
158	0715BJDL	Jul 2015	Municipality	Beijing	PRC	Beijing City	Demolition Lawyer
159	0715BJPL	Jul 2015	Municipality	Beijing	PRC	Beijing City	Property Rights Lawyer
160	1215BJPL-1	Dec 2015	Municipality	Beijing	PRC	Beijing City	Property Rights Lawyer
161	1215BJPL-2	Dec 2015	Municipality	Beijing	PRC	Beijing City	Property Rights Lawyer
162	1215BJPL-3	Dec 2015	Municipality	Beijing	PRC	Beijing City	Property Rights Lawyer
163	1215BJPL-4	Dec 2015	Municipality	Beijing	PRC	Beijing City	Property Rights Lawyer
164	0516HSHSB	May 2016	Municipality	Shanghai	PRC	H District, Shanghai City	Self-employed Business
165	0516HSHFW	May 2016	Municipality	Shanghai	PRC	H District, Shanghai City	Factory Worker
166	0516HSHPE	May 2016	Municipality	Shanghai	PRC	H District, Shanghai City	Private Company Employee
167	0516PSHRE	May 2016	Municipality	Shanghai	PRC	State-Owned Enterprise under Food Supervision Administration, P District, Shanghai City	Retired Employee

Interview No.	Abbr. (MMYY–LO–PO)	Date	Admin Level	Province/ Municipality	Country	Institution	Position/Occupation	Detail
168	0516PSHCH-F50	May 2016	Municipality	Shanghai	PRC	P District, Shanghai City	*Chaiqian* Household	
169	0516PSHSB	May 2016	Municipality	Shanghai	PRC	P District, Shanghai City	Self-employed Business	
170	0516XSHGA	May 2016	Municipality	Shanghai	PRC	The Municipal Bureau of Housing Management, X District, Shanghai City	Government Auditor	
171	0516YSHRW	May 2016	Municipality	Shanghai	PRC	Y District, Shanghai City	Retired Worker	
172	0516YSHST	May 2016	Municipality	Shanghai	PRC	Y District, Shanghai City	School Teacher	
173	0516YSHRE	May 2016	Municipality	Shanghai	PRC	Y District, Shanghai City	Retired Employee	
174	0616BJDL	Jun 2016	Municipality	Beijing	PRC	Beijing City	Demolition Lawyer	
175	0717TGGVP-M40-1	Jul 2017	Municipality	Guangdong	PRC	X Village, T District, Guangzhou City	Village Petitioner	
176	0717TGGFG11-50-1	Jul 2017	Municipality	Guangdong	PRC	X Village, T District, Guangzhou City	Villager	Focus Group 11
177	0717TGGFG11-50-2	Jul 2017	Municipality	Guangdong	PRC	X Village, T District, Guangzhou City	Villager	Focus Group 11
178	0717TGGFG11-50-3	Jul 2017	Municipality	Guangdong	PRC	X Village, T District, Guangzhou City	Villager	Focus Group 11
179	0717TGGVP-M40-2	Jul 2017	Municipality	Guangdong	PRC	X Village, T District, Guangzhou City	Village Petitioner	
180	0717TGGVG-M50	Jul 2017	Municipality	Guangdong	PRC	X Village, T District, Guangzhou City	Villager	
181	0717BTJOA-M3040	Jul 2017	Village	Tianjin	PRC	T Village, B District, Tianjin City	Online Activist	
182	0717BTJVR-M50	Jul 2017	Village	Tianjin	PRC	T Village, B District, Tianjin City	Village Representative	
183	0717BTJVP-70	Jul 2017	Village	Tianjin	PRC	T Village, B District, Tianjin City	Village Petitioner	
184	0717BTJVG-60-1	Jul 2017	Village	Tianjin	PRC	T Village, B District, Tianjin City	Villager	
185	0717BTJVG-60-2	Jul 2017	Village	Tianjin	PRC	T Village, B District, Tianjin City	Villager	
185	0717BTJVG-60-3	Jul 2017	Village	Tianjin	PRC	T Village, B District, Tianjin City	Villager	
186	0717BTJVA-M30	Jul 2017	Village	Tianjin	PRC	T Village, B District, Tianjin City	Village Activist	
187	0718SHAO	Jul 2018	Municipality	Shanghai	PRC	Complaints and Proposals Administration, Shanghai City	Administration Official	
188	0718SHBO	Jul 2018	Municipality	Shanghai	PRC	Housing Administration Bureau, Shanghai City	Bureau Official	

189	0718SHCO	Jul 2018	Municipality	Shanghai	PRC	Construction Committee, Shanghai City	Committee Official	
190	0718SHIC	Jul 2018	Municipality	Shanghai	PRC	National Public Radio, X District, Shanghai	Foreign Correspondent	
191	0718XSHIW-M70	Jul 2018	Municipality	Shanghai	PRC	X District, Shanghai City	Laid-off Worker	
192	0718JSHDM	Jul 2018	Municipality	Shanghai	PRC	2nd Demolition Company, J District, Shanghai City	Deputy Manager	
193	0718JSHEP	Jul 2018	Municipality	Shanghai	PRC	2nd Demolition Company, J District, Shanghai City	Employee	
194	0718JSHSC	Jul 2018	Municipality	Shanghai	·PRC	Housing Management Bureau, J District, Shanghai City	Section Chief	
195	0718JSHFG12-F50-1	Jul 2018	Municipality	Shanghai	PRC	J District, Shanghai City	Resident	Focus Group 12
196	0718JSHFG12-F50-2	Jul 2018	Municipality	Shanghai	PRC	J District, Shanghai City	Resident	Focus Group 12
197	0718JSHFG12-F50-3	Jul 2018	Municipality	Shanghai	PRC	J District, Shanghai City	Resident	Focus Group 12
198	0718JSHFG12-F50-4	Jul 2018	Municipality	Shanghai	PRC	J District, Shanghai City	Resident	Focus Group 12
199	0718JSHFG12-F50-5	Jul 2018	Municipality	Shanghai	PRC	J District, Shanghai City	Resident	Focus Group 12
200	0718JSHFG-F50-6	Jul 2018	Municipality	Shanghai	PRC	J District, Shanghai City.	Resident	Focus Group 12
201	0718JSHVG-1	Jul 2018	Municipality	Shanghai	PRC	X Village, S Township, J District, Shanghai City	Villager	
202	0718JSHVG-2	Jul 2018	Municipality	Shanghai	PRC	X Village, S Township, J District, Shanghai City	Villager	
203	0718JSHVG-3	Jul 2018	Municipality	Shanghai	PRC	X Village, S Township, J District, Shanghai City	Villager	
204	0718JSHVG-4	Jul 2018	Municipality	Shanghai	PRC	X Village, S Township, J District, Shanghai City	Villager	
205	0718JSHVG-5	Jul 2018	Municipality	Shanghai	PRC	X Village, S Township, J District, Shanghai City	Villager	
206	0718JSHVG-6	Jul 2018	Municipality	Shanghai	PRC	X Village, S Township, J District, Shanghai City	Villager	

Interview No.	Abbr. (MMYY-LO-PO)	Date	Admin Level	Province/ Municipality	Country	Institution	Position/Occupation	Detail
207	0718JSHVG-7	Jul 2018	Municipality	Shanghai	PRC	X Village, S Township, J District, Shanghai City	Villager	
208	0718JSHVG-8	Jul 2018	Municipality	Shanghai	PRC	X Village, S Township, J District, Shanghai City	Villager	
209	0718PSHGM-1	Jul 2018	Municipality	Shanghai	PRC	1st House Expropriation Firm, P District, Shanghai City	General Manager	
210	0718PSHGM-2	Jul 2018	Municipality	Shanghai	PRC	1st House Expropriation Firm, P District, Shanghai City	General Manager	
211	0718PSHSC	Jul 2018	Municipality	Shanghai	PRC	Demolition Bureau, P District, Shanghai City	Section Chief	
212	0718BJDL	Jul 2018	Municipality	Beijing	PRC	Beijing City	Demolition Lawyer	
213	0519QCSST-M	May 2019	District	Sichuan	PRC	S Street Work Committee, Q District, Chengdu City	Secretary	
214	0519QCSDS-F	May 2019	District	Sichuan	PRC	S Street Work Committee, Q District, Chengdu City	Deputy Secretary	
215	0519QCSPS-F	May 2019	District	Sichuan	PRC	Q Community, Q District, Chengdu City	Party Secretary	
216	0519QCSCD-F	May 2019	District	Sichuan	PRC	Q Community, Q District, Chengdu City	Cadre	
217	0519QCSCD-M-1	May 2019	District	Sichuan	PRC	Q Community, Q District, Chengdu City	Cadre	
218	0519QCSCD-M-2	May 2019	District	Sichuan	PRC	Q Community, Q District, Chengdu City	Cadre	
219	0519QCSFO-F	May 2019	District	Sichuan	PRC	Q Community, Q District, Chengdu City	Financial Officer	

No.	Code	Date	Level	Province	Country	Location	Role
220	0519QCSRC-F	May 2019	District	Sichuan	PRC	S Street, Q District, Chengdu City	Retired Cadre
221	0519QCSNH-F	May 2019	District	Sichuan	PRC	S Street, Q District, Chengdu City	Nail Household
222	0519QCSNH-M-1	May 2019	District	Sichuan	PRC	S Street, Q District, Chengdu City	Nail Household
223	0519QCSNH-M-2	May 2019	District	Sichuan	PRC	S Street, Q District, Chengdu City	Nail Household
224	0519QCSGD-F	May 2019	District	Sichuan	PRC	*Chaiqian* Working Group, B Shedu, S Street, Q District, Chengdu City	Group Director
225	0719JCSVM	Jul 2019	District	Sichuan	PRC	Chengdu City Construction Investment & Management Group Co. Ltd	Vice General Manager
226	0719JCSEP	Jul 2019	District	Sichuan	PRC	Chengdu City Construction Investment & Management Group Co. Ltd	Employee
227	0719JCSRD-F	Jul 2019	County	Sichuan	PRC	J County, Chengdu City	Resident
228	0719JCSRD-M	Jul 2019	County	Sichuan	PRC	J County, Chengdu City	Resident
229	0719JCSCH-M	Jul 2019	County	Sichuan	PRC	J County, Chengdu City	*Chaiqian* Household
230	0719JCSCH	Jul 2019	County	Sichuan	PRC	J County, Chengdu City	*Chaiqian* Household
231	0719WCSPS	Jul 2019	Village	Sichuan	PRC	W Village, S Township, Chengdu City	Party Secretary
232	0719JCSCH-F50	Jul 2019	District	Sichuan	PRC	J District, Chengdu City	*Chaiqian* Household
233	0919QCSPS-F	Sep 2019	District	Sichuan	PRC	Q Community, Q District, Chengdu City	Party Secretary
234	0919QCSPS-M	Sep 2019	District	Sichuan	PRC	K Community, Q District, Chengdu City	Party Secretary
235	0919QCSCD	Sep 2019	District	Sichuan	PRC	F Street Office, Q District, Chengdu City	Cadre
236	1019QCSPS-F	Oct 2019	District	Sichuan	PRC	Q Community, Q District, Chengdu City	Party Secretary
237	1019QCSPM	Oct 2019	District	Sichuan	PRC	Q Community, Q District, Chengdu City	Party Committee Member

Media-Sourced Event Dataset

Description of Datasets, Data Sources, and Methodology

Social Unrest in China (SUIC)

The Social Unrest in China (SUIC) is a hand-coded protest-event dataset that covers incidents from 1995 through to the 2010s, and is being continuously updated. To collect cases of mass incidents or protest events, trained student-coders searched English and Chinese-language news sites, such as South China Morning Post, China Economic Times (中国经济时报), Oriental Morning Daily (东方早报), Legal Daily（法制日报）and a range of human rights news sources, namely, Radio Free Asia, Chinese Human Rights Defenders, and Boxun.

Radio Free Asia is a private, nonprofit corporation, funded by the US Congress that delivers uncensored domestic news to China and other authoritarian countries in Asia with poor media environments. All broadcasts are in local languages. The Chinese Human Rights Defenders is an online blog that records cases of human rights abuses in China. It relies on citizen journalists and volunteers to report incidents of human rights abuses and social unrest in China. In comparison with other websites, this dataset is relatively unbiased toward larger events. Boxun is an aggregation website that is partially funded by the National Endowment of Democracy. Most articles appearing on the Boxun website are filed by registered citizen-journalists（博讯公民记者）. Any online users can register with the website to become citizen-journalists to report on social incidents they have witnessed or come across or of which they were a victim. Boxun also has an editorial team whose members file news reports. It also reshares news reports filed by other news agencies.

The search terms included 抗议 (protests), 静坐 (sit-ins), 骚乱 or 暴动 (riots), 围堵 (blocking e.g., streets), 镇压 (repression), 举牌 (carrying posters), 拉横幅 or 打横幅 (holding banners), 撒传单 (distributing leaflets), 绝食 (hunger strike), 示威 (demonstrations), and 民怨 or 喊冤 (grievance).

To ensure a comprehensive search, coders used media articles with a higher level of detail and avoided case duplications across various sites. For example, if one news article reports on a case that is already included in the dataset, this article will not be included as a separate entry. Instead, any further details provided will be included in the coded variables. In other words, each entry in the SUIC dataset refers to a different incident.

The SUIC dataset is also subject to several media-related caveats. To the extent that media reports are biased toward larger incidents and those that lead to more property damage and casualties, the SUIC dataset is predisposed to such media orientations. Another potentially significant drawback is the development of the internet and independent journalism in China, which has resulted in a higher density of cases reported in the more recent years covered by the dataset, and those that took place in urban locales.

Additional Tables and
Graphs for Chapter 3

Table D.1 Number of Counted Presence for Each Agent Type (N = 5067)

Agents	Number of Presence
Government Officials	1028
State Security	1002
Thugs	973
Hired Agents	760
Private Companies	331
Grassroots Government Officials	336
Grassroots Nongovernment Officials	346
Quasistate Security	235

Table D.2 Cross-Tabulation: Repressive Strategies vs. Agent Type

	Govt	State security	Thugs	of which: (Hired agents)	(Private companies)	Grassroots govt	Grassroots nongovt	Quasistate security	Strategy Total
Disrupt	701	606	666	535	211	236	217	166	2592
% within "disrupt"	27%	23%	26%	21%	8%	9%	8%	6%	100%
Injure	571	684	728	606	228	203	200	165	2551
% within "injure"	22%	27%	29%	24%	9%	8%	8%	6%	100%
Kill	40	48	55	42	27	11	17	10	181
% within "kill"	22%	27%	30%	23%	15%	6%	9%	6%	100%
Restrict liberty	399	532	315	250	102	121	126	96	1589
% within "restrict liberty"	25%	33%	20%	16%	6%	8%	8%	6%	100%
Covert	175	127	140	95	54	68	85	26	621
% within "covert"	28%	20%	23%	15%	9%	11%	14%	4%	100%

Table D.3 Repressive Strategies Given Agent Type

	Disrupt	Injure	Kill	Restrict Liberty	Covert
	(1)	(2)	(3)	(4)	(5)
State Security	0.012	0.749***	0.239	1.272***	−0.357***
	(0.095)	(0.099)	(0.218)	(0.096)	(0.126)
Quasistate Security	0.443***	0.381**	−0.035	−0.174	−0.440*
	(0.154)	(0.157)	(0.348)	(0.148)	(0.225)
Grassroots Government Officials	0.463***	0.021	−0.314	0.014	0.450***
	(0.135)	(0.132)	(0.332)	(0.131)	(0.156)
Grassroots Nongovernment Officials	0.345***	−0.070	0.148	0.132	0.828***
	(0.133)	(0.134)	(0.282)	(0.132)	(0.149)
Government Officials	0.620***	−0.059	0.042	0.151	0.230*
	(0.097)	(0.098)	(0.221)	(0.096)	(0.126)
Thugs (hired or private)	0.631***	1.250***	0.622***	−0.255***	−0.143
	(0.097)	(0.102)	(0.221)	(0.096)	(0.125)
Rural	−0.093	0.607***	0.393*	−0.090	−0.278**
	(0.095)	(0.098)	(0.229)	(0.097)	(0.126)
Pre2012	−0.313***	0.140	0.642***	−0.216**	0.309**
	(0.098)	(0.103)	(0.217)	(0.102)	(0.128)
Constant	−0.043	−0.779***	−4.017***	−0.967***	−1.734***
	(0.123)	(0.127)	(0.307)	(0.124)	(0.158)
N	2,184	2,184	2,184	2,184	2,184
Log Likelihood	−1,390.582	−1,327.615	−376.607	−1,344.908	−910.182
AIC	2,799.163	2,673.229	771.214	2,707.816	1,838.364

*$p < .1$; **$p < .05$; ***$p < .01$

Table D.4 Citizen Nonviolent Responses Given Agent Type

	Protest	Petition	Legal Mobilization
	(1)	(2)	(3)
State Security	0.862***	−0.223**	−0.430***
	(0.101)	(0.095)	(0.149)
Quasistate Security	−0.316*	−0.421***	−0.601**
	(0.164)	(0.161)	(0.29)
Grassroots Govt	−0.464***	0.255**	0.382**
	(0.148)	(0.127)	(0.182)
Grassroots Nongovt	−0.17	0.425***	0.293
	(0.142)	(0.127)	(0.192)
Government Officials	0.022	0.174*	0.364**
	(0.102)	(0.096)	(0.146)
Thugs	−0.194*	−0.198**	0.126
	(0.102)	(0.096)	(0.144)
Rural	0.149	−0.374***	−0.651***
	(0.102)	(0.096)	(0.145)
Pre2012	0.104	−0.05	−0.566***
	(0.106)	(0.101)	(0.168)
Constant	−1.188***	−0.272**	−1.680***
	(0.132)	(0.121)	(0.178)
N	2,105	2,105	2,105
Log Likelihood	−1,235.31	−1,360.34	−722.79
AIC	2,488.62	2,738.68	1,463.58

*p < .1; **p < .05; ***p < .01

Table D.5 Citizen Violent Responses Given Agent Type

	Destroy property	Self-harm	Harm agent
	(1)	(2)	(3)
State Security	0.514***	−0.153	0.830***
	(0.189)	(0.175)	(0.178)
Quasistate Security	0.091	0.574**	0.457**
	(0.277)	(0.238)	(0.230)
Grassroots Government	−0.350	0.272	0.024
	(0.296)	(0.225)	(0.230)
Grassroots Nongovernment	0.525**	0.277	−0.680**
	(0.220)	(0.230)	(0.266)
Government Officials	−0.482**	0.593***	−0.325*
	(0.195)	(0.178)	(0.175)
Thugs	0.029	−0.189	0.322*
	(0.186)	(0.176)	(0.170)
Rural	0.106	−0.216	1.105***
	(0.190)	(0.176)	(0.195)
Pre2012	1.198***	0.803***	0.996***
	(0.185)	(0.173)	(0.168)
Constant	−3.396***	−3.056***	−4.015***
	(0.256)	(0.229)	(0.261)
N	2,105	2,105	2,107
Log Likelihood	−471.201	−530.906	−533.406
AIC	960.402	1,079.813	1,084.813

$^*p < .1; ^{**}p < .05; ^{***}p < .01$

Table D.6 Citizen Responses Given Repressive Strategies

	Protest	Petition	Legal Mobilization	Destroy Property	Self-harm	Harm agent
	(1)	(2)	(3)	(4)	(5)	(6)
Disrupt	−0.255**	0.231**	0.217	0.049	0.394**	−0.473***
	(0.101)	(0.099)	(0.154)	(0.192)	(0.189)	(0.171)
Injure	0.078	−0.175*	−0.493***	0.017	−0.255	0.884***
	(0.103)	(0.096)	(0.142)	(0.195)	(0.175)	(0.217)
Kill	0.496**	−0.552**	0.232	0.561	0.054	0.371
	(0.224)	(0.257)	(0.350)	(0.345)	(0.409)	(0.328)
Restrict	0.289***	0.274***	0.187	0.116	0.108	−0.290
	(0.099)	(0.095)	(0.143)	(0.187)	(0.175)	(0.177)
Covert	−0.006	0.284**	0.312*	−0.282	0.198	−0.570**
	(0.138)	(0.130)	(0.187)	(0.275)	(0.229)	(0.286)
Rural	0.13	−0.287***	−0.573***	0.202	−0.204	1.003***
	(0.099)	(0.093)	(0.140)	(0.187)	(0.171)	(0.195)
Pre2012	0.166	−0.046	−0.627***	1.301***	0.790***	0.985***
	(0.104)	(0.100)	(0.167)	(0.186)	(0.171)	(0.170)
Constant	−0.987***	−0.535***	−1.573***	−3.442***	−2.914***	−3.716***
	(0.139)	(0.132)	(0.192)	(0.281)	(0.250)	(0.294)
N	2,105	2,105	2,105	2,105	2,105	2,107
Log Likelihood	1,276.95	1,365.85	−729.706	473.519	−537.830	−528.083
AIC	2,569.90	2,747.69	1,475.41	963.039	1,091.660	1,072.165

$^*p < .1; ^{**}p < .05; ^{***}p < .01$

Table D.7 Marginal Probability Effects of Agents on Repressive Strategies

Dependent Variable	Mean Expected Probability (1) (Thugs = 0; all other agents = 0; controls held at means)	95% confidence interval		Mean Expected Probability (2) (Thugs = 1; All other agents = 0; controls held at means)	95% confidence interval		Mean Marginal Probability (All other agents and controls = 0)	95% confidence interval	
		Lower bound	Upper bound		Lower bound	Upper bound		Lower bound	Upper bound
Thugs									
Disrupt	0.451	0.401	0.504	0.612	0.569	0.654	0.160	0.115	0.207
Injure	0.400	0.348	0.453	0.693	0.652	0.733	0.294	0.243	0.340
Kill	0.027	0.016	0.046	0.049	0.033	0.071	0.022	0.006	0.040
Restrict	0.262	0.222	0.304	0.215	0.183	0.251	-0.047	-0.081	-0.012
Covert	0.144	0.112	0.181	0.129	0.103	0.159	-0.015	-0.046	0.014
State Security									
Disrupt	0.451	0.402	0.502	0.446	0.401	0.496	-0.004	-0.046	0.042
Injure	0.400	0.346	0.452	0.580	0.532	0.628	0.180	0.131	0.228
Kill	0.027	0.015	0.042	0.034	0.021	0.053	0.008	-0.006	0.023
Restrict	0.262	0.223	0.306	0.563	0.514	0.609	0.300	0.259	0.345
Covert	0.143	0.113	0.179	0.105	0.081	0.132	-0.038	-0.068	-0.012
Quasistate Security									
Disrupt	0.453	0.403	0.507	0.560	0.469	0.646	0.107	0.031	0.184
Injure	0.401	0.353	0.453	0.487	0.397	0.579	0.086	0.001	0.172
Kill	0.027	0.016	0.043	0.031	0.012	0.061	0.003	-0.014	0.030
Restrict	0.261	0.220	0.307	0.224	0.168	0.290	-0.037	-0.089	0.018

(continued)

Table D.7 Continued

Dependent Variable	Mean Expected Probability (1) (Thugs = 0; all other agents = 0; controls held at means)	95% confidence interval		Mean Expected Probability (2) (Thugs = 1; All other agents = 0; controls held at means)	95% confidence interval		Mean Marginal Probability (All other agents and controls = 0)	95% confidence interval	
		Lower bound	Upper bound		Lower bound	Upper bound		Lower bound	Upper bound
Covert	0.143	0.113	0.179	0.099	0.061	0.149	-0.044	-0.085	0.002
Government Officials									
Disrupt	0.453	0.402	0.505	0.602	0.556	0.645	0.149	0.102	0.197
Injure	0.401	0.351	0.454	0.390	0.343	0.436	-0.012	-0.061	0.034
Kill	0.027	0.016	0.044	0.028	0.017	0.043	0.001	-0.013	0.014
Restrict	0.261	0.221	0.307	0.278	0.242	0.322	0.017	-0.024	0.055
Covert	0.143	0.113	0.181	0.179	0.146	0.213	0.036	0.002	0.069
Grassroots Government Officials									
Disrupt	0.451	0.396	0.502	0.570	0.491	0.646	0.119	0.050	0.189
Injure	0.400	0.351	0.453	0.406	0.330	0.481	0.006	-0.059	0.072
Kill	0.027	0.016	0.043	0.016	0.006	0.035	-0.011	-0.024	0.005
Restrict	0.262	0.224	0.308	0.261	0.205	0.322	-0.001	-0.049	0.050
Covert	0.143	0.112	0.180	0.211	0.154	0.271	0.068	0.023	0.119
Grassroots Nongovernment Officials									
Disrupt	0.453	0.399	0.508	0.538	0.468	0.608	0.085	0.016	0.152
Injure	0.400	0.350	0.454	0.389	0.322	0.461	-0.010	-0.072	0.060
Kill	0.026	0.015	0.042	0.033	0.016	0.060	0.006	-0.009	0.026
Restrict	0.261	0.220	0.302	0.281	0.223	0.344	0.020	-0.032	0.076
Covert	0.144	0.113	0.180	0.280	0.217	0.349	0.135	0.075	0.194

Table D.8 Marginal Probability Effects of Agents on Violent and Nonviolent Citizen Responses

Dependent Variable	Mean Expected Probability (1) (Thugs = 0; all other agents = 0; controls held at means)	95% confidence interval		Mean Expected Probability (2) (Thugs = 1; All other agents = 0; controls held at means)	95% confidence interval		Mean Marginal Probability (All other agents and controls = 0)	95% confidence interval	
		Lower bound	Upper bound		Lower bound	Upper bound		Lower bound	Upper bound
Thugs									
Protest	0.253	0.212	0.296	0.216	0.180	0.250	-0.037	-0.074	0.001
Petition	0.383	0.338	0.432	0.337	0.295	0.376	-0.046	-0.090	-0.001
Legal Mobilization	0.097	0.072	0.127	0.109	0.083	0.138	0.012	-0.015	0.037
Damage Properties	0.049	0.032	0.071	0.049	0.033	0.069	0.000	-0.017	0.017
Self-harm	0.050	0.035	0.070	0.043	0.030	0.061	-0.007	-0.024	0.007
Harm Agents	0.046	0.030	0.065	0.063	0.044	0.084	0.017	0.001	0.034
State Security									
Protest	0.251	0.207	0.293	0.449	0.398	0.496	0.198	0.153	0.242
Petition	0.383	0.334	0.429	0.326	0.286	0.369	-0.057	-0.101	-0.012
Legal Mobilization	0.097	0.072	0.128	0.065	0.047	0.087	-0.032	-0.058	-0.011
Damage Properties	0.049	0.031	0.071	0.085	0.061	0.116	0.036	0.015	0.062
Self-harm	0.051	0.034	0.073	0.045	0.030	0.065	-0.005	-0.021	0.009
Harm Agents	0.046	0.030	0.065	0.098	0.073	0.129	0.052	0.030	0.080
Quasistate Security									
Protest	0.253	0.213	0.298	0.204	0.148	0.270	-0.049	-0.101	0.002
Petition	0.382	0.332	0.433	0.294	0.224	0.368	-0.089	-0.152	-0.025
Legal Mobilization	0.096	0.070	0.128	0.058	0.030	0.102	-0.039	-0.069	-0.001
Damage Properties	0.049	0.032	0.072	0.056	0.029	0.099	0.008	-0.017	0.042
Self-harm	0.051	0.035	0.072	0.085	0.048	0.138	0.034	0.003	0.079

(continued)

Table D.8 Continued

Dependent Variable	Mean Expected Probability (1) (Thugs = 0; all other agents = 0; controls held at means)	95% confidence interval		Mean Expected Probability (2) (Thugs = 1; All other agents = 0; controls held at means)	95% confidence interval		Mean Marginal Probability (All other agents and controls = 0)	95% confidence interval	
		Lower bound	Upper bound		Lower bound	Upper bound		Lower bound	Upper bound
Harm Agents	0.046	0.030	0.066	0.073	0.042	0.114	0.027	0.001	0.060
Government Officials									
Protest	0.254	0.212	0.301	0.254	0.217	0.293	0.000	-0.035	0.038
Petition	0.383	0.334	0.435	0.430	0.386	0.473	0.046	-0.004	0.094
Legal Mobilization	0.098	0.074	0.124	0.140	0.112	0.169	0.042	0.013	0.071
Damage Properties	0.048	0.031	0.071	0.029	0.018	0.042	-0.020	-0.039	-0.006
Self-harm	0.051	0.035	0.072	0.086	0.063	0.115	0.035	0.013	0.059
Harm Agents	0.046	0.031	0.069	0.033	0.021	0.050	-0.013	-0.027	0.000
Grassroots Government Officials									
Protest	0.253	0.212	0.298	0.179	0.132	0.236	-0.074	-0.118	-0.028
Petition	0.382	0.335	0.432	0.441	0.369	0.514	0.059	0.001	0.124
Legal Mobilization	0.096	0.073	0.126	0.138	0.095	0.195	0.042	0.003	0.088
Damage Properties	0.049	0.031	0.072	0.036	0.018	0.064	-0.013	-0.034	0.013
Self-harm	0.051	0.035	0.072	0.071	0.042	0.108	0.020	-0.005	0.048
Harm Agents	0.046	0.030	0.065	0.049	0.028	0.078	0.003	-0.017	0.028
Grassroots Nongovernment Officials									
Protest	0.254	0.214	0.298	0.223	0.179	0.280	-0.030	-0.080	0.020
Petition	0.382	0.334	0.432	0.484	0.419	0.554	0.102	0.044	0.165
Legal Mobilization	0.097	0.071	0.126	0.127	0.085	0.184	0.030	-0.009	0.076
Damage Properties	0.049	0.032	0.072	0.076	0.046	0.115	0.028	0.002	0.060
Self-harm	0.050	0.034	0.069	0.066	0.040	0.103	0.016	-0.008	0.048
Harm Agents	0.046	0.030	0.067	0.025	0.013	0.042	-0.021	-0.040	-0.005

Table D.9 Distribution of Nonviolent Strategies by Agent Types (Percentages in parentheses)

	Collective punishment	Welfare suspension	Thought work	Financial rewards	Misc	All strategies
Government officials	47 (76%)	6 (55%)	16 (41%)	6 (29%)	10 (36%)	85 (53%)
Grassroots govt officials	6 (10%)	0 (0%)	12 (31%)	4 (19%)	6 (21%)	28 (17%)
Grassroots nongovt officials	5 (8%)	5 (45%)	10 (26%)	3 (14%)	3 (11%)	26 (16%)
Thugs	2 (3%)	0 (0%)	0 (0%)	1 (5%)	7 (25%)	10 (6%)
Real estate developers	0 (0%)	0 (0%)	0 (0%)	7 (33%)	1 (4%)	8 (5%)
Other	2 (3%)	0 (0%)	1 (3%)	0 (0%)	1 (4%)	4 (2%)
All agents	62	11	39	21	28	161

Source: Author's collection of media data.

Notes

Chapter 1

1. Interview 0516HSHPE and 0516PSHCH-F50.
2. Interview 0516YSHRW; 0516YSHST; and 0516YSHRE.
3. For instance, the growth experience of the Asian Tigers—particularly South Korea and Singapore—illustrates the capacity of these governments to create a pliant workforce by keeping wages low and banning collective bargaining, outcomes that favor capital owners and large business conglomerates. Pinochet's Chile similarly banned unions and passed strict labor laws that restricted collective bargaining, which resulted in high income inequality between capitalists and laborers.
4. In 2010, land-related disputes accounted for an estimated 45–65 percent of the 180,000 total social unrest incidents that occurred in China that year. See Ong (2015a).
5. A 1.2 million-acre increase in urban construction has occurred annually. The rezoning of this land from rural to urban usage and resultant expropriation from peasants can be inferred. The central government aims to make nearly half a billion more people urban residents in the next 25 to 30 years, and urbanization is not expected to slow until it reaches 70 to 75 percent of the total population.
6. India is one of the two comparative cases studied in Chapter 7. Its urban population growth rate fell from its peak of 3.9 percent in 1972 to 2.3 percent in 2019 to reach an overall urbanization rate of 34 percent.
7. The term "outsourcing" originated in the literature of the economics of industrial production. Outsourcing is "the procurement of products or services from sources that are external to the organization. Firms should consider outsourcing when it is believed that certain support functions can be completed faster, cheaper, or better by an outside organization" (Lankford and Parsa 1999, 310). Also see Bhagwati, Panagiriya, and Srinivasan (2004) and Grossman and Helpman (2005).
8. I first coined the term "everyday repression" in Ong (2015b).
9. See Ong (2018a) and (2018b).
10. For research on the central and local governments' diverging interests in containing protests, see Yongshun Cai (2010) and Lianjiang Li, Liu, and O'Brien (2012).
11. Thus, adding the central state to the existing analysis of the "state" will complicate the concept without providing any additional analytical leverage.
12. This holds true irrespective of whether the relations are conceptualized as in Joel Migdal's state-in-society term or Peter Evans' notion of the state's "embedded autonomy" within the society. See Evans (1995) and Migdal (1988, 2001).

13. For a similarly broad conception of social control, see Hassan (2020), who includes bureaucratic management as a means of controlling society.
14. Loveman (2005) has argued along the same line about symbolic power of the state.
15. This is intrinsically the democratic peace theory in a domestic context. See Davenport (2007b).
16. Ong (2015b) and Ong (2018b).
17. I recognize the flourishing and well-established literature on mafias in countries like Italy, Russia, and Japan; for instance, see Galeotti (2018); Gambetta (1993); Hill (2003); and Volkov (2002b). To be sure, mafias are distinctive from TFH; see Chapter 3 for more detail.

Chapter 2

1. By contrast, Almond and Powell (1966) have defined "state capabilities" in terms of the following five dimensions: extractive, regulative, distributive, symbolic, and responsive capabilities.
2. Skinner and Winckler (1969) have applied the concept to an analysis of agricultural cycles in China.
3. Gerschewski (2013) has argued that legitimation along with repression and co-optation are the three pillars of stability in autocratic regimes. See also Dukalskis and Gerschewski (2017) and Tannenberg et al. (2021).
4. Some scholars, such as Schatz and Maltseva (2012) and Viterna (2006), have evoked the term "persuasion," but it carries a meaning different from the one used here.
5. In *State of Repression*, Blaydes (2018) has also similarly differentiated active cooperation from acquiescence as different forms of compliance.
6. C.f. Chen and Greitens (2021) who argue that legibility depends not only on state capacity to collect information, but also integrate it.
7. Tianjian Shi (2015) has proposed a "cultural logic" in explaining political participation and trust in the authorities, drawing on survey data collected in mainland China.
8. For empirical evidence in support of this thesis, see W. Tang (2016), who argued that egalitarian communal living in villages and work-unit housing compounds, as an integral part of the socialist legacy, has promoted interpersonal trust. This has in turn enhanced citizen participation in the regime, which enjoys legitimacy.
9. Section 2.3 builds on my earlier work on everyday repression. See Ong (2015b).
10. It is not uncommon for the militias to harass and extort citizens and illegally detain people they are supposed to protect. See Butler, Gluch, and Mitchell (2007); Callaghy (1984); and Mueller (2000).
11. These dimensions of repression are outlined in Earl (2003).
12. TFH are not necessarily covert repressive agents like those involved in human rights abuses, but the acts they commit are often covert in nature or in intention. For agents involved in human rights violations, see Loveman (1998) and della Porta (1995).

13. Unfunded mandates were made worse by the 1994 fiscal recentralization. See Bernstein and Lü (2003) and C. Wong (2000).

14. By monopolizing land sale, local governments can acquire collective-owned land from farmers at low rates, convert it into state-owned land, and sell the user rights at multifold prices to private developers. See Hsing (2010) and Ong (2014).

15. For the use of thugs in the collection of population fines, see Hardee-Cleaveland and Banister (1988).

16. Note that observability of actions here refers to the physicality of actions, not intentionality.

17. Oppenheimer's *The Act of Killing* portrayed the Suharto regime in Indonesia, making use of a far-right paramilitary organization known as Pancasila Youth and young hoodlums who scalped movie-ticket to massacre at least a million civilians loosely labeled "Communists." Also see Alvarez (2006, 17); Article 19 (1997); Carey, Colaresi, and Mitchell (2015); Kine (2014); Mazzei (2009); Rafter (2014, 258); Roessler (2005, 209); and Stanley (1996).

18. Local officials are usually investigated for corruption as a violation of Party rules and are then subject to criminal investigation and prosecution if found guilty. See Yongshun Cai (2014).

19. Since the fiscal decentralization reform in the 1980s and subsequent recentralization of power to collect revenue in 1994, local state capacity to spend on public goods, including policing, have declined. Formal bureaucratic expenditures have also declined with fiscal recentralization introduced in 1994, leaving government agencies to seek out alternative informal financing, such as taking bribes or imposing fees. See William and Godson (2002) and P. Wang (2017).

20. Some social brokers are also known as "activists" in the existing literature, but they are distinct from student or youth activists who take part in revolutions or collective actions. For examples of the former usage of "activists," see Perry (2011); Solomon (1969); and Guo and Sun (2014).

21. See Guo (2012).

22. Fulbrook (2005) looks at the lives of ordinary East Germans, arguing that the GRD was not all oppression and rule by fear. It involved many its citizens in its political structures and processes, but in no way did it come close to the level of involvement of mass organizations in China.

23. *Druzhinniki* were volunteers recruited from the society to serve as auxiliary police, but "Soviet citizens were often unwilling to donate their time for boring patrols and intrusive raids to verify the internal passports of other citizens." See *Russia Update* (2015) and Shelley (1996, 86).

24. At one end of the spectrum was South Korea's developmental state, which could effectively pursue state goals relatively unconstrained by societal force, but Zaire's predatory state with opposite traits sat at the other end of the spectrum. See Evans (1995).

25. A state's central capabilities can be indicated by competent bureaucracy, fiscal endowment, size of army, and number of police. See Mann (1984).

26. Jeffery Herbst (2000) studies reasons that some African countries face challenges in asserting "authority over distance."

27. See Ziblatt (2006) for a study on state formation in Italy and Germany; Scott (2010) on the highland tribes in Southeast Asia; and Koss and Sato (2016) on contemporary China.

28. Scholars have concluded they are positively and negatively associated or exhibit an inverted-U relationship. See Davenport and Inman (2012); Lichbach (1987); Moore (1998); Muller and Opp (1986); Pierskalla (2010); and Rasler (1996).

29. Alisha Holland (2017) has argued that forbearance, such as a government's nonenforcement of cleaning up street vending, is driven by a deliberate attempt to win votes from poorer groups.

30. The meaning of persuasion as a tool of control in existing studies differs from my interpretation of it. Schatz and Maltseva (2012) use the term to mean government proactive framing of controversial issues in the manner to ensure regime survival. Viterna (2006) argues women could be "pulled," "pushed," and "persuaded" to join the Salvadoran Guerrilla Army. The context here is being persuaded to mobilize, not to comply with state directives. For use of the term in China's context, see Brady (2008) on propaganda and Repnikova & Fang (2018) on digital authoritarianism.

31. However, ideology, in terms of Xi Jinping Thought (习近平思想), is enjoying resurgence under the presidency of Xi, who has also abolished the term limits of the office. In their survey work, Pan and Xu find that educated and higher-income urban citizens tend to embrace political liberalism and espouse nontraditional values, the opposite of what the CCP is promoting. See Pan and Xu (2018).

32. One possible exception is *Ruling by Other Means*, an edited volume that examines state-mobilized social movements in a range of countries, including China. See Ekiert, Perry, and Yan (2020).

33. As they argue, "deceptively ad hoc and arbitrary, dishing out cash payments or other material benefits in exchange for compliance has become a patterned and routinized response to popular unrest." See C.K. Lee and Zhang (2013, 1486).

34. See Perry (2002b) and (2019).

35. The content analysis was based on selected keyword frequencies in government regulations issued by the central government and those of the major field sites (Shanghai, Chengdu, and Zhengzhou). The regulations were sourced from the Peking University Legal Treasures (*Beida Fabao*). See Appendix A for more details.

36. Douglass North, John Wallis, and Barry Weingast have made a similar argument with the state's capacity to monopolize and control the use of violence. In *Violence and Social Orders* (2009) and subsequently in the *Shadow of Violence* (2012, 344), they argue that countries with limited access order often experience slower growth or economic collapse, precipitated by violence. Only in open-access-order societies, in which the governments have credible commitments to control the use of violence through the military and police, can the rule of law be enforced impartially for all citizens. They consider China to be a mature and successful limited-access-order society, in which the dominant (ruling) coalition limits competition and establishes rents to maintain its rule and prevent violence.

37. Albertus, Fenner, and Slater (2018, 9–12) argue that resource redistribution can undercut rivals and enmesh citizens in relationships of dependence, contributing to

regime durability. Their focus on the political economy of redistribution complements this book's analyses of repression and state power.

38. The large, rich, classic literature of developmental states offers examinations of states' bureaucratic capacity, state-business relations, and industrial policies (Haggard 2018; J. Wong 2004). More recent work, such as that of Looney (2020), deals with how some East Asian countries have successfully mobilized the society for rural development.

Chapter 3

1. This builds on my earlier work on everyday repression; see Ong (2015b).
2. Holland (2017) has argued for forbearance, such as government nonenforcement of street vending cleanup, as driven by a deliberate attempt to win votes from poorer groups.
3. Notably, external agents' undisciplined violence could sometimes be a benefit rather than a cost to the hiring party. Avant (2005a, 225) argues the possible functional expediency of the United States' use of private security companies instead of sending the military to conduct human rights abuses in Abu Ghraib because professional military values prevent them from committing the violent acts carried out by those companies.
4. Avant (2005a, 81) has made a similar argument with respect to strong and weak states' engagement of private security companies.
5. This differentiates TFH from other nonstate violent agents, such as the ultranationalist skinheads in Russia, who committed violent crimes against immigrants for the sake of ethnic cleansing. See Harding (2009).
6. Interview No. 0812GKYVG-F50-1.
7. Interview No. 0812GKYVG-F50-1. Note that the use of insider-outsiders (those who are not from immediate localities but still know the region well) was also present in the case of the Ku Klux Klan, which used members of neighboring klaverns to conduct violence against victims. See Cunningham (2004).
8. Illegal fees were extracted to finance local infrastructural projects. See Hurst et al. (2014).
9. For instance, reports of violent events at the subnational level in Africa are found to be associated with cellphone coverage across the continent. See Pierskalla and Hollenbach (2013).
10. For instance, U.S. media with different partisan orientation has been found to depict the same events in a diverging manner. See Davenport (2010).
11. See Table D.1 in Appendix D for number of each agent's presence.
12. The full cross-tabulation table can be found in Table D.2 in Appendix D.
13. Regression results for the binominal logit models appear in Table D.3 in Appendix D.
14. These models imply correlation rather than causality because reverse causality cannot be ruled out. Specific agent types could be deployed with completing certain

actions in mind in the end because they were deemed the most suitable or effective for those jobs.

15. The mean marginal effects for thugs are the calculated differences between a) and b) where a) is the mean expected probabilities of repressive strategies when thugs = 1, all other agents = 0, and control variables are held at means; and b) is the mean expected probabilities of repressive measures when thugs = 0, all other agents = 0, and control variables held at means. The control variables are rural–urban location and the year 2012, when the new regulation on housing demolition was passed. The probabilities are simulated using the Zelig package, comparing baseline conditions (all agents = 0) and the treatment condition (agent x = 1, other agents = 0) with all other control variables equal. See King, Tomz, and Wittenburg (2000); Kuhn (1980); and Rowe (2009).

16. Collective petitioning that involves more than five people is deemed illegal, but the petition itself is an institution that has a strong historical presence in China. "Petition" here refers to both legal and illegal ones.

17. Findings for the binomial logit models appear in Table D.4 in Appendix D.

18. These mean marginal effects are calculated the same way as they are in Figure 3.4.

19. For details on marginal probability of agents on citizen responses, see Table D.8 in Appendix D.

20. These are the marginal probabilities for the other agents, that is, thugs (0.215), quasistate security (0.204), grassroots government (0.179), and grassroots nongovernment officials (0.223). See Table D.8 in Appendix D. The finding for the police's lack of effectiveness in deterring protests does not necessarily contradict a recent study that shows the concentration of police resources in policing protests rather than crime prevention; see Scoggins (2021).

21. 63 of 92 cases of self-harm in the dataset took the form of self-immolation.

22. The simulation here is based on the binomial logit models reported in Table D.5 in Appendix D. The marginal probabilities reported here appear in Table D.8 in Appendix D.

23. Collective petitioning involving five or more people has since the mid-2010s been declared illegal; so has "skip-level" petitioning (越级上访), that is, citizens petitioning at administrative levels above those available for their place of residence.

24. For a contrasting view, see Mattingly (2019).

25. The likelihood of pursuing petition and legal mobilization is affected by location, with urban residents typically having better access to institutional channels of conflict resolution.

26. Self-immolation tends to be associated with practices of Hindus and Buddhists, for example, the self-immolation protests of Buddhists against the government in South Vietnam and the Tibetan Buddhists in China.

27. In recent years, a growing number of studies have drawn on emotions to explain participation in civil wars and armed mobilization as well as how the collective actions have been overcome. See Costalli and Ruggeri (2015); Pearlman (2013); Rodgers (2010, 273); Wood (2003); and Nugent (2020).

Chapter 4

1. In this respect, the case studies in this chapter are not a representative sample of TFH violence in that most third-party thuggish violence is humdrum and low-grade and carried out covertly to avert public attention.
2. "Failure" in this respect refers to instances in which TFH do not bring the expected benefit of plausible deniability because the nature of violence was not low-grade, pedestrian, or covert.
3. Three small districts (小区) in the intersection of Wuyuan Road, Changle Road, and Wulumuqizhong Road were designated for renewal which started in 2002. Source: Interview 0718XSHLW-M70.
4. A new law passed in 2011 has made real estate companies' involvement in demolition works illegal.
5. Interview 0718XSHLW-M70.
6. Interview 0718XSHLW-M70.
7. Interview 0718XSHLW-M70.
8. Interview 0718XSHLW-M70.
9. The human costs of demolition and relocation in Shanghai during the 1990s have also been vividly captured by Shao (2013). For additional information on the destruction of old neighborhoods in Shanghai, see also J. Li (2015).
10. Flower Village is a pseudonym.
11. Villagers received about 40,000 RMB/*mu* (92,400 USD/hectare), whereas total compensation was 120,000 RMB/*mu* (277,200 USD/hectare). Source: Interview 0812GKYVG-M60.
12. 1 *mu* is equivalent to 0.06667 hectare.
13. Interview 0812GKYVG-M60.
14. Interview 0812GKYVG-M70.
15. Interview 0812GKYVG-M70.
16. Interview 0812GKYVG-M60.
17. Interview 0812GKYVG-M60.
18. Interview 0812GKYVG-F. Also, see X. Zhu (2012).
19. Interviews 0812BKYVG-M and 0812BKYVG-F.
20. Interview 0812GKYVG-M60. This is further supported by Cheng (2011) and X. Zhu (2012).
21. Interview 0812GKYVG-M60.
22. Interviews 0812GKYVG-M60 and 0812GKYVG-F. Also, see X. Zhu (2012).
23. Interview 0812GKYFG-F50.
24. Interview 0812GKYFG-F50.
25. Interview 0812GKYVR-M40.
26. Interview 0812GKYVG-M60.
27. Interviews 0812GKYVG-M60; 0812GKYVG-M70; and 0812GKYVG-F.
28. Interview 0812GKYVG-M60.

29. Cunningham (2012, 263) observed that the KKK mobilized members of klaverns from neighboring counties to carry out violent acts instead of locals in order to reduce the likelihood of identification by witnesses.
30. Both Lo and Liu had attained only a middle school education. Lo was a retired cadre from a state-owned factory, and Liu had been a businessman.
31. Names of villages are withheld for to preserve anonymity.
32. Sunzi Village is a pseudonym.
33. A plot of collective-owned village land had been leased to a private entrepreneur, who ran an auto repair shop. A few years earlier, the village authority unilaterally terminated the lease agreement in order to take back the land for development. When the owner refused to comply, the village authority cut off their utility supply and sent in thugs to threaten personal safety of the technicians and harass his clients (Interview 0614SZHAW-M40). In the name of building low-cost housing for retirees, the village authority had built low-rise apartments with "small property rights" on a plot of collective-owned land and sold them to private individuals. But the proceeds never registered on the village budgets, and the villagers did not benefit from the sale or low-cost housing (Interview 0614SZHRV-M60) Also, see Radio Free Asia (2012).
34. Interview 0614SZHFG1.
35. The footage was made into a Youku (2012) video.
36. Interview 0614SZHBO-M50.
37. Interview 0614SZHFG2.
38. Lunar Village is a pseudonym.
39. Interview 0614LZHFG1.
40. Interview 0614LZHFG1.
41. Interview 0614LZHVG-M60.
42. The gangsters, who reportedly spoke nonlocal dialects, were hired from the northeast and paid a daily rate of 100 RMB.
43. The names of these districts are all psuedonyms. Interviews 0614RZHPL-M50; 0614RZHVG-F40 (Ran); 0614ZZHVG-M40 (Zhai); and 0614ZZHVR-M50 (Xin). Also see Qiao (2010).
44. This section is partly drawn from Ong (2018a, 2018b).
45. Interview # 0614XZHPS-M40.
46. For examples of media reports on this, see Jacobs (2012a, 2009) and Long and Yang (2010).
47. Interview # 0714FBJPT-M.
48. Interview # 0714FBJVP-F.
49. For practical reasons, a field site was chosen only after a known large-scale protest incident had occurred, precluding random selection.

Chapter 5

1. These categories are ideal types that inform analysis, but in reality one or more of these categories may overlap; for example, an individual who is a social broker can be an economic broker at the same time.

2. Organization members may not know about the payment to their leaders or organizational brokers. They expect the party endorsed by their leaders to provide local public goods or specialized policies after the election if their group shows its collective loyalty. By way of contrast, voters expect to receive a personal payment from party brokers after an election, but they expect collective benefits from the organizational brokers. Hence, voters are monitored individually in party brokerage but collectively in organizational brokerage. See Holland and Palmer-Rubin (2015).

3. Brokers are market makers in the sense that their brokerage allows for the market of economic transactions to take place, without which the buyer and seller would not be matched.

4. These are informal institutions by the definition of Helmke and Levitsky (2004).

5. A close cousin is Duara's argument about those holding the cultural nexus of power in rural society. See Duara (1988, 43).

6. Pioneering works that show a strong association between civic trust and democracy include Almond and Sidney (1963); Bernhard (1993); di Palma (1991); and Putnam (1995).

7. For instance, see Almond and Sidney (1963) and Inglehart and Warren (1999).

8. The interests of the multiple parties represented by political brokers have been shown in existing work on rural and urban China. See J. Wang (2017) and Read (2012).

9. Even though the election of the director takes place every few years, the candidates are prescreened by the street offices, hampering genuine competition. See Tomba (2014).

10. For instance, similar institutions can be found in Taiwan and Indonesia. See Read (2012).

11. Some block captains volunteered to sign birth-control responsibility letters with RCs, meaning that they took on the responsibility of monitoring unwanted pregnancies in the neighborhoods. See Read (2012, 185).

12. Interviews 0715WCSDD and 0715JCSCD-M30. This pattern may, however, vary in another city or region.

13. While the community officers in affluent Beijing gated communities (小区) may act as the state's nerve endings, those in Shenyang neighborhoods populated by unemployed and laid-off workers are tasked directly by the state to provide welfare, manage contention, and maintain stability. The role of the latter is more interventionist than the former. See Read (2012) and Tomba (2014).

14. Interview 0715WCSDD.

15. Below the brigade (village) are the production brigade (生产大队) and production team (生产队). The latter became the unit of economic planning after the disastrous Great Leap Forward, taking power away from the commune (township). See Unger (2002).

16. They had overtaken the brokerage role of the imperial rural gentry and the entrepreneurial brokers of the late Qing period.

17. The target-based responsibility system set various evaluation criteria against which rural cadres are evaluated. It predisposes them to devote more energy to tasks that raise local economic growth rather than improve people's livelihood. The two objectives overlap but are not necessarily equal. See Ong (2012a) and Whiting (2001).

18. Since 2019, village Party secretaries also serve as village heads, and members of village and Party committees are no longer separated, but overlap. See Xinhuanet (2019b).

19. In anthropological literature gift-giving is perceived as producing *guanxi* to achieve the instrumental goals of self-enrichment. I see instrumental goals here as persuading community members to obey the state's instructions and comply with its policies. See Kipnis (1997); Yan (1996); and Yang (2016).

20. Per Mattingly (2019) brokers here also differentiate themselves from informal institutions, which include informal civil society organizations, village committees, lineage groups, and folk religious organizations. Village committees are political brokers in this context, whereas informal civil society organizations fall outside the purview of this book.

21. Interview 0715JCSGD.

22. Interview 0715JCSGD.

23. The Chaoyang Masses are not unique, but they are the most publicized. Other volunteer groups that have arisen in Beijing include the Xicheng aunties (西城大妈), Haidian Internet users, and Shijingshan Old Neighbors. See L. Zhang (2017).

24. The financial rewards range between 1,000 and 10,000 RMB ($148–$1,488), accordingly to Yuan and Yu (2017).

25. Interviews 0715JCSCD-M30; 0715JCSCD; 0715WCSDD; 0715QCSRC; and 0715DCSGD.

26. Interviews 0715JCSCD-M30 and 0715JCSCD.

27. Interviews 0715WCSDD; 0715QCSRC; and 0715DCSGD.

28. Interviews 0715WCSDD; 0715QCSRC; and 0715DCSGD.

29. For a study of how work teams were and are deployed in a comprehensive range of historical and contemporary campaigns in China for the purpose of mass mobilization, see Perry (2002b).

30. Interview 0715JCSRD-M.

31. For studies on the Party-state's grassroots machinery, see Barnett (1967) and Koss (2018).

32. "Aunties" (大妈), a respectful term for older women in the community, carries no connotation of blood relations.

33. The rationale of punishment by implication was the Confucian belief that held the family as society's most fundamental unit (家族本位). Family members typically included a spouse and sons living in the same household. Co-officials included coworkers at the same administrative levels as the offender and those above and below them. See N. Chen (1987).

34. Tianjian Shi (2015) has demonstrated that culture has an independent effect on citizen behavior and political outcome, exogenous of institutions.

35. Interviews 0718JSHSC. This point is also substantiated by the case studies in Chapter 4.

36. Interview 0718JSHDM.

37. Interviews 0919QCSPS-F and 0919QCSPS-M.

38. Interview 0717TGGVG.

39. Interviews 0718PSHSC and 0718PSHGM.

40. Interviews 0718PSHSC and 0718PSHGM.
41. The content analysis was based on frequencies of selected key words found in government regulations issued by the central government and the municipalities of Shanghai, Chengdu, and Zhengzhou, which were the major field sites. The regulations were sourced from the Peking University Legal Treasures (*Beida Fabao* 北大法宝). See Appendix A for more details.
42. These percentages are proportions of total documents issued by the central government.
43. Usually, each media report contains only one case. Thus, these were 159 separate incidents involving the use of nonviolent strategies in land grabs and housing demolition.
44. Note that definition of "urban" is quite broad. I have adopted the official parameters that include all cities, prefectures, counties, and urban townships.
45. Violent agents, namely the police and quasistate security, are visibly absent here.
46. Although in a different country setting, these findings could be contrasted with what Blaydes (2018, 52) finds with individual and collective punishments in communities with low and high social cohesion in Iraq. Blaydes finds individual targeted punishment in a low socially cohesive setting leads to public noncooperation, whereas collective punishment in a high socially cohesive environment leads to nationalist rebellions.

Chapter 6

1. Original quotation: "以死相挟是弱者最后的武器，只有在毫无办法走投无路的情况下，才会使用这样的极端手段。……我们不难再次看到普通人在政府面前的绝对劣势……到底是谁害死了唐福珍呢？真的是她自己么?" (*Nanfang Daily* 2009).
2. This was formally written in the Party constitution during the seventh Party Congress in 1945. Mao described the relationship between the Party and the masses like that "between fish and water." See Mao (1957).
3. It was to prevent crime and preempt escalation of social conflicts (矛盾不上交，就地解决). See Z. Zhu (2018).
4. In the Chinese context, mass mobilization (群众动员) implies "state-sponsored efforts to storm and eventually overwhelm strong but vulnerable barriers to the progress of socialism through intensive mass mobilization of active commitment." See Bennett (1976, 18).
5. Interview 0715DCSGD.
6. Interview 0919QCSPS-F.
7. In other localities in Chengdu, grid management has been outsourced to private companies.
8. Interview 0715DCSGD.
9. Interview 0715DCSGD.

10. Interview 0715JCSRD-M.

11. "Aunties" (大妈), a respectful term for older women in the community, carries no connotation of blood relations.

12. "自改委是全国创新，不仅体现在能很好地处理拆迁问题上，还提现在如何尊重群众意见的民主模式，民间的智慧是无穷的." This is the version of *zigaiwei* endorsed and promoted by CCTV.

13. Interview 0715JCSRD-M. See also Huaian Changan Net (2014).

14. Interview 0715JCSRD-M.

15. Interview 0715JCSGD. See *Tianya* (2015a).

16. Interview 0719JCSVM. See also Kuo (2019).

17. Interviews 0719JCSVM and 0719JCSEP.

18. Interview 0715JCSCD.

19. Mediation in imperial China was always performed by authoritative or semiauthoritative figures—leaders of clans or towns or older people who enjoyed social status in the community—who were a class or rank above the disputing parties. In imperial China, mediation was a way for the central government to resolve disputes by drawing on local resources. It was an institution that allowed the central government to take advantage of informal local authorities to resolve disputes and maintain a stable social order. See H. Zhang (2018, 136).

20. As society evolves, resolutions of increasingly complex disputes often require mediators having appropriate legal knowledge. This had caused a decline in significance of people's mediation in the 1980s and 1990s, partly because of a lack of legally qualified grassroots mediators.

21. Colloquially, the quip is "Small issues don't leave the community; big issues don't leave the subdistrict" (小事不出社区，大事不出街道). See Halegua (2005, 730).

22. Interviews 0718PSHSC; 0718PSHGM; 0718JSHDM; 0718JSHEP; and 0718JSHSC.

23. Interviews 1019QCSPS-F and 1019QCSPM. See also Yuanyuan Cai, Xiong, and Ren (2011).

24. Interviews 1019QCSPS-F and 1019QCSPM. Also see H. Cai (2008) and Yuanyuan Cai, Xiong, and Ren (2011).

25. Interviews 1019QCSPS-F and 1019QCSPM.

26. Interview 0718JSHFG-F50.

27. Interview 0718JSHFG-F50.

28. Interview 0718JSHFG-F50.

29. Interview 0718JSHFG-F50.

30. This section is largely drawn from my published paper; see Ong (2019a).

31. In China, the term "*huangniu*" is generally associated with ticket scalpers, that is, individuals who acquire scarce products or services by colluding with insiders and sell them at higher prices to would-be buyers. They help people to secure appointments with top medical specialists in major Chinese cities and purchase coveted admission tickets.

32. Interview 0516YSHRW.

33. Interview 0516YSHRW.

34. Interview 0516YSHRW.
35. In Shanghai, the space is complicated by the dual criteria according to which compensation is determined: the number of household members to be resettled and the size of the existing premise, whichever is more favorable to the families. Despite the guidelines on compensation, demolition officers are still the final arbiters of the application of the rules.
36. Interview 0516YSHPT. Once a family has consented, their relevant information, such as the size of the household and premises, will be posted on a public billboard. Officially, this is aimed at improving the transparency of relocation projects, given their contentious nature and susceptibility to corruption. Unofficially, it is also intended to put pressure on the remaining families who have yet to sign the agreements.
37. Interview 0516YSHRW.
38. Interview 0516YSHRE.
39. Separately, what differentiates knowing someone in the demolition office and a *huangniu* is whether the person charges for the service. A person becomes a *huangniu* when she or he seeks a cut in return for his service.
40. For the former meaning, see Gold, Guthrie, and Wank (2002) and Yang (2002).
41. Interview 0516XSHGA.
42. Interview 0516XSHGA. With the assistance of a well-connected *huangniu*, families who run a business and live on the same property can also increase repayments by counting residential space as the area designated for business, qualifying them for higher payouts.
43. Interviews 0516YSHRW; 0516YSHST; and 0516YSHRE.
44. Interview 0516XSHGA.
45. Interview 0516XSHGA.
46. Interview 0516XSHGA.
47. This fact was also confirmed by in interviews 0516YSHRW and 0516YSHST.
48. Interview 0516YSHST.
49. Interview 0516YSHRW.
50. Information, such as the assessed price of each property, size of family and of residential space, types of resettled housing allocated, list of poor households granted special attention, families who have consented, and bonuses awarded to those who had signed the agreements, is posted on public notice boards.
51. Interview 0516XSHGA.

Chapter 7

1. The youth groups under the home ministry's control gave Rhee direct access to the nonstate violent groups, which were deployed to undermine the political bases of his challengers. After 1956 the youth gangs were also involved in electoral violence and attacks against student protestors. See Mobrand (2016).

2. Korean society is traditionally rooted in Confucian philosophy, which emphasizes the role of the individual in the context of one's social networks, not as an autonomous unit. See Seo and Kim (2015).

3. It was not hesitant in using harassment, violence, terror, and mass arrest to deal with political dissenters and those supportive of the communist North. See Vu (2007).

4. In the spring of 1960, however, when the Rhee regime staged a blatantly rigged election accompanied by political terrorism in the name of fighting communism, a protest movement made up of university students forcefully emerged and gathered substantial momentum in Seoul. See Q.-Y. Kim (1996).

5. Criminals were mobilized alongside the formal coercive agents, namely the military and the National Intelligence Service. For more on Korea's formal coercive apparatus under Rhee and Park, see Greitens (2016).

6. Chun corporatized the national trade union and tightened labor laws to allow for representation by only one labor union for each workplace. The developmental Korean state had a clientelist relationship with the chaebols, the big business conglomerates it partnered with to pursue growth-oriented policies (Billet 1990; Sunhyuk Kim, Han, and Jang 2008).

7. The agenda items usually included topics like "greeting and making dialogues among neighbors" and "finding common matters of concern." See Seo and Kim (2015, 74).

8. This discourse of morality played a crucial role in "shaping the dominant ideology of the regime, socializing and reproducing discursive and moral practices associated with it." See Seo and Kim (2015, 78).

9. Jong Youl Lee (2000, 5) states that "trucks would come early in the morning to take families to their new location. The old units were then bulldozed by wrecking crews to prevent their being reoccupied."

10. The program legalized only six percent of Seoul's squatter settlements by 1973. See Porteux and Kim (2016, 376).

11. By 1987 Korean society had grown increasingly discontent with the regime's authoritarian approach. In student protests commemorating the 1980 Gwangju massacre, protestors called for President Chun's resignation and an end to authoritarian rule. The Reagan administration pressured Chun to relax his tight grip on power, and a democratization plan was announced. See Ra (2014).

12. One example is the case of the Sang Kye Dong evictions. In preparation for the 1988 Olympics, the area became slated for redevelopment as a new city with 57,000 apartments. When hundreds of local residents organized to resist this redevelopment, they were subjected to violent attacks, involving hundreds of riot police and hundreds of men hired by the construction company to intimidate residents (The Asian Coalition for Housing Rights 1989, 92).

13. Through this policy, around 100 sites were redeveloped and 48,000 buildings accommodating 720,000 people were destroyed. See L. K. Davis (2011).

14. To put civil resistance in perspective, Chang (2015) has argued that protest activities in the 1970s laid the groundwork for the democracy movement and civil society in the 1980s.

15. This section is partly drawn from my primary interviews conducted during field research in India in July 2015 and a published paper. See Ong (2019b).

16. Closely associated with the Hindu religion, caste is a system that classifies and ranks people from birth. The system rankings continue to shape behavior and interactions among members of the society but in a more subtle manner now than earlier. For instance, see Heitzman and Worden (1996).

17. India's total urban population grew from 285 million in 2001 to 377 million in 2011 and to just over 471 million in 2019. The urban population growth rate peaked at an all-time high of 3.9 percent in 1972 and gradually declined to 2.3 percent in 2019 (Mohan and Dasgupta 2004; Nandy 2015; World Bank 2018).

18. Interview 0715NDDOC. The interviewee was an advisor to the Congress government's Minister of Rural Development.

19. The requirements are 80 percent of landowners for private projects and from 60 percent of owners for public–private partnership projects. The Act also sets land compensation at four times the market value of recent pre-acquisition transactions in rural areas and twice the market value in urban areas. See Ramesh and Khan (2015).

20. The word often used to describe them is "prabhav," which translates to "hold" as in "grip on the neighborhood." See Berenschot (2011).

21. More available in Berenschot (2009).

22. Political parties rely critically on grassroots brokers, who are locally embedded activists and leaders from the upper castes of villages and communities. Their social status allows them to command authority and elicit cooperation and trust of the communities, key to shaping voting behavior. See Thachil (2011).

23. Interview 0715NDDPL. Its 2007 march, garnering support from 25,000 farmers, contributed to the promulgation of the Forest Rights Act.

24. Interview 0715NDDPL.

25. Interview 0715NDDPO.

Chapter 8

1. Tom Grundy, editor of *Hong Kong Free Press*, makes a persuasive argument on the intended self-censorship effect of the National Security Law. See Grundy (2020) and Lau (2019).

2. However, Lianjiang Li (2020) argues that distrust for the central government indicates a preference for regime change.

3. The KGB was split into several agencies, including separate ones for foreign intelligence, domestic intelligence, counterintelligence, etc., because Gorbachev and later Yeltsin feared the organization's capacity to mount a coup. Despite the effort to neutralize the former KGB, the agency's main successor, the FSB, steadily increased its influence throughout the 1990s. In contrast, the Ministry of Internal Affairs, which controls ordinary police, remained organizationally similar following the transition. See Taylor (2011).

4. The courts were not only corrupt but also underfunded and backlogged, meaning that settling a ruling could take years (Galeotti 2018, 112, 115). Formal legal institutions were seen by firms as "slow, corrupt, or incapable of enforcing court rulings" (Gans-Morse 2012, 272). Business partners were unreliable and frequently reneged on contracts (Volkov 2002a, 44). The police, for their part, tended to carry an outdated Soviet mindset of private entrepreneurs and did not consider them worthy of protection (Volkov 1999, 742).

5. For instance, Solntsevo, a criminal organization that became one of the largest in Russia, established itself as a "pseudo-state agency for the enforcement of contracts," by collecting unpaid debts and winning damages for broken contracts. See Galeotti (2018, 147–148).

6. Although some argue that coercive institutions played such a leading role under Putin that they had become an influential political force independent of Putin (Holmes 2008, 1023), others suggest the prevalence of FSB officials may simply be a reflection of patrimonial appointments derived from Putin's own background in the security apparatus instead of a cohesive political grouping (Taylor 2011, 56–57).

7. Fights between competing criminal groups, street shootings, and murders declined significantly in the 2000s in stark contrast to the decade before. See Cheloukhine (2008, 370) and Holmes (2008, 1014). Likewise, the day-to-day encounters of businesses and criminals decreased as indicated in a 2010 survey of small businesses, which showed less than eight percent had contact with criminal protection rackets in the previous three years, marking a drastic decrease from the 1990s. See Gans-Morse (2012, 268–269).

8. State capacity never returned to the level of the Soviet era in large part because of endemic corruption and patron-client ties with criminals and other economic elites.

9. The warning was issued in a closed-door meeting of the Central Commission for Discipline Inspection. See J. Shi (2018).

10. According to the CCP's 2018 Notice, "Launching the Special Criminal Syndicate Combat" (根据中共的 《关于开展扫黑除恶专项斗争的通知》), the 12 groups targeted are (1) underground forces that threaten political security, especially regime security, and institutional security and penetrate into the political arena; (2) forces that control the grassroots governance, including the evil forces that destroy grassroots elections, monopolize rural resources, and embezzle collective assets; (3) those who use the clan and clan forces to dominate the countryside and the Party, including village tyrants who harm the people; (4) evil forces involved in land acquisition, land rental, land demolition, construction of projects, instigation, etc.; (5) evil forces involved in forcing projects, malicious bidding, illegal land occupation in the construction site, transportation, mineral resources sector, fishing and other industries and fields; (6) evil forces that bully consumers and sellers, forcibly sell, and collect illicit protection fees in commercial markets, wholesale markets, stations, docks, tourist attractions, and other places; (7) evil forces that manipulate and manage criminal activities, such as prostitution, gambling, and drug dealing; (8) those involved in illegal usury and violent debt collection; (9) evil forces that intervene in civil disputes and act as an underworld force of "underground law enforcement teams"; (10) evil

forces that infiltrate and develop overseas triad societies and cross-border criminal underworld forces; (11) evil forces that engage in activities in the *Sanmiao* market, sand mining, and other industries, disrupting legal production and operation and disrupting normal market order; and (12) manipulators and organizers behind the scenes who violate the regulations on the petitioning system, harass, extort, organize, and instigate petitioners to illegally file petitions and unreasonable petitions; organizers and manipulators who seriously disrupt the order of the unit and the social order (Xinhua Net, 2019a).

11. For instance, in Liaoning province, 36 black societies and 83 dark forces had been destroyed from January 2018 to the end of April 2019, with the confiscated property valued at 16.1 billion RMB. See P. Wang (2019).

Bibliography

Acemoglu, Daron, and James A. Robinson. 2012. *Why Nations Fail: The Origins of Power, Prosperity and Poverty*. New York, NY: Crown.

Acemoglu, Daron, and James A. Robinson. 2019. *The Narrow Corridor: States, Societies, and the Fate of Liberty*. New York, NY: Penguin Press.

Ahram, Ariel. 2016. "Pro-Government Militias and the Repertoires of Illicit State Violence." *Studies in Conflict and Terrorism* 39 (3): 207–26.

Albertus, Michael, Sofia Fenner, and Dan Slater. 2018. *Coercive Distribution*. Cambridge, UK: Cambridge University Press.

Albertus, Michael, and Victor Menaldo. 2012. "Coercive Capacity and the Prospects for Democratization." *Comparative Politics* 44 (2): 151–69.

Almond, Gabriel A., and G. Bingham Powell, Jr. 1966. *Comparative Politics: A Developmental Approach*. Boston, MA: Little, Brown.

Almond, Gabriel A., and Verba Sidney. 1963. *The Civic Culture: Political Attitudes and Democracy in Five Nations*. Princeton, NJ: Princeton University Press.

Alvarez, Alex. 2006. "Militias and Genocide." *War Crimes, Genocide, & Crimes against Humanity* 2 (1): 1–33.

Amnesty International. 2012. "Standing Their Ground: Thousands Face Violent Eviction in China." London, UK: Amnesty International.

Arendt, Hannah. 1958. *The Origins of Totalitarianism*. New York, NY: Meridian Books.

Article 19. 1997. "Deadly Marionettes: State-Sponsored Violence in Africa." http://www.article19.org/pdfs/publications/africa-deadly-marionettes.pdf.

Atkinson-Sheppard, Sally, and Hannah Hayward. 2019. "Conceptual Similarities; Distinct Difference: Exploring 'the Gang' in Mainland China." *The British Journal of Criminology* 59 (3): 614–33. https://doi.org/10.1093/bjc/azy051.

Atwal, Maya, and Edwin Bacon. 2012. "The Youth Movement Nashi: Contentious Politics, Civil Society, and Party Politics." *East European Politics* 28 (3): 256–66. https://doi.org/10.1080/21599165.2012.691424.

Auerbach, Adam M., and Tariq Thachil. 2018. "How Clients Select Brokers: Competition and Choice in India's Slums." *American Political Science Review* 112 (4): 775–91.

Auyero, Javier. 2001. *Poor People's Politics: Peronist Survival Networks and the Legacy of Evita*. Durham, NC: Duke University Press.

Avant, Deborah. 2005a. *The Market for Force: The Consequences of Privatizing Security*. Cambridge, UK: Cambridge University Press.

Avant, Deborah. 2005b. "Private Security Companies." *New Political Economy* 10 (1): 121–31.

Averill, Stephen C. 2006. *Revolution in the Highlands: China's Jinggangshan Base Area*. Lanham, MD: Rowman & Littlefield.

Baldwin, Kate. 2013. "Why Vote with the Chief? Political Connections and Public Goods Provision in Zambia." *American Journal of Political Science* 57 (4): 794–809.

Barnett, A. Doak. 1967. *Cadres, Bureaucracy, and Political Power in Communist China*. New York, NY: Columbia University Press.

Beetham, David. 1991. *The Legitimation of Power*. Basingstoke, UK: Macmillan.

Bellin, Eva. 2004. "The Robustness of Authoritarianism in the Middle East: Exceptionalism in Comparative Perspective." *Comparative Politics* 36 (2): 139–57. https://doi.org/10.2307/4150140.

Bennett, Gordon. 1976. *Yundong: Mass Campaigns in Chinese Communist Leadership*. Berkeley, CA: University of California.

Berenschot, Ward. 2009. "Rioting as Maintaining Relations: Hindu–Muslim Violence and Political Mediation in Gujarat, India." *Civil Wars* 11 (4): 414–34.

Berenschot, Ward. 2010. "Everyday Mediation: The Politics of Public Service Delivery in Gujarat, India: Everyday Mediation: Public Service Delivery in Gujarat." *Development and Change* 41 (5): 883–905. https://doi.org/10.1111/j.1467-7660.2010.01660.x.

Berenschot, Ward. 2011. "On the Usefulness of Goondas in Indian Politics: 'Moneypower' and 'Musclepower' in a Gujarati Locality." *South Asia: Journal of South Asian Studies* 34 (2): 255–75. https://doi.org/10.1080/00856401.2011.582669.

Berenschot, Ward. 2015. "Clientelism, Trust Networks, and India's Identity Politics: Conveying Closeness in Gujarat." *Critical Asian Studies* 47 (1): 24–43.

Berenschot, Ward. 2019. "Informal Democratization: Brokers, Access to Public Services and Democratic Accountability in Indonesia and India." *Democratization* 26 (2): 208–24. https://doi.org/10.1080/13510347.2018.1512590.

Berenschot, Ward, and Sarthak Bagchi. 2019. "Comparing Brokers in India: Informal Networks and Access to Public Services in Bihar and Gujarat." *Journal of Contemporary Asia* 50 (3): 457–77. https://doi.org/10.1080/00472336.2019.1605535.

Berman, Sheri. 1997. "Civil Society and the Collapse of the Weimar Republic." *World Politics* 49 (3): 401–29.

Bernhard, Michael. 1993. "Civil Society and Democratic Transition in East Central Europe." *Political Science Quarterly* 108 (2): 307–26.

Bernstein, Thomas P., and Xiaobo Lü. 2003. *Taxation without Representation in Contemporary Rural China*. New York, NY: Cambridge University Press.

Bhagwati, Jagdish, Arvind Panagariya, and T.N Srinivasan. 2004. "The Muddles over Outsourcing." *Journal of Economic Perspectives* 18 (4): 93–114. https://doi.org/10.1257/0895330042632753.

Biddulph, Sarah. 2015. *The Stability Imperative: Human Rights and Law in China*. Vancouver, BC: University of British Columbia Press.

Biggs, Michael. 2016. "Size Matters: Quantifying Protest by Counting Participants." *Sociological Methods and Research* 47 (3): 1–33.

Billet, Bret L. 1990. "South Korea at the Crossroads: An Evolving Democracy or Authoritarianism Revisited?" *Asian Survey* 30 (3): 300–11.

Blaydes, Lisa. 2018. *State of Repression: Iraq under Saddam Hussein*. Princeton, NJ: Princeton University Press.

Bohara, Alok K., Neil J. Mitchell, Mani Nepal, and Nejem Raheem. 2008. "Human Rights Violations, Corruption, and the Policy of Repression." *Policy Studies Journal* 36 (1): 1–18.

Bourdieu, Pierre. 1986. "The Forms of Capital." In *Handbook of Theory of Research for the Sociology of Education*, edited by John Richardson, 46–58. New York, NY: Greenwood Press.

Brady, Anne-Marie. 2008. *Marketing Dictatorship: Propaganda and Thought Work in Contemporary China*. Lanham, MD: Rowman & Littlefield.

Brady, Anne-Marie. 2009. "Mass Persuasion as a Means of Legitimation and China's Popular Authoritarianism." *American Behavioral Scientist* 53 (3): 434–57. https://doi.org/10.1177/0002764209338802.

Brass, Paul R. 1997. *Theft of an Idol: Text and Context in the Representation of Collective Violence.* Princeton, NJ: Princeton University Press.

Brehm, John, and Emerson M. S. Niou. 1997. "Police Patrol versus Self-Policing: A Comparative Analysis of the Control Systems Used in the Former Soviet Union and Communist China." *Journal of Theoretical Politics* 9 (1): 107–30. https://doi.org/10.1177/0951692897009001010.

Broadhurst, Roderic. 2012. "Black Societies and Triad-like Organized Crime in China." In *Routledge Handbook of Transnational Organized Crime*, edited by Stan Gilmour and Felia Allum. 151–71. New York, NY: Routledge.

Brysk, Alison. 2014. "Perpetrators of 'Private Wrongs': Non-State Actors, Violence Against Women, and Responsiveness to Transnational Human Rights Campaigns." Paper presented at 2014 International Studies Association Annual Meeting. Toronto, Canada.

Butler, Christopher K., Tali Gluch, and Neil Mitchell. 2007. "Security Forces and Sexual Violence: A Cross-National Analysis of a Principle-Agent Argument." *Journal of Peace Research* 44 (6): 669–87.

Cai, Hong. 2008. "Rural Land Disputes and the Mediation Mechanisms 农村土地纠纷及其解决机制研究." *Law Review* (法学评论) (2): 143–50.

Cai, Yongshun. 2010. *Collective Resistance in China: Why Popular Protests Succeed or Fail.* Stanford, CA: Stanford University Press.

Cai, Yongshun. 2014. *State and Agents in China: Disciplining Government Officials.* Stanford, CA: Stanford University Press.

Cai, Yongshun, and Lin Zhu. 2013. "Disciplining Local Officials in China: The Case of Conflict Management." *The China Journal* 70 (July): 98–119.

Cai, Yuanyuan, Xingguo Xiong, and Xiaogang Ren. 2011. "An Analysis of Village Committee's Role in Mediating Rural Housing Demolition Conflicts 浅析村委会在农村房屋拆迁纠纷中的调解职能." *Legal System and Society* (法制与社会)(32): 266–67.

Callaghy, Thomas. 1984. *The State–Society Struggle: Zaire in Comparative Perspective.* New York, NY: Columbia University Press.

Campbell, Bruce B., and Arthur D. Brenner, eds. 2002. *Death Squads in Global Perspective: Murder with Deniability.* New York, NY: Palgrave Macmillan.

Carey, Sabine C., Michael P. Colaresi, and Neil J. Mitchell. 2015. "Governments, Informal Links to Militias, and Accountability." *Journal of Conflict Resolution* 59 (5): 850–76.

Carr-Harris, Jill. 2005. "Struggle-Dialogue: Tools for Land Movements in India." New Delhi: Ekta Parishad.

Cassidy, John. 2009. *How Markets Fail: The Logic of Economic Calamities.* New York, NY: Farrar, Straus and Giroux.

CCTV News. 2000. "民政部关于在全国推进城市社区建设的意见 [Opinions of the Ministry of Civil Affairs on Advancing the Construction of Urban Communities Nationwide]." CCTV News. http://www.cctv.com/news/china/20001212/366.html.

CECC. 2017. "Corruption and Weak Property Protections Fuel Protests in Rural China: The Case of Wukan Village." Commission Analysis. The Congressional-Executive Commission on China. https://www.cecc.gov/publications/commission-analysis/corruption-and-weak-property-protections-fuel-protests-in-rural-0.

Chang, Paul Y. 2015. *Protest Dialects: State Repression and South Koreasis/corruption-and-weak-pro–1979*. Stanford, CA: Stanford University Press.

Chatterjee, Partha. 2004. *The Politics of the Governed: Reflections on Popular Politics in Most of the World*. New York, NY: Columbia University Press.

Cheloukhine, Serguei. 2008. "The Roots of Russian Organized Crime: From Old-Fashioned Professionals to the Organized Criminal Groups of Today." *Crime, Law and Social Change* 50 (4): 353–74. https://doi.org/10.1007/s10611-008-9117-5.

Chen, Baifeng. 2018. "乡村'混混'介入的基层治理生态 [Grassroots Governance Ecology of Rural 'Mixed' Intervention]." 思想战线 *[Thinking]* 44 (5): 114–27.

Chen, Huirong. 2015. "State Power and Village Cadres in Contemporary China: The Case of Rural Land Transfer in Shandong Province." *Journal of Contemporary China* 24 (95): 778–97.

Chen, Huirong, and Sheena Greitens. 2021. "Information Capacity and Social Order: The Local Politics of Information Integration in China." *Governance: An International Journal of Policy, Administration, and Institutions*, April. https://doi.org/10.1111/gove.12592.

Chen, Naihua. 1987. "关于秦汉刑事连坐的若干问题 [Several Questions on the Criminal Lianzuo System in Qin and Han Dynasty]." *Journal of Shandong Normal University*, no. 6: 1–6.

Chen, Yung-fa. 1986. *Making Revolution: The Communist Movement in Eastern and Central China, 1937–1945*. Berkeley, CA: University of California Press.

Chen, Zhong Xiao Lu, and Jun Yi Cui. 2009. "'Chaiqian Buchang Xinxi Gongkai Zhihuo' [The Question Surrounding The Disclosure of Information Regarding Compensation for Housing Demolition and Relocation]." *Caijing Wang*, July 17, 2009.

Cheng, Xinhao. 2011. "村庄的夕阳: 小村拆迁中的家庭关系与老人生活 [Villages at Sunset: Family Relations and Life for Seniors amidst Village Demolition]." Master's Dissertation, Peking University, Department of Sociology.

Chengdu Daily. 2012. "央视记者蹲点10个月 全程记录曹家巷自治改造 [CCTV Reporters Spent Ten Months Recording the Whole Process of Caojiaxiang Self-Governed Reconstruction]." *Chengdu Daily*, December 30, 2012. http://news.ifeng.com/gundong/detail_2012_12/30/20668793_0.shtml.

Cheskin, Ammon, and Luke March. 2015. "State–Society Relations in Contemporary Russia: New Forms of Political and Social Contention." *East European Politics* 31 (3): 261–73.

Chesterman, Simon, and Chia Lehnhart, eds. 2007. *From Mercenaries to Markets: The Rise and Regulation of Private Military Companies*. Oxford, UK: Oxford University Press.

Chin, Ko-lin, and Roy Godson. 2006. "Organized Crime and the Political-Criminal Nexus in China." *Trends in Organized Crime* 9 (3): 5–44.

China Daily. 2011. "China Issues New Regulations on House Expropriation." *China Daily*, January 22, 2011. http://www.chinadaily.com.cn/china/2011-01/22/content_11900 647.htm.

China Labour Watch. 2010. "The Strike Wave." *China Labour Watch*. http://www.chinalab orwatch.org/newscast/60.

China Law Translate. 2021. "Crackdown on Underworld Forces." *China Law Translate*. 2021. https://www.chinalawtranslate.com/criminal-procedure-2/%E6%89%AB%E9 %BB%91%E9%99%A4%E6%81%B6%E4%B8%93%E9%A1%B9%E6%96%97%E4 %BA%89/.

Costalli, Stefano, and Andrea Ruggeri. 2015. "Indignation, Ideologies, and Armed Mobilization: Civil War in Italy, 1943–45." *International Security* 40 (2): 119–57. https://doi.org/10.1162/ISEC_a_00218.

Crawford, Neta C. 2009. "Homo Politicus and Argument (Nearly) All the Way Down: Persuasion in Politics." *Perspectives on Politics* 7 (1): 103–24. https://doi.org/10.1017/S1537592709090136.

Cunningham, David. 2004. *There's Something Happening Here: The New Left, the Klan, and FBI Counterintelligence.* Berkeley, CA: University of California Press.

Cunningham, David. 2012. *Klansville, U.S.A.: The Rise and Fall of the Civil Rights-Era Ku Klux Klan.* Oxford, UK: Oxford University Press.

Davenport, Christian. 2007a. "State Repression and Political Order." *Annual Review of Political Science* 10 (1): 1–23. https://doi.org/10.1146/annurev.polisci.10.101405.143216.

Davenport, Christian. 2007b. *State Repression and the Domestic Democratic Peace.* Cambridge, UK: Cambridge University Press.

Davenport, Christian. 2010. *Media Bias, Perspective, and State Repression: The Black Panther Party.* Cambridge, UK: Cambridge University Press.

Davenport, Christian, and Patrick Ball. 2002. "Views to a Kill." *Journal of Conflict Resolution* 46 (3): 427–50.

Davenport, Christian, and Molly Inman. 2012. "The State of State Repression Research Since the 1990s." *Terrorism and Political Violence* 24 (4): 619–34. https://doi.org/10.1080/09546553.2012.700619.

Davis, Lisa Kim. 2011. "International Events and Mass Evictions: A Longer View." *International Journal of Urban and Regional Research* 35 (3): 582–99. https://doi.org/10.1111/j.1468-2427.2010.00970.x.

Decalo, Samuel. 1998. *The Stable Minority: Civilian Rule in Africa, 1960–1990.* Gainesville, FL: FAP Books.

Deng, Yanhua. 2017. "'Autonomous Redevelopment': Moving the Masses to Remove Nail Households." *Modern China* 43 (5): 494–522. https://doi.org/10.1177/0097700416683901.

Deng, Yanhua, and Kevin O'Brien. 2013. "Relational Repression in China: Using Social Ties to Demobilize Protesters." *The China Quarterly* 215 (September): 533–52.

Deng, Yanhua, Kevin On in n, and Li Zhang. 2020. "How Grassroots Cadres Broker Land Taking in Urbanizing China." *The Journal of Peasant Studies* 47 (6): 1233f Pe

Donaghy, Maureen M. 2018. *Democratizing Urban Development: Community Organizations for Housing Across the United States and Brazil.* Philadelphia, PA: Temple University Press.

Duara, Prasenjit. 1988. *Culture, Power, and the State: Rural North China, 1900–1942.* Stanford, CA: Stanford University Press.

Dukalskis, Alexander, and Johannes Gerschewski. 2017. "What Autocracies Say (and What Citizens Hear): Proposing Four Mechanisms of Autocratic Legitimation." *Contemporary Politics* 23 (3): 251–68.

Earl, Jennifer. 2003. "Tanks, Tear Gas, and Taxes: Toward a Theory of Movement Repression." *Sociological Theory* 21 (1): 44–68.

Earl, Jennifer, Andrew Martin, John D McCarthy, and Sarah A Soule. 2004. "The Use of Newspaper Data in the Study of Collective Action." *Annual Review of Sociology* 30: 65–80.

Earl, Jennifer, Sarah A. Soule, and John D. McCarthy. 2003. "Protest under Fire? Explaining the Policing of Protest." *American Sociological Review* 68 (4): 581–606.

Ekiert, Grzegorz, Elizabeth J. Perry, and Xiaojun Yan, eds. 2020. *Ruling by Other Means: State-Mobilized Movements*. Cambridge, UK: Cambridge University Press.

Etzioni, Amitai. 1975. *A Comparative Analysis of Complex Organizations: On Power, Involvement, and Their Correlates*. New York, NY: The Free Press.

Evans, Peter. 1995. *Embedded Autonomy: States and Industrial Transformation*. Princeton, NJ: Princeton University Press.

Fazhi. 2019. "'扫黑除恶' 在扫除什么？法官、扫黑办主任和政法教师这样说" [What's the 'Sweeping Black Campaign' Getting Rid Of?]." *Initium Media*, August 21, 2019. https://theinitium.com/article/20190822-mainland-nationwide-campaign-against-gang-crime-and-evil/.

Francisco, Ronald A. 1995. "The Relationship Between Coercion and Protests: An Empirical Evaluation in Three Coercive States." *Journal of Conflict Resolution* 39 (2): 263–82.

Fu, Diana. 2018. *Mobilizing without the Masses: Control and Contention in China*. Cambridge, UK: Cambridge University Press.

Fulbrook, Mary. 2005. *The People's State: East German Society from Hitler to Honecker*. New Haven, CT; London, UK: Yale University Press.

Galeotti, Mark. 2018. *The Vory: Russia's Super Mafia*. New Haven, CT; London, UK: Yale University Press.

Gallagher, Mary. 2004. "China: The Limits of Civil Society in a Late Leninist State." In *Civil Society and Political Change in Asia: Expanding and Contracting Democratic Space*, edited by M. Alagappa, 419–52. Stanford, CA: Stanford University Press.

Gambetta, Diego. 1993. *The Sicilian Mafia: The Business of Private Protection*. Cambridge, MA: Harvard University Press.

Gandhi, Jennifer. 2008. *Political Institutions under Dictatorship*. Cambridge, UK; New York, NY: Cambridge University Press.

Gandhi, Jennifer, and Ellen Lust-Okar. 2009. "Elections Under Authoritarianism." *Annual Review of Political Science* 12 (June): 403–22.

Gans-Morse, Jordan. 2012. "Threats to Property Rights in Russia: From Private Coercion to State Aggression." *Post-Soviet Affairs* 28 (3): 263–95.

Gartner, Scott S., and Patrick M. Regan. 1996. "Threat and Repression: The Non-Linear Relationship between Government and Opposition Violence." *Journal of Peace Research* 33 (3): 273–87.

Geddes, Barbara, Joseph Wright, and Erica Frantz. 2018. *How Dictatorships Work: Power, Personalization, and Collapse*. Cambridge, UK; New York, NY: Cambridge University Press.

Gerschewski, Johannes. 2013. "The Three Pillars of Stability: Legitimation, Repression, and Co-Optation in Autocratic Regimes." *Democratization* 20 (1): 13–38. https://doi.org/10.1080/13510347.2013.738860.

Gilley, Bruce. 2006. "The Meaning and Measure of State Legitimacy: Results for 72 Countries." *European Journal of Political Research* 45 (3): 499–525. https://doi.org/10.1111/j.1475-6765.2006.00307.x.

Global Times. 2013. "China's Xi Stresses Conflict Resolution through Rule of Law." *Global Times*, October 11, 2013. http://www.globaltimes.cn/content/817246.shtml.

Gold, Thomas, Doug Guthrie, and David Wank, eds. 2002. *Social Connections in China: Institutions, Culture, and the Changing Nature of Guanxi*. Cambridge, UK: Cambridge University Press.

Gould, Roger V. 1989. "Power and Social Structure in Community Elites." *Social Forces* 68 (2): 531–52. https://doi.org/10.2307/2579259.

Greitens, Sheena. 2016. *Dictators and Their Secret Police: Coercive Institutions and State Violence.* Cambridge, UK: Cambridge University Press.

Greitens, Sheena. 2020. "The Saohei Campaign: Protection Umbrellas, and China's Challenging Political-Legal Apparatus." *China Leadership Monitor* 65: 1–18.

Greitens, Sheena, Myunghee Lee, and Emir Yazici. 2020. "Understanding China's 'Preventive Repression' in Xinjiang." The Brookings Institution. https://www.brookings.edu/blog/order-from-chaos/2020/03/04/understanding-chinas-preventive-repression-in-xinjiang/.

Greitens, Sheena, and Rory Truex. 2020. "Repressive Experiences among China Scholars: New Evidence from Survey Data." *The China Quarterly* 242 (June): 349–75.

Grossman, Gene M., and Elhanan Helpman. 2005. "Outsourcing in a Global Economy." *The Review of Economic Studies* 72 (1): 135–59. https://doi.org/10.1111/0034-6527.00327.

Grundy, Tom. 2020. "Hong Kong's National Security Laws Are Designed to Make the Media Self-Censor." *The Guardian*, July 14, 2020. https://www.theguardian.com/world/2020/jul/14/hong-kongs-national-security-laws-are-designed-to-make-the-media-self-censor?utm_source=dlvr.it&utm_medium=twitter.

Guang, Lei, Margaret Roberts, Yiqing Xu, and Jiannan Zhao. 2020. "Pandemic Sees Increase in Chinese Support for Regime, Decrease in Views Towards the U.S." The China Data Lab, UC San Diego's School of Global Policy and Strategy. http://chinadatalab.ucsd.edu/viz-blog/pandemic-sees-increase-in-chinese-support-for-regime-decrease-in-views-towards-us/.

Gui, Xiaowei. 2017. "How 'Power-Interest Networks' Have Shaped Anti-Demolition Protests in Grassroots China." *China: An International Journal* 15 (4): 69–89.

Gueorguiev, Dimitar. 2021. *Retrofitting Leninism: Participation without Democracy in China.* New York, NY: Oxford University Press.

Gueorguiev, Dimitar, Li Shao, and Charles Crabtree. 2017. "Blurred Lines: Uncertainty and Self-Censorship in China." *SSRN Electronic Journal*, January.

Guo, Shengli, and Xiaoyi Sun. 2014. "Loyalist-Activist Networks and Institutional Identification in Urban Neighbourhoods." In *Neighbourhood Governance in Urban China*, edited by Ngai-Ming Yip, 90–112. Cheltenham, UK; Northampton, MA: Edward Elgar Publishing.

Guo, Xuezhi. 2012. *China's Security State: Philosophy, Evolution, and Politics.* Cambridge, UK: Cambridge University Press.

Haggard, Stephan. 2018. *Developmental States.* Cambridge, UK: Cambridge University Press.

Halegua, Aaron. 2005. "Reforming the People's Mediation System in Urban China." *Hong Kong Law Journal* 35 (3): 715–50.

Hamilton, Clive, and Mareike Ohlberg. 2020. *Hidden Hand: Exposing How the Chinese Communist Party Is Reshaping the World.* London, UK: Oneworld.

Han, Jun. 2009. *Zhongguo Nongcun Tudi Wenti Diaocha [An Investigation of Rural Land Issues in China].* Shanghai, China: Shanghai Yuandong Chubanshe.

Hanser, Amy. 2016. "Street Politics: Street Vendors and Urban Governance in China." *The China Quarterly* 226 (June): 363–82. https://doi.org/10.1017/S0305741016000278.

Hardee-Cleaveland, Karen, and Judith Banister. 1988. "Fertility Policy and Implementation in China, 1986–88." *Population and Development Review* 14 (2): 245–86.

Harding, Luke. 2009. "Putin's Worst Nightmare." *The Guardian*, February 8, 2009. https://www.theguardian.com/world/2009/feb/08/russia-race.

Hartog, Eva. 2016. "A Kremlin Youth Movement Goes Rogue." *The Moscow Times*, April 8, 2016. https://www.themoscowtimes.com/2016/04/08/a-kremlin-youth-movement-goes-rogue-a52435.

Hassan, Mai. 2020. *Regime Threats and State Solutions: Bureaucratic Loyalty and Embeddedness in Kenya*. Cambridge Studies in Comparative Politics. Cambridge, UK: Cambridge University Press.

Hau, Matthias vom. 2015. "State Theory: Four Analytical Traditions." In *The Oxford Handbook of Transformations of the State*, edited by Stephan Leibfried, Evelyne Huber, Matthew Lange, Jonah D. Levy, and John D. Stephens. Oxford, UK: Oxford University Press. https://doi.org/10.1093/oxfordhb/9780199691586.013.7.

Heitzman, James, and Robert L. Worden, eds. 1996. *India: A Country Study*. 5th ed. Area Handbook Series 550–21. Washington, D.C: Federal Research Division, Library of Congress.

Helmke, Gretchen, and Steven Levitsky. 2004. "Informal Institutions and Comparative Politics: A Research Agenda." *Perspectives on Politics* 2 (4): 725–40. https://doi.org/10.1017/S1537592704040472.

Hemment, Julie. 2020. "Occupy Youth! State-Mobilized Contention in the Putin Era (or, What Was Nashi and What Comes Next?)." In *Ruling by Other Means: State-Mobilized Movements*, edited by Grzegorz Ekiert, Elizabeth J. Perry, and Xiaojun Yan, 166–92. Cambridge, UK: Cambridge University Press.

Herbst, Jeffrey. 2000. *States and Power in Africa: Comparative Lessons in Authority and Control*. Princeton, NJ: Princeton University Press.

Heurlin, Christopher. 2016. *Responsive Authoritarianism in China: Land, Protests, and Policy Making*. New York, NY: Cambridge University Press.

Hill, Peter B. E. 2003. *The Japanese Mafia: Yakuza, Law, and the State*. Oxford, UK: Oxford University Press.

Hirschfeld, Katherine. 2015. *Gangster States: Organized Crime, Kleptocracy and Political Collapse*. New York, NY: Palgrave Macmillan.

Holland, Alisha C. 2017. *Forbearance as Redistribution: The Politics of Informal Welfare in Latin America*. Cambridge, UK: Cambridge University Press.

Holland, Alisha C., and Brian Palmer-Rubin. 2015. "Beyond the Machine: Clientelist Brokers and Interest Organizations in Latin America." *Comparative Political Studies* 48 (9): 1186–223.

Holmes, Leslie. 2008. "Corruption and Organised Crime in Putin's Russia." *Europe–Asia Studies* 60 (6): 1011–31.

Hsing, You-tien. 2010. *The Great Urban Transformation: Politics of Land and Property in China*. New York, NY: Oxford University Press.

Huaian Changan Net. 2014. "赴四川成都考察学习调研报告 [Investigation Report on the Field Trip to Chengdu, Sichuan]." Government Website. Huaian Changan Net. October 10, 2014. http://zfw.huaian.gov.cn/tszs/content/5e38cfba485981e50148f7eea29e6554.html.

Huang, Haifeng. 2015. "Propaganda as Signaling." *Comparative Politics* 47 (4): 419–37.

Huang, Youqin. 2006. "Collectivism, Political Control, and Gating in Chinese Cities." *Urban Geography* 27 (6): 507–25.

Human Rights Watch. 2009. "An Alleyway in Hell." Human Rights Watch. http://www.hrw.org/sites/default/files/reports/china1109webwcover_1.pdf.

Hurst, William, Mingxing Liu, Yongdong Liu, and Ran Tao. 2014. "Reassessing Collective Petitioning in Rural China: Civic Engagement, Extra-State Violence, and Regional Variation." *Comparative Politics* 46 (4): 459–78.

iFeng News. 2017. "吴天君被判11年，曾主导野蛮拆迁惹惊天血案 [Wu Tianjun Sentenced to 11 Years." *IFeng News*, August 5, 2017. http://inews.ifeng.com/51570457/news.shtml?&back&back.

Inglehart, Robert, and Mark E. Warren. 1999. "Trust, Well-Being and Democracy." In *Democracy and Trust*, edited by Mark E. Warren, 88–120. Cambridge, UK: Cambridge University Press.

Jackson, Jonathan, Aziz Z. Huq, Tom R. Tyler, and Ben Bradford. 2013. "Monopolizing Force? Police Legitimacy and Public Attitudes Toward the Acceptability of Violence." *Psychology Public Policy and Law* 19 (4): 479–97.

Jacobs, Andrew. 2009. "Seeking Justice, Chinese Land in Secret Jails." *The New York Times*, August 3, 2009. http://www.nytimes.com/2009/03/09/world/asia/09jails.html.

Jacobs, Andrew. 2012a. "Chinese Media Retreat After Reports of Unexpected 'Black Jail' Verdict." *The New York Times*, March 12, 2012. http://cn.nytimes.com/china/20121 203/c03detain/en-us/.

Jacobs, Andrew. 2012b. "Artist Ai Weiwei Loses Appeal Over Tax Evasion Case." *The New York Times*, July 20, 2012. https://www.nytimes.com/2012/07/21/world/asia/chin ese-artist-loses-appeal-in-tax-evasion-case.html.

Jasper, James M. 2011. "Emotions and Social Movements: Twenty Years of Theory and Research." *Annual Review of Sociology* 37 (1): 285–303. https://doi.org/10.1146/annu rev-soc-081309-150015.

Jasper, James M. 2018. *The Emotions of Protest*. Chicago, IL: University of Chicago Press.

Jenkins, Rob. 2011. "The Politics of India's Special Economic Zones." In *Understanding India's Political Economy: A Great Transformation?*, edited by Sanjay Ruparelia, Sanjay Reddy, John Harriss, and Stuart Corbridge, 49–66. London, UK; New York, NY: Routledge.

Jenkins, Rob, Loraine Kennedy, and Partha Mukhopadhyay, eds. 2014. *Power, Policy, and Protest: The Politics of India's Special Economic Zones*. New Delhi, India: Oxford University Press.

Jiang, Shengsan, Shouying Liu, and Qing Li. 2010. *Zhongguo Tudi Zhidu Gaige [Land Reform in China]*. Shanghai, China: Shanghai Sanlian Shudian.

Jiang, Steven. 2015. "Zhou Yongkang: From Apex of Power to Caged 'tiger' in China." *CNN*, June 11, 2015. https://www.cnn.com/2014/12/05/world/asia/china-zhou-yongk ang/index.html.

Johnson, Ian. 2013. "Picking Death Over Eviction." *New York Times*, September 9, 2013. https://cn.nytimes.com/china/20130909/c09chinaurban/en-us/.

Joo, Yu-Min. 2019. *Megacity Seoul: Urbanization and the Development of Modern South Korea*. Abingdon, UK; New York, NY: Routledge.

Joske, Alex. 2020. "The Party Speaks for You: Foreign Interference and the Chinese Communist Party's United Front System." Australian Strategic Policy Institute. https://www.aspi.org.au/report/party-speaks-you.

Jowett, Garth S., and Victoria O'Donnell. 2014. *Propaganda and Persuasion*. 6th ed. Thousand Oaks, CA: SAGE.

Kaiman, Jonathan. 2013. "China's Southern Weekly Newspaper Reappears after Censorship Standoff." *The Guardian*, January 10, 2013. https://www.theguardian.com/world/2013/jan/10/china-censorship-souther-weekly-reappears.

Kalyvas, Stathis. 2006. *The Logic of Violence in Civil War*. New York, NY: Cambridge University Press.

Kelkar, Govind S. 1978. "The Chinese Experience of Political Campaigns and Mass Mobilization." *Social Scientist* 7 (5): 45–63. https://doi.org/10.2307/3516725.

Kennedy, Loraine. 2019. "The Politics of Land Acquisition in Haryana: Managing Dominant Caste Interests in the Name of Development." *Journal of Contemporary Asia*, 1–18. https://doi.org/10.1080/00472336.2019.1651885.

Kim, Quee-Young. 1996. "From Protest to Change of Regime: The 4-19 Revolt and the Fall of the Rhee Regime in South Korea." *Social Forces* 74 (4): 1179–1208. https://doi.org/10.2307/2580348.

Kim, Soo-hyun. 2010. "Issues of Squatters and Eviction in Seoul: From the Perspectives of the Dual Roles of the State." *City, Culture and Society* 1 (3): 135–43.

Kim, Sunhyuk, Chonghee Han, and Jiho Jang. 2008. "State–Society Relations in South Korea after Democratization: Is the Strong State Defunct?" *Pacific Focus* 23 (2): 252–70.

Kim, Sunil, and Jonson N. Porteux. 2019. "Adapting Violence for State Survival and Legitimacy: The Resilience and Dynamism of Political Repression in a Democratizing South Korea." *Democratization* 26 (4): 730–50.

Kine, Phelim. 2014. "Indonesia's Act of Denial." *Al Jazeera English*, March 1, 2014. http://america.aljazeera.com/opinions/2014/3/indonesia-s-act-ofdenial.html.

King, Gary, Michael Tomz, and Jason Wittenberg. 2000. "Making the Most of Statistical Analyses: Improving Interpretation and Presentation." *American Journal of Political Science* 44: 341–55.

Kipnis, Andrew. 1997. *Producing Guanxi: Sentiment, Self, and Subculture in a North China Village*. Durham, NC: Duke University Press.

Kipnis, Andrew. 2002. "Practices of Guanxi Production and Practices of Ganqing Avoidance." In *Social Connections in China: Institutions, Culture, and the Changing Nature of Guanxi*, edited by Thomas Gold, Doug Guthrie, and David Wank, 21–34. Cambridge, UK: Cambridge University Press.

Kohli, Atul. 1994. "Where Do High-Growth Political Economies Come from? The Japanese Lineage in South Korean Development." *World Development* 22 (9): 1269–93.

Kolo, Vincent. 2010. "Honda Strike—A Turning Point for China's Labor Movement." *Socialist Alternative*. https://www.socialistalternative.org/2010/06/22/honda-strike.

Koo, Hagen. 1993. "Strong State and Contentious Society." In *State and Society in Contemporary Korea*, edited by Hagen Koo, 231–50. Ithaca, NY; London, UK: Cornell University Press.

Koss, Daniel. 2018. *Where the Party Rules: The Rank and File of China's Communist State*. Cambridge, UK: Cambridge University Press.

Koss, Daniel, and Hiroshi Sato. 2016. "A Micro-Geography of State Extractive Power: The Case of Rural China." *Studies in Comparative International Development* 51 (4): 389–410.

Koter, Dominika. 2013. "King Makers: Local Leaders and Ethnic Politics in Africa." *World Politics* 65 (2): 187–232.

Kuhn, Philip A. 1980. *Rebellion and Its Enemies in Late Imperial China: Militarization and Social Structure 1796–1864*. Cambridge, MA: Harvard University Press.

Kung, James, Yongshun Cai, and Xiulin Sun. 2009. "Rural Cadres and Governance in China: Incentive, Institution and Accountability." *The China Journal* 62 (July): 61–77.

Kuo, Lily. 2019. "Inside Chengdu: Can China's Megacity Version of the Garden City Work?" *The Guardian*, February 4, 2019. https://www.theguardian.com/cities/2019/feb/04/if-we-have-to-leave-we-leave-the-downside-of-life-in-chinas-park-city.

Kuo, Lily. 2020. "Ms Du, Door Sensors and Me: Life with a Beijing Covid-19 Quarantine Handler." *The Guardian*, May 1, 2020. https://www.theguardian.com/world/2020/may/01/life-with-a-beijing-covid-19-quarantine-handler-coronavirus?CMP=share_btn_tw.

La Grange, Adrienne, and Hee Nam Jung. 2004. "The Commodification of Land and Housing: The Case of South Korea." *Housing Studies* 19 (4): 557–80. https://doi.org/10.1080/0267303042000221963.

Lankford, William M, and Faramarz Parsa. 1999. "Outsourcing: A Primer." *Management Decision* 37 (4): 310–16. https://doi.org/10.1108/00251749910269357.

Lau, Chris. 2019. "Hong Kong Law Scholar Benny Tai, Serving Jail Term for Co-Founding 2014 Occupy Protests, Gets Bail." *South China Morning Post*, August 15, 2019. https://www.scmp.com/news/hong-kong/politics/article/3022869/hong-kong-law-scholar-benny-tai-serving-jail-term-co.

Leander, Anna. 2005. "The Market for Force and Public Security: The Destabilizing Consequences of Private Military Companies." *Journal of Peace Research* 42 (5): 605–22.

Lee, Ching Kwan. 2007. *Against the Law: Labor Protests in China's Rustbelt and Sunbelt*. Berkeley, CA: University of California Press.

Lee, Ching Kwan, and Yonghong Zhang. 2013. "The Power of Instability: Unraveling the Microfoundations of Bargained Authoritarianism in China." *American Journal of Sociology* 118 (6): 1475–1508.

Lee, Jong Youl. 2000. "The Practice of Urban Renewal in Seoul, Korea: Mode, Governance, and Sustainability." Presented at the the 2nd International Critical Geography Conference, Taegu, Korea, August 9. https://citeseerx.ist.psu.edu/viewdoc/download?doi=10.1.1.565.2005&rep=rep1&type=pdf.

Lee, Lynn. 2017. "Wukan: The End of a Democratic Uprising in China." *Al Jazeera*, June 10, 2017. https://www.aljazeera.com/indepth/features/2017/05/wukan-democratic-uprising-china-170531091411268.html.

Lee, Yoonkyung. 2019. "Neo-Liberal Methods of Labour Repression: Privatised Violence and Dispossessive Litigation in Korea." *Journal of Contemporary Asia* 51 (3): 20–37.

Levi, Margaret. 1988. *Of Rule and Revenue*. Berkeley, CA: University of California Press.

Levi, Margaret, Audrey Sacks, and Tom Tyler. 2009. "Conceptualizing Legitimacy, Measuring Legitimating Beliefs." *American Behavioral Scientist* 53 (3): 354–75.

Levien, Michael. 2011. "Special Economic Zones and Accumulation by Dispossession in India." *Journal of Agrarian Change* 11 (4): 454–83.

Levien, Michael. 2013. "The Politics of Dispossession Theorizing India's 'Land Wars.'" *Politics & Society* 41 (3): 351–94. https://doi.org/10.1177/0032329213493751.

Levien, Michael. 2015. "Social Capital as Obstacle to Development: Brokering Land, Norms, and Trust in Rural India." *World Development* 74 (C): 77–92. https://doi.org/10.1016/j.worlddev.2015.04.012.

Li, Jie. 2015. *Shanghai Homes: Palimpsests of Private Life*. Global Chinese Culture. New York, NY: Columbia University Press.

Li, Lianjiang. 2020. "Distrust in Government and Preference for Regime Change in China." *Political Studies*, 326–43. https://doi.org/10.1177/0032321719892166.

Li, Lianjiang, Mingxing Liu, and Kevin J. O'Brien. 2012. "Petitioning Beijing: The High Tide of 2003–2006." *The China Quarterly* 210 (June): 313–34.

Li, Lianjiang, and Kevin J. O'Brien. 2008. "Protest Leadership in Rural China." *The China Quarterly* 193: 1–23.

Li, Lifeng. 2014. "群众运动与乡村治理-1945-1976年中国基层政治的一个解释框架【Mass Movements and Rural Governance: An Explanatory Framework on the Grass-Roots Politics in China】, 1945–1976." *Jiangsu Social Sciences* (江苏社会科学), no. 1: 218–30.

Li, Ling. 2018. "The Moral Economy of Guanxi and the Market of Corruption: Networks, Brokers and Corruption in China's Courts." *International Political Science Review* 39 (5): 634–46. https://doi.org/10.1177/0192512118791585.

Li, Xingping, Zonghui Zhang, and Yijin Zhang. 2005. "'模拟拆迁':浦江县旧城改造的启迪" [Simulated Demolition": Lessons from the Reconstruction of Pujiang County]." *Development of Small Cities & Towns* (小城镇建设), no. 6: 100–104.

Liang, Jing. 2018. "'扫黑 考验习近平的治国理念和执政能力' ["The Sweeping Campaign" Is a Challenge to Xi Jinping's Governance Ideologies and Capability]." *Radio Free Asia*, January 30, 2018. https://www.rfa.org/cantonese/commentaries/lj/com-01302018080449.html.

Liang, Zhiping. 2002. "法辨: 中国法的过去, 现在与未来" [Interpretation of Law, the Past, Current, and Future of Law in China]. Beijing, China: China University of Political Science and Law Press.

Liao, Xingmiu, and Wen-Hsuan Tsai. 2019. "Managing Irregular Petitions in China: Two Types of Social Control Strategy Within the Authoritarian System." *Journal of East Asian Studies* 19: 1–18.

Lichbach, Mark Irving. 1987. "Deterrence of Escalation? The Puzzle of Aggregate Studies of Repression and Dissent." *Journal of Conflict Resolution* 31: 266–97.

Lieberthal, Kenneth. 1973. "The Suppression of Secret Societies in Post-Liberation Tientsin." *The China Quarterly* 54 (June): 242–66.

Lifton, Robert J. 1956. "'Thought Reform' of Western Civilians in Chinese Communist Prisons." *Psychiatry* 19: 173–95.

Lim, Jae-Cheon. 2015. *Leader Symbols and Personality Cult in North Korea: The Leader State*. New York, NY: Routledge.

Liu, Chang. 2007. *Peasants and Revolution in Rural China: Rural Political Change in the North China Plain and the Yangzi Delta, 1850–1949*. London, UK; New York, NY: Routledge.

Liu, Shouying. 2019. "Land Issues in China's Urban-Rural Stage of Development." In *The Fundamental Dynamic Effect on Reform and Opening in China*, edited by Binhong Shao, 68–104. Leiden, The Netherlands; Boston, MA: Brill. https://doi.org/10.1163/9789004417229_005.

Liu, Yu. 2010. "Maoist Discourse and the Mobilization of Emotions in Revolutionary China." *Modern China* 36 (3): 329–62. https://doi.org/10.1177/0097700409360015.

Long, Zhi, and Yipei Yang. 2010. "'Nanfang Dushibao: Anyuanding: Beijing Jiefang "Heijianyu" Diaocha' [Southern Metropolitan Daily: Anyuanding: An Investigation of Beijing 'Black Jails' for Petition-Stopping]." *Nanfang Dushibao [Southern Metropolis Daily]*, September 24, 2010.

Looney, Kristen E. 2020. *Mobilizing for Development: The Modernization of Rural East Asia*. New York, NY: Cornell University Press.

Loveman, Mara. 1998. "High-Risk Collective Action: Defending Human Rights in Chile, Uruguay, and Argentina." *American Journal of Sociology* 104 (2): 477–525. https://doi.org/10.1086/210045.

Loveman, Mara. 2005. "The Modern State and the Primitive Accumulation of Symbolic Power." *American Journal of Sociology* 110 (6): 1651–83. https://doi.org/10.1086/428688.

Lu, Yao, and Ran Tao. 2017. "Organizational Structure and Collective Action: Lineage Networks, Semiautonomous Civic Associations, and Collective Resistance in Rural China." *American Journal of Sociology* 122 (6): 1726–74.

Lu, Yao, Wenjuan Zheng, and Wei Wang. 2017. "Migration and Popular Resistance in Rural China: Wukan and Beyond." *The China Quarterly* 229 (March): 1–22. https://doi.org/10.1017/S0305741016001582.

Luo, Changping. 2004. "'拆迁引发姐妹同日离婚' [Demolition Caused Sisters Divorced on the Same Day]." *The Beijing News*, May 8, 2004. http://www.bjnews.com.cn/news/2011/11/09/163185.html.

Maizland, Lindsay. 2020. "China's Repression of Uighurs in Xinjiang." Council on Foreign Relations. https://www.cfr.org/backgrounder/chinas-repression-uighurs-xinjiang.

Mann, Michael. 1984. "The Autonomous Power of the State: Its Origins, Mechanisms and Results." *European Journal of Sociology / Archives Européennes de Sociologie* 25 (2): 185–213. https://doi.org/10.1017/S0003975600004239.

Mann, Michael. 1993. *The Sources of Social Power, Volume: The Rise of Classes and Nation States, 1760–1914*. Cambridge, UK: Cambridge University Press.

Mao, Zedong. 1957. "The Situation in the Summer of 1957." Marxists Internet Archive. Selected Works of Mao Zedong Volume 5. https://www.marxists.org/reference/archive/mao/selected-works/volume-5/mswv5_66.htm.

Mares, Isabela, and Lauren Young. 2016. "Buying, Expropriating, and Stealing Votes." *Annual Review of Political Science* 19: 267–88.

Mares, Isabela, and Lauren E. Young. 2019. *Conditionality and Coercion: Electoral Clientelism in Eastern Europe*. Oxford, UK: Oxford University Press.

Marten, Kimberly. 2006. "Warlordism in Comparative Perspective." *International Security* 31 (3): 41–73.

Marten, Kimberly. 2012. *Warlords: Strong-Arm Brokers in Weak States*. Ithaca, NY: Cornell University Press.

Martin, Brian G. 1995. "The Green Gang and the Guomindang State: Du Yuesheng and the Politics of Shanghai, 1927–37." *The Journal of Asian Studies* 54 (1): 64–92

Mattingly, Daniel C. 2019. *The Art of Political Control in China*. Cambridge, UK: Cambridge University Press.

Mazzei, Julie. 2009. *Death Squads or Self-Defense Forces?: How Paramilitary Groups Emerge and Threaten Democracy in Latin America*. Chapel Hill, NC: University of North Carolina Press.

McAdam, Douglas, Sidney Tarrow, and Charles Tilly. 2001. *Dynamics of Contention*. Cambridge, UK: Cambridge University Press.

McCarthy, John D., and Clark McPhail. 1998. "The Institutionalization of Protest in the United States." In *The Social Movement Society: Contentious Politics for a New Century*, edited by David S. Meyer and Sidney Tarrow, 83–110. Lanham, MD: Rowman and Littlefield.

McConnell, Terrance C. 1981. "Moral Blackmail." *Ethics* 91 (4): 544–67.

Mehta, Mona G. 2013. "Networks of Death and Militant Vegetarianism: The Mechanics of Communal Violence in Gujarat." *India Review* 12 (2): 108–17.

Mertha, Andrew. 2008. *China's Water Warriors: Citizen Action and Policy Change*. Ithaca, NY: Cornell University Press.

Micklethwait, John, and Adrian Wooldridge. 2014. *The Fourth Revolution: The Global Race to Reinvent the State*. New York, NY: Penguin Press.

Micklethwait, John, and Adrian Wooldridge. 2020. "The Virus Should Wake Up the West." *Bloomberg*, April 12, 2020. https://www.bloomberg.com/opinion/articles/2020-04-13/coronavirus-pandemic-is-wake-up-call-to-reinvent-the-state.

Migdal, Joel S. 1988. *Strong Societies and Weak States: State-Society Relations and State Capabilities in the Third World*. Princeton, NJ: Princeton University Press.

Migdal, Joel S. 2001. *State in Society: Studying How States and Societies Transform and Constitute One Another*. New York, NY: Cambridge University Press.

Miller, Gary J. 2005. "The Political Evolution of Principal-Agent Models." *Annual Review of Political Science* 8 (June): 203–25.

Mitchell, Neil J. 2004. *Agents of Atrocity: Leaders, Followers, and the Violation of Human Rights in Civil War*. New York, NY: Palgrave Macmillan.

Mobrand, Erik. 2016. "The Street Leaders of Seoul and the Foundations of the South Korean Political Order." *Modern Asian Studies* 50 (2): 636–74.

Mohan, Rakesh, and Shubhagato Dasgupta. 2004. "Urban Development in India in the 21st Century: Policies for Accelerating Urban Growth." Stanford King Center on Global Development Working Paper No.231.

Moore, Will H. 1998. "Repression and Dissent: Substitution, Context, and Timing." *American Journal of Political Science* 42 (3): 851–73.

Mozur, Paul. 2020. "China, Desperate to Stop Coronavirus, Turns Neighbor Against Neighbor." *The New York Times*, February 3, 2020. https://www.nytimes.com/2020/02/03/business/china-coronavirus-wuhan-surveillance.html.

Mueller, John. 2000. "The Banality of 'Ethnic War.'" *International Security* 25 (1): 42–70.

Muller, Edward N., and Karl-Dieter Opp. 1986. "Rational Choice and Rebellious Collective Action." *The American Political Science Review* 80 (2): 471–88.

Nandy, S.N. 2015. "Urbanization in India—Past, Present and Future Consequences." *Urban India* 35 (2): 8–24.

Nanfang Daily. 2009. "'唐福珍死于愤怒 愤怒源于无力感' [Tang Fuzhen Died of Anger, Her Anger Originated in the Feeling of Powerlessness]." *Nanfang Daily*, December 3, 2009, sec. AA02. https://web.archive.org/web/20091205153433/http:/gcontent.nddaily.com/1/d9/1d94108e907bb831/Blog/f08/fa9af8.html.

Newton, Kenneth. 1999. "Social and Political Trust in Established Democracies." In *Critical Citizens: Global Support for Democratic Government*, edited by Pippa Norris, 169–87. Oxford, UK: Oxford University Press.

Newton, Kenneth, and Pippa Norris. 2000. "Confidence in Public Institutions: Faith, Culture, or Performance?" In *Why People Don't Trust Government*, edited by Joseph Nye, Philip Zelikow, and David King, 52–73. Cambridge, MA: Harvard University Press.

North, Douglass C., John Joseph Wallis, Steven B. Webb, and Barry R. Weingast, eds. 2012. *In the Shadow of Violence: Politics, Economics, and the Problem of Development*. Cambridge, UK: Cambridge University Press.

North, Douglass C., John Joseph Wallis, and Barry R. Weingast. 2009. *Violence and Social Orders*. Cambridge, UK: Cambridge University Press.

Nugent, Elizabeth R. 2020. "The Psychology of Repression and Polarization." *World Politics* 72 (2): 291–334.

O'Brien, Kevin J., and Lianjiang Li. 2006. *Rightful Resistance in Rural China*. New York, NY: Cambridge University Press.

O'Brien, Kevin J, and Yanhua Deng. 2015. "The Reach of the State: Work Units, Family Ties and 'Harmonious Demolition.'" *The China Journal* 74: 1–17.

Oh, Jennifer S. 2012. "Strong State and Strong Civil Society in Contemporary South Korea: Challenges to Democratic Governance." *Asian Survey* 52 (3): 528–49. https://doi.org/10.1525/as.2012.52.3.528.

Oi, Jean C. 1989. *State and Peasant in Contemporary China: The Political Economy of Village Government*. Berkeley, CA: University of California Press.

Olson, Mancur. 1993. "Dictatorship, Democracy, and Development." *American Political Science Review* 87 (September): 567–76.

Ong, Lynette H. 2006. "The Political Economy of Township Government Debt, Township Enterprises and Rural Financial Institutions in China." *The China Quarterly* 186: 377–400.

Ong, Lynette H. 2012a. *Prosper or Perish: The Political Economy of Credit and Fiscal Systems in Rural China*. Ithaca, NY: Cornell University Press.

Ong, Lynette H. 2012b. "Indebted Dragon—The Risky Strategy Behind China's Construction Economy." *Foreign Affairs*, November 27, 2012. https://www.foreignaffairs.com/articles/china/2012-11-27/indebted-dragon.

Ong, Lynette H. 2014. "State-Led Urbanization in China: Skyscrapers, Land Revenue and 'Concentrated Villages.'" *The China Quarterly* 217: 162–79.

Ong, Lynette H. 2015a. "Reports of Social Unrest: Basic Characteristics, Trends and Patterns, 2003-12." In *Handbook of the Politics of China*, edited by David SG Goodman and Edward Edgar, 345–60. Edward Elgar Publishing.

Ong, Lynette H. 2015b. "'Thugs-for-Hire': State Coercion and 'Everyday Repression' in China." *SSRN Electronic Journal*, Harvard Yenching Workshop. https://doi.org/10.2139/ssrn.2609999.

Ong, Lynette H. 2018a. "Thugs and Outsourcing of State Repression in China." *The China Journal* 80: 94–110. https://doi.org/10.1086/696156.

Ong, Lynette H. 2018b. "'Thugs-for-Hire': Subcontracting of State Coercion and State Capacity in China." *Perspectives on Politics* 16 (3): 680–95. https://doi.org/10.1017/S1537592718000981.

Ong, Lynette H. 2019a. "Engaging Huangniu (Brokers): Commodification of State-Society Bargaining in China." *Journal of Contemporary China* 28 (116): 293–307. https://doi.org/10.1080/10670564.2018.1511398.

Ong, Lynette H. 2019b. "'Land Grabbing' in an Autocracy and a Multi-Party Democracy: China and India Compared." *Journal of Contemporary Asia* 50 (3): 361–79. https://doi.org/10.1080/00472336.2019.1569253.

Ong, Lynette H., and Donglin Han. 2019. "What Drives People to Protest in an Authoritarian Country? Resources and Rewards vs Risks of Protests in Urban and Rural China." *Political Studies* 67 (1): 224–48. https://doi.org/10.1177/0032321718763558.

Ong, Lynette. 2021. "Xi Jinping's 'Sweeping Black' Campaign." Urban Violence Research Network. April 27, 2021. https://urbanviolence.org/xi-jinpings-sweeping-black-campaign-strong/.

O'Shaughnessy, Nicholas. 2016. *Selling Hitler: Propaganda and the Nazi Brand*. London, UK: C. Hurst & Co.

Palma, Giuseppe di. 1991. "Legitimation from the Top to Civil Society: Politico-Cultural Change in Eastern Europe." *World Politics* 44 (1): 49–80.

Pan, Jennifer. 2020. *Welfare for Autocrats: How Social Assistance in China Cares for Its Rulers*. New York, NY: Oxford University Press.

Pan, Jennifer, and Yiqing Xu. 2018. "China's Ideological Spectrum." *The Journal of Politics* 80 (1): 254–73.

Pearlman, Wendy. 2013. "Emotions and the Microfoundations of the Arab Uprisings." *Perspectives on Politics* 11 (2): 387–409. https://doi.org/10.1017/S153759271 3001072.

Pei, Minxin. 2006. *China's Trapped Transition: The Limits of Developmental Autocracy*. Cambridge, MA: Harvard University Press.

Perry, Elizabeth J. 1980. *Rebels and Revolutionaries in North China, 1845–1945*. Stanford, CA: Stanford University Press.

Perry, Elizabeth J. 1985. "Rural Violence in Socialist China." *China Quarterly*, no. 103: 414–40.

Perry, Elizabeth J. 2002a. *Challenging the Mandate of Heaven: Social Protest and State Power in China*. Armonk, NY: ME Sharpe.

Perry, Elizabeth J. 2002b. "Moving The Masses: Emotion Work In The Chinese Revolution." *Mobilization: An International Quarterly* 7 (2): 111–28.

Perry, Elizabeth J. 2007. "Studying Chinese Politics: Farewell to Revolution?" *China Journal* 57: 1–22.

Perry, Elizabeth J. 2011. "From Mass Campaigns to Managed Campaigns: Constructing a 'New Socialist Countryside.'" In *Mao's Invisible Hand: The Political Foundations of Adaptive Governance in China*, edited by Elizabeth J. Perry and Sebastian Heilmann, 30–61. Cambridge, MA: Harvard University Asia Center.

Perry, Elizabeth J. 2019. "Making Communism Work: Sinicizing a Soviet Governance Practice." *Comparative Studies in Society and History* 61 (3): 535–62.

Pierskalla, Jan H. 2010. "Protest, Deterrence, and Escalation: The Strategic Calculus of Government Repression." *Journal of Conflict Resolution* 54 (1): 117–45.

Pierskalla, Jan H., and Florian M. Hollenbach. 2013. "Technology and Collective Action: The Effect of Cell Phone Coverage on Political Violence in Africa." *American Political Science Review* 107 (2): 207–24.

Poe, Steven C. 2004. "The Decision to Repress: An Integrative Theoretical Approach to the Research on Human Rights and Repression." In *Understanding Human Rights Violations: New Systematic Studies*, edited by Sabine C. Carey and Steven C. Poe, 16–38. Aldershot, UK: Ashgate.

Porta, Donatella della. 1995. *Social Movements, Political Violence, and the State*. New York, NY: Cambridge University Press.

Portes, Alejandro. 2000. "The Two Meanings of Social Capital." *Sociological Forum* 15 (1): 1–12.

Porteux, Jonson, and Sunil Kim. 2016. "Public Ordering of Private Coercion: Urban Redevelopment and Democratization in Korea." *Journal of East Asian Studies* 16 (3): 371–90.

Posner, Richard A. 1983. *The Economics of Justice*. Cambridge, MA; London, UK: Harvard University Press.

Putnam, Robert D. 1995. "Bowling Alone: America's Declining Social Capital." *Journal of Democracy* 6 (1): 65–78.

Putnam, Robert D., Robert Leonardi, and Raffaella Nanetti. 1993. *Making Democracy Work: Civic Traditions in Modern Italy*. Princeton, NJ: Princeton University Press.

Qiao, Long. 2010. "Villagers Got Beaten up during the Forced Demolition of Zhutun Village, Zhengzhou," December 20, 2010. https://www.rfa.org/mandarin/yataibaodao/zheng-12202010094833.html.

Qiaoan, Runya, and Jessica Teets. 2019. "Responsive Authoritarianism in China—A Review of Responsiveness in Xi and Hu Administrations." *Journal of Chinese Political Science* 25 (1): 139–53.

Ra, Jong-Yil. 2014. "After Chun Doo-Hwan: The Progress of Democratization and the Residue of Authoritarianism in South Korea." In *Democracy or Alternative Political Systems in Asia: After the Strongmen*, edited by Hsin-Huang Michael Hsiao, 58–78. New York, NY: Routledge.

Radio Free Asia. 2011. "'城中村改造半夜拆房 三百打手村民受伤' [Chengzhongcun Demolished at Midnight, 300 Gangsters Injuered Villagers]." *Radio Free Asia*, August 31, 2011. https://www.rfa.org/mandarin/yataibaodao/c-08312011111724.html.

Radio Free Asia. 2012. "'河南郑州村民被强拆集体抗议 城中村改造不理百姓生计' [Villagers Protested against Forced Demolition, Chengzhongcun Transformation Ignores of the Wellbeing of the People]." *Radio Free Asia*, September 2012. https://www.rfa.org/mandarin/yataibaodao/hn-09192012112033.html.

Radio Free Asia. 2013. "Top Chinese Reporter Fired as Thugs Attack Film Crew." *Radio Free Asia*, March 1, 2013. https://www.rfa.org/english/news/china/reporter-03012013135209.html.

Radio Free Asia. 2014. "'郑州千人堵路抗议城中村强拆' [Thousands of People in Zhengzhou Protest against Forced Demolition of Chengzhongcun by Blocking the Streets]." *Radio Free Asia*, March 7, 2014. https://www.rfa.org/mandarin/yataibaodao/renquanfazhi/yf1-03072014103802.html?searchterm:utf8:ustring=%E9%83%91%E5%B7%9E.

Radio Free Asia. 2018. "'蔡奇北京"清除低端人口"是习近平全国"扫黑除恶"的前奏' [Cai Qi's Campaign of 'Clearing out the Low-End Population' in Beijing Was a Prelude to Xi Jinping's Nationwide 'Sweeping Black Campaign']." *Radio Free Asia*, February 2, 2018. https://www.rfa.org/mandarin/zhuanlan/yehuazhongnanhai/gx-02022018141457.html.

Rafter, Nicole. 2014. "Film Review. Joshua Oppenheimer (Dir.), The Act of Killing, 2012." *Theoretical Criminology* 18 (2): 257–60.

Ramesh, Jairam, and Muhammad Ali Khan. 2015. *Legislating for Justice: The Making of the 2013 Land Acquisition Law*. New Delhi, India: Oxford University Press.

Ramzy, Austin, and Chris Buckley. 2019. "'Absolutely No Mercy': Leaked Files Expose How China Organized Mass Detentions of Muslims." *New York Times*, November 16, 2019. https://www.nytimes.com/interactive/2019/11/16/world/asia/china-xinjiang-documents.html.

Ranganathan, Malini. 2014. "'Mafias' in the Waterscape: Urban Informality and Everyday Public Authority in Bangalore." *Water Alternatives* 7 (1): 89–105.

Rasler, Karen. 1996. "Concessions, Repression, and Political Protest in the Iranian Revolution." *American Sociological Review* 61 (1): 132–52.

Rauta, Vladimir. 2016. "Proxy Agents, Auxiliary Forces, and Sovereign Defection: Assessing the Outcomes of Using Non-State Actors in Civil Conflicts." *Southeast European and Black Sea Studies* 16 (1): 91–111.

Read, Benjamin. 2012. *Roots of the State: Neighborhood Organization and Social Networks in Beijing and Taipei*. Stanford, CA: Stanford University Press.

Repnikova, Maria, and Kecheng Fang. 2018. ion and Sorian Participatory Persuasion 2.0: Netizens as Thought Work Collaborators in China." *Journal of Contemporary China* 27 (113): 763–79.

Rithmire, Meg E. 2015. *Land Bargains and Chinese Capitalism: The Politics of Property Rights under Reform.* New York, NY: Cambridge University Press.

Ritter, Emily H. 2014. "Policy Disputes, Political Survival, and the Onset and Severity of State Repression." *Journal of Conflict Resolution* 58 (1): 143–68.

Rodgers, Kathleen. 2010. "'Anger Is Why We're All Here': Mobilizing and Managing Emotions in a Professional Activist Organization." *Social Movement Studies* 9 (3): 273–91.

Roessler, Philip G. 2005. "Donor-Induced Democratization and the Privatization of State Violence in Kenya and Rwanda." *Comparative Politics* 37 (2): 207–27. https://doi.org/10.2307/20072883.

Rowe, William T. 2009. *China's Last Empire: The Great Qing.* Cambridge, MA; London, UK: Harvard University Press.

Russia Update. 2015. "Druzhinniki Volunteer Police Patrols, a Staple of Soviet Era, Revived in Russia." *Russia Update,* May 13, 2015. https://pressimus.com/Interpreter_Mag/press/8317.

Schatz, Edward, and Elena Maltseva. 2012. "Kazakhstan's Authoritarian 'Persuasion.'" *Post-Soviet Affairs* 28 (1): 45–65. https://doi.org/10.2747/1060-586X.28.1.45.

Schedler, Andreas. 2002. "Elections Without Democracy: The Menu of Manipulation." *Journal of Democracy* 13 (2): 36–50.

Schmitz, Rob. 2016. *Street of Eternal Happiness: Big City Dreams Along a Shanghai Road.* Crown.

Schoenhals, Michael. 2012. *Spying for the People: Mao's Secret Agents, 1949–1967.* Cambridge: Cambridge University Press.

Schoon, Eric W. 2014. "The Asymmetry of Legitimacy: Analyzing the Legitimation of Violence in 30 Cases of Insurgent Revolution." *Social Forces* 93 (2): 779–801.

Scoggins, Suzanne E. 2018. "Policing Modern China." *China Law and Society Review* 3 (2): 79–117. https://doi.org/10.1163/25427466-00302001.

Scoggins, Suzanne. 2021. *Policing China: Street-Level Cops in the Shadow of Protest.* Ithaca, NY: Cornell University Press.

Scoggins, Suzanne E., and Kevin J O'Brien. 2016. "China's Unhappy Police." *Asian Survey* 56 (2): 225–42.

Scott, James C. 1985. *Weapons of the Weak: Everyday Forms of Peasant Resistance.* New Haven, CT; London, UK: Yale University Press.

Scott, James C. 1989. "Everyday Forms of Resistance." *Copenhagen Journal of Asian Studies* 4 (1): 33–62.

Scott, James C. 1998. *Seeing Like a State: How Certain Schemes to Improve the Human Condition Have Failed.* New Haven, CT: Yale University Press.

Scott, James C. 2010. *The Art of Not Being Governed: An Anarchist History of Upland Southeast Asia.* New Haven, CT: Yale University Press.

Seawright, Jason, and John Gerring. 2008. "Case Selection Techniques in Case Study Research: A Menu of Qualitative and Quantitative Options." *Political Research Quarterly* 61 (2): 294–308. https://doi.org/10.1177/1065912907313077.

Seo, Jungmin, and Sungmoon Kim. 2015. "Civil Society under Authoritarian Rule: Bansanghoe and Extraordinary Everyday-Ness in Korean Neighborhoods." *Korea Journal* 55 (1): 59–85.

Shao, Qin. 2013. *Shanghai Gone: Domicide and Defiance in a Chinese Megacity*. State and Society in East Asia. Lanham: Rowman & Littlefield Publishers, Inc.

Sharafutdinova, Gulnaz. 2014. "The Pussy Riot Affair and Putin's Démarche from Sovereign Democracy to Sovereign Morality." *Nationalities Papers* 42 (4): 615–21. https://doi.org/10.1080/00905992.2014.917075.

Shelley, Louise I. 1996. *Policing Soviet Society : The Evolution of State Control*. London, UK; New York, NY: Routledge.

Shi, Jiangtao. 2018. "Xi Jinping Puts China's Mafia in Cross Hairs, but Fears of Judicial Abuse Remain." *South China Morning Post*, January 26, 2018. https://www.scmp.com/print/news/china/policies-politics/article/2130629/xi-puts-chinas-mafia-cross-hairs-fears-judicial-abuse.

Shi, Tianjian. 2015. *The Cultural Logic of Politics in Mainland China and Taiwan*. New York, NY: Cambridge University Press.

Shi, Yu. 2020. "The Son of Wu Tianjun, 'King of Political and Legal Affairs' in Henan, Was Sentenced 中国河南'政法王'吴天君之子获刑." *DW News*, January 6, 2020. https://www.dwnews.com/%E4%B8%AD%E5%9B%BD/60163629/.

Shin, Hyun Bang. 2018. "Urban Movements and the Genealogy of Urban Rights Discourses: The Case of Urban Protesters against Redevelopment and Displacement in Seoul, South Korea." *Annals of the American Association of Geographers* 108 (2): 356–69. https://doi.org/10.1080/24694452.2017.1392844.

Shue, Vivienne. 1988. *The Reach of the State: Sketches of the Chinese Body Politics*. Stanford, CA: Stanford University Press.

Simmel, George. 1950. "The Triad." In *The Sociology of Georg Simmel*, edited by Kurt H. Wolff, 145–62. New York, NY: Free Press.

Sina News. 2015. "Qiu He's 'Relatives and Friends' in Kunming 仇和在昆明的'亲友团.'" *Sina News*, March 24, 2015. https://news.sina.com.cn/c/2015-03-24/172631640250.shtml.

Sinha, Aseema. 2005. "Political Foundations of Market-Enhancing Federalism: Theoretical Lessons from India and China." *Comparative Politics* 37 (2): 337–56.

Skinner, G. William, and Edwin A. Winckler. 1969. "Compliance Succession in Rural Communist China: A Cylical Theory." In *A Sociological Reader on Complex Organizations*, edited by Amitai Etzioni, 410–38. New York, NY: Holt, Rinehart & Winston.

Sohu News. 2007. "'Shanghai "Dongqian Zhongjie" Fuchu Shuimian—Jiehun Lihun Yici Zhuan Liuwan' [Shanghai Relocation Agents Are Revealed: Earn 60,000 Every Marriage and Divorce]." *Sohu News*, December 17, 2007.

Soifer, Hillel D. 2008. "State Infrastructural Power: Approaches to Conceptualization and Measurement." *Studies in Comparative International Development* 43 (3–4): 231–51.

Soifer, Hillel D., and Matthias vom Hau. 2008. "Unpacking the Strength of the State: The Utility of State Infrastructural Power." *Studies in Comparative International Development* 43 (3–4): 219–30. https://doi.org/10.1007/s12116-008-9030-z.

Solodovnik, Svetlana. 2014. "Russia: The Official Church Chooses the State." *Russian Politics & Law* 52 (3): 38–66. https://doi.org/10.2753/RUP1061-1940520302.

Solomon, Richard H. 1969. "On Activism and Activists: Maoist Conceptions of Motivation and Political Role Linking State to Society." *The China Quarterly* 39 (September): 76–114.

Song, Fuli. 2015. "'大同的耿式难题' [Geng's Dilemma in Datong]." *Tencent*. March 2, 2015. https://datong.house.qq.com/a/20150302/049510.htm.

Spence, Michael, and Richard Zeckhauser. 1971. "Insurance, Information, and Individual Action." *American Economic Review* 61 (2): 380–87.

Spires, Anthony J. 2020. "Regulation as Political Control: China's First Charity Law and Its Implications for Civil Society." *Nonprofit and Voluntary Sector Quarterly* 49 (3): 571–88.

Staniland, Paul. 2012. "Organizing Insurgency: Networks, Resources, and Rebellion in South Asia." *International Security* 37 (1): 142–76.

Stanley, William. 1996. *The Protection Racket State: Elite Politics, Military Extortion, and Civil War in El Salvador*. Philadelphia, PA: Temple University Press.

Steinhardt, H. Christoph. 2012. "How Is High Trust in China Possible? Comparing the Origins of Generalized Trust in Three Chinese Societies." *Political Studies* 60 (2): 434–54. https://doi.org/10.1111/j.1467-9248.2011.00909.x.

Stephenson, Svetlana. 2017. "It Takes Two to Tango: The State and Organized Crime in Russia." *Current Sociology* 65 (3): 411–26. https://doi.org/10.1177/0011392116681384.

Stern, Gary H., and Ron J. Feldman. 2004. *Too Big To Fail: The Hazards of Bank Bailouts*. Washington, DC: Brookings Institution Press.

Stokes, Susan C., Thad Dunning, Marcelo Nazareno, and Valeria Brusco. 2013. *Brokers, Voters, and Clientelism: The Puzzle of Distributive Politics*. Cambridge, UK: Cambridge University Press.

Stovel, Katherine, and Lynette Shaw. 2012. "Brokerage." *Annual Review of Sociology* 38: 139–58.

Su, Yang. 2011. *Collective Killings in Rural China during the Cultural Revolution*. Cambridge, UK; New York, NY: Cambridge University Press.

Su, Zheng, and Tianguang Meng. 2016. "Selective Responsiveness: Online Public Demands and Government Responsiveness in Authoritarian China." *Social Science Research* 59 (September): 52–67.

Sud, Nikita. 2014a. "The Men in the Middle: A Missing Dimension in Global Land Deals." *The Journal of Peasant Studies* 41 (4): 593–612. https://doi.org/10.1080/03066 150.2014.920329.

Sud, Nikita. 2014b. "Governing India's Land." *World Development* 60 (8): 43–56. https:// doi.org/10.1016/j.worlddev.2014.03.015.

Suh, Dae-Sook. 1995. *Kim Il Sung: The North Korean Leader*. New York, NY: Columbia University Press.

Svolik, Milan W. 2012. "Contracting on Violence: The Moral Hazard in Authoritarian Repression and Military Intervention in Politics." *Journal of Conflict Resolution* 57 (5): 765–94. https://doi.org/10.1177/0022002712449327.

Tang, Beibei. 2015. "'Not Rural but Not Urban': Community Governance in China's Urban Villages." *The China Quarterly* 223 (September): 724–44. https://doi.org/10.1017/ S0305741015000843.

Tang, Beibei. 2019. "Grid Governance in China's Urban Middle-Class Neighbourhoods." *The China Quarterly* 241: 43–61. https://doi.org/10.1017/S0305741019000821.

Tang, Jane. 2020. "Residents of China's Shandong Left Homeless by Suspended Rural Resettlement Plan." Translated by Luisetta Mudie. *Radio Free Asia*, July 27, 2020. https://www.rfa.org/english/news/china/shandong-homeless-07272020092442.html.

Tang, Wenfang. 2016. *Populist Authoritarianism: Chinese Political Culture and Regime Sustainability*. New York, NY: Oxford University Press.

Tannenberg, Marcus, Michael Bernhard, Johannes Gerschewski, Anna Lührmann, and Christian von Soest. 2021. "Claiming the Right to Rule: Regime Legitimation Strategies from 1900 to 2019." *European Political Science Review* 13 (1): 77–94.

Tarrow, Sidney. 2011. *Power in Movement: Social Movements and Contentious Politics*. 3rd ed. Cambridge, MA: Cambridge University Press.

Taylor, Brian D. 2011. *State Building in Putin's Russia: Policing and Coercion after Communism*. Cambridge, UK: Cambridge University Press.

Teets, Jessica C. 2014. *Civil Society under Authoritarianism: The China Model*. New York, NY: Cambridge University Press.

Teiwes, Frederick C. 1993. *Politics and Purges in China: Rectification and the Decline of Party Norms, 1950–65*. Armonk, NY: M. E. Sharpe.

Thachil, Tariq. 2011. "Embedded Mobilization: Nonstate Service Provision as Electoral Strategy in India." *World Politics* 63 (3): 434–69. https://doi.org/10.1017/S0043887711000116.

Thachil, Tariq. 2014. *Elite Parties, Poor Voters: How Social Services Win Votes in India*. New York, NY: Cambridge University Press.

The Asian Coalition for Housing Rights. 1989. "Evictions in Seoul, South Korea: The Asian Coalition for Housing Rights." *Environment and Urbanization* 1 (1): 89–94. https://doi.org/10.1177/095624788900100112.

The Economist. 2020. "Building up the Pillars of State: Rich Countries Try Radical Economic Policies to Counter COVID-19." *The Economist*, March 26, 2020. https://www.economist.com/briefing/2020/03/26/rich-countries-try-radical-economic-policies-to-counter-covid-19.

The Paper [澎拜新闻]. 2017. "'吴天君被查 主政郑州期间大搞拆迁绰号"一指没,"' [澎拜新闻]." *The Paper [澎拜新闻]*, February 3, 2017. https://www.thepaper.cn/newsDetail_forward_1613071.

The State Council of the People's Republic of China. 2011. "国有土地上房屋征收与补偿条例' [Ordinance on Requisition and Compensation of Houses on State Land]." The State Council of the People's Republic of China. http://www.gov.cn/zwgk/2011-01/21/content_1790111.htm.

Tian, Xianhong. 2010. "从威权到谋利-农民上访行为逻辑变迁的一个解释框架From Right-Protection to Benefit-Seeking: A Frame of Explanation for the Changing Logic behind Farmer Petition." *Open Times*（开放时代）, no. 6: 24–38.

Tianya BBS. 2013. "'关于上海市闸北区振沪动迁组涉嫌贪污问题的举报' [Reporting of the Zhenhu Demolition Group in Zhabei District, Shanghai, Suspected of Corruption]." *Tianya BBS*. http://bbs.tianya.cn/m/post-828-441189-1.shtml?from=singlemessage&isappinstalled=0.

Tianya BBS. 2015a. "徇私舞弊，暴力拆迁---成都市抚琴街3号院拆迁重大情况反映！[Playing Favoritism and Committing Irregularities, Forced Demolition--The Case of Fuqin Street, Chengdu]." *Tianya BBS*. http://bbs.tianya.cn/post-828-1076359-1.shtml.

Tianya BBS. 2015b. "成都市抚琴街3号院附条件自主改造项目 已签约住户集体声明' [Collective Statement by Signatories of the Self Renovation Project at Courtyard No. 3 at Fuqin Street, Chengdu]." *Tianya BBS*. http://bbs.tianya.cn/post-828-1084288-1.shtml.

Tilly, Charles. 1978. *From Mobilization to Revolution*. New York, NY: McGraw-Hill.

Tilly, Charles. 2003. *Politics of Collective Violence*. Cambridge, UK; New York, NY: Cambridge University Press.

Time Weekly. 2011. "'浙商320亿昆明项目悬疑 新螺蛳湾的空壳道场' The Uncertain Future of Zhejiang Merchants' 32 Billion Project in Kunming: The Empty Luosiwan International Trade City." *Time Weekly*, September 7, 2011. http://www.time-weekly.com/html/20110907/13931_1.html.

Tocqueville, Alexis de. 1835. "CHAPTER 7: Of the Omnipotence of the Majority in the United States and Its Effects." In *Democracy in America*, edited by Eduardo Nolla, vol. 2, 402–26. Indianapolis, IN: Liberty Fund.

Tomba, Luigi. 2014. *The Government Next Door: Neighborhood Politics in Urban China*. Ithaca, NY; London, UK: Cornell University Press.

Tsai, Lily. 2007. *Accountability Without Democracy: Solidary Groups and Public Goods Provision in Rural China*. Cambridge Studies on Comparative Politics. New York, NY: Cambridge University Press.

Tyler, Tom R. 2006a. *Why People Obey the Law*. Princeton, NJ: Princeton University Press.

Tyler, Tom R. 2006b. "Psychological Perspectives on Legitimacy and Legitimation." *Annual Review of Psychology* 57 (1): 375–400. https://doi.org/10.1146/annurev. psych.57.102904.190038.

Tyler, Tom R. 2011a. "Trust and Legitimacy in the USA and Europe." *European Journal of Criminology* 8 (4): 254–66.

Tyler, Tom R. 2011b. *Why People Cooperate: The Role of Social Motivations*. Princeton, NJ: Princeton University Press.

Tyler, Tom R., and Yuen J. Huo. 2002. *Trust in the Law*. New York, NY: Russell Sage.

Tynen, Sarah. 2019. "State Territorialization through Shequ Community Centres: Bureaucratic Confusion in Xinjiang, China." *Territory, Politics, Governance*, July. https://doi.org/10.1080/21622671.2019.1643778.

Unger, Jonathan. 2002. *The Transformation of Rural China*. Armonk, NY: M.E. Sharpe.

Vadlamanti, Krishna Chaitya, and Haider Khan. 2013. "Competing for Investments in Special Economic Zones? An Empirical Investigation on Indian States, 1998–2010." In *Invisible India: Hidden Risks within an Emerging Superpower*, edited by Jason Miklian and Ashid Kolas, 184–203. London, UK: Routledge.

Van Slyke, Lyman P. 1967. *Enemies and Friends: The United Front in Chinese Communist History*. Stanford, CA: Stanford University Press.

Varese, Federico, ed. 2010. *Organized Crime: Critical Concepts in Criminology*. London, UK; New York, NY: Routledge.

Viterna, Jocelyn S. 2006. "Pulled, Pushed, and Persuaded: Explaining Women's Mobilization into the Salvadoran Guerrilla Army." *American Journal of Sociology* 112 (1): 1–45. https://doi.org/10.1086/502690.

Volkov, Vadim. 1999. "Violent Entrepreneurship in Post-Communist Russia." *Europe-Asia Studies* 51 (5): 741–54.

Volkov, Vadim. 2002a. *Violent Entrepreneurs : The Use of Force in the Making of Russian Capitalism*. Ithaca, NY: Cornell University Press.

Volkov, Vadim. 2002b. "Violent Entrepreneurship in Post-Communist Russia." In *Beyond State Crisis? Post-Colonial Africa and Post-Soviet Eurasia in Comparative Perspective*, edited by Mark R. Beissinger and Crawford Young, 81–104. Washington: Woodrow Wilson Center Press.

Vu, Tuong. 2007. "State Formation and the Origins of the Developmental States in South Korea and Indonesia." *Studies in Comparative International Development* 41 (4): 27–56.

Walder, Andrew G. 2019. *Agents of Disorder: Inside China's Cultural Revolution*. Cambridge, MA: The Belknap Press of Harvard University Press.

Wales, Oscar. 2016. "Skinheads and Nashi: What Are the Reasons for the Rise of Nationalism amongst Russian Youth in the Post-Soviet Period?" *Slovo* 28 (2): 106–30.

Wang, Cailiang. 2012. "'2011中国拆迁年度报告'" Beijing Cailiang Law Firm.

Wang, Cailiang. 2016. "推进PPP模式 法律不能缺位." *Caixin Blog* (blog). September 5, 2016. http://wangcailiang.blog.caixin.com/archives/151080.

Wang, Cailiang. 2018a. "'律师解读: 扫黑除恶' [A Lawyer's Analysis: The Sweeping Black Campaign]." Sina Weibo. January 25, 2018. https://card.weibo.com/article/m/show/id/2309404200169976555509.

Wang, Cailiang. 2018b. "'嘉禾事件十年再反思' [Ten Years after the Jiahe Incident]." Wechat Official Account. September 6, 2018. https://mp.weixin.qq.com/s/xx6YIUyXuM2jTJh9M0CP5g.

Wang, Di. 2018. *Violence and Order on the Chengdu Plain: The Story of a Secret Brotherhood in Rural China, 1939–1949*. Stanford, CA: Stanford University Press.

Wang, Di, and Sida Liu. 2021. "Doing Ethnography on Social Media: A Methodological Reflection on the Study of Online Groups in China." *Qualitative Inquiry* 27 (8–9): 977–87, May.

Wang, Juan. 2012. "Shifting Boundaries between the State and Society: Village Cadres as New Activists in Collective Petition." *The China Quarterly* 211 (September): 697–717. https://doi.org/10.1017/S0305741012000872.

Wang, Juan. 2017. *The Sinews of State Power: The Rise and Demise of The Cohesive Local State in Rural China*. New York, NY: Oxford University Press.

Wang, Maya. 2020. "More Evidence of China's Horrific Abuses in Xinjiang: But Little Action Holding Beijing Accountable." *Human Rights Watch*, February 20, 2020. https://www.hrw.org/news/2020/02/20/more-evidence-chinas-horrific-abuses-xinjiang.

Wang, Peng. 2017. *The Chinese Mafia: Organized Crime, Corruption, and Extra-Legal Protection*. Oxford, UK: Oxford University Press.

Wang, Peng. 2019. "Politics of Crime Control: How Campaign-Style Law Enforcement Sustains Authoritarian Rule in China." *The British Journal of Criminology* 60 (2): 422–43. https://doi.org/10.1093/bjc/azz065.

Weber, Max. 1965. *Politics As a Vocation*. Philadelphia, PA: Fortress Press.

Wedeen, Lisa. 2015. *Ambiguities of Domination: Politics, Rhetoric, and Symbols in Contemporary Syria*. Chicago, IL: University of Chicago Press.

Weidmann, Nils. 2016. "A Closer Look at Reporting Bias in Conflict Event Data." *American Journal of Political Science* 60 (1): 206–18.

Weingast, Barry R., and Mark J. Moran. 1983. "Bureaucratic Discretion or Congressional Control? Regulatory Policymaking by the Federal Trade Commission." *Journal of Political Economy* 91 (5): 765–800.

Weinstein, Jeremy M. 2007. *Inside Rebellion: The Politics of Insurgent Violence*. Cambridge, UK: Cambridge University Press.

Weinstein, Liza. 2008. "Mumbai's Development Mafias: Globalization, Organized Crime and Land Development." *International Journal of Urban and Regional Research* 32 (1): 22–39. https://doi.org/10.1111/j.1468-2427.2008.00766.x.

Whiting, Susan. 2001. *Power and Wealth in Rural China: The Political Economy of Institutional Change*. New York, NY: Cambridge University Press.

Whyte, Martin King, and William L. Parish. 1984. *Urban Life in Contemporary China*. Chicago, IL: University of Chicago Press.

wickedonna2. 2014. "Thousands of Villagers Resisted Government-Led Forced Demolition in Laoyachen, Zhengzhou on March 6th." Tumblr. 2014. https://wickedonna2.tumblr.com/post/78770967097.

Williams, Phil, and Roy Godson. 2002. "Anticipating Organized and Transnational Crime." *Crime, Law and Social Change* 37 (4): 311–55.

Wintrobe, Ronald. 1998. *The Political Economy of Dictatorship*. Cambridge, UK; New York, NY: Cambridge University Press.

Wong, Christine. 2000. "Central-Local Relations Revisited: The 1994 Tax-Sharing Reform and Public Expenditure Management in China." *China Perspectives*, no. 31: 52–63.

Wong, Joseph. 2004. "The Adaptive Developmental State in East Asia." *Journal of East Asian Studies* 4 (3): 345–62.

Wong, Siu Wai, Bo-sin Tang, and Jinlong Liu. 2019. "Village Elections, Grassroots Governance and the Restructuring of State Power: An Empirical Study in Southern Peri-Urban China." *The China Quarterly*, 241: 1–21. https://doi.org/10.1017/S03057 41019000808.

Wood, Elisabeth. 2003. *Insurgent Collective Action and Civil War in El Salvador*. New York, NY: Cambridge University Press.

Wood, Elisabeth. 2008. "The Social Processes of Civil War: The Wartime Transformation of Social Networks." *Annual Review of Political Science* 11: 539–61.

World Bank. 2018. "Urban Population (% of Total Population)—India." 2018. https://data.worldbank.org/indicator/SP.URB.TOTL.IN.ZS?locations=IN.

Wu, Jiebing, Yong Li, and Chengcheng Song. 2020. "Temporal Dynamics of Political Trust in China: A Cohort Analysis." *China Information* 34 (1): 109–36. https://doi.org/10.1177/0920203X19852917.

Xia, Ming. 2006. "Assessing and Explaining the Resurgence of China's Criminal Underworld." *Global Crime* 7 (2): 151–75. https://doi.org/10.1080/17440570601014420.

Xinhua Net. 2012. "调查骗拆迁补偿款乱象：'黄牛'自己掏钱抢盖房子' [Investigation into the Chaos of Demolition Compensation Fraud: 'Huangniu' Used Their Own Money to Build Extra Shacks]." *Xinhua Net*, December 20, 2012. http://www.xinhuanet.com//politics/2012-12/20/c_124121944.htm.

Xinhua Net. 2019a. "中央扫黑除恶专项斗争第一轮督导整改落实情况公布' [The Central Committee's Annoucement of the First-Round Supervision, Rectification and Implementation of Launching the Special Criminal Syndicate Combat]." *Xinhua Net*, January 31, 2019. http://www.xinhuanet.com/2019-01/31/c_1124072249.htm.

Xinhua Net. 2019b. "'中共中央印发《中国共产党农村基层组织工作条例》'作条 [Central Committee of CCP Publishes Regulations on CCP Rural Grassroots-Level Organization Work]. *Xinhua Net*, January 10, 2019. http://www.xinhuanet.com/2019-01/10/c_1123973918.htm.

Yan, Yunxiang. 1996. "The Culture of Guanxi in a North China Village." *China Journal* 35: 1–25.

Yang, Mayfair Mei-hui. 2002. "Rebuttal: The Resilience of Guanxi and Its New Deployments: A Critique of Some New Guanxi Scholarship." *The China Quarterly*, no. 170: 459–76.

Yang, Mayfair Mei-hui. 2016. *Gifts, Favors, and Banquets: The Art of Social Relationships in China*. Kindle Edition. Ithaca, NY; London, UK: Cornell University Press.

Youku. 2012. 郑州市沙门村事件*Shamen Village Incident in Zhengzhou*. https://v.youku.com/v_show/id_XNDU4NzUwNTQ4.html.

Yuan, Lu, and Yan Yu. 2017. "The Eagle-Eyed Elderly Keeping Beijing Safe." *Sixth Tone*, August 4, 2017. https://www.sixthtone.com/news/1000628/the-eagle-eyed-elderly-keeping-beijing-safe.

Zhang, Changdong. 2019. "Asymmetric Mutual Dependence between the State and Capitalists in China." *Politics & Society* 47 (2): 149–76. https://doi.org/10.1177/00323 29219833282.

Zhang, Hongye. 2018. "Why Chinese People Tend to Be Mediated by Authority." *American Journal of Mediation* 11: 131–62.

Zhang, Liping. 2017. "Police Target Celebrity Drug District With Crime-Busting App." *Sixth Tone*, February 15, 2017. https://www.sixthtone.com/news/1937/police-target-celebrity-drug-district-with-crimebusting-app.

Zhang, Weiying, and Feng Deng. 2003. "信息，激励与连带责任-对中国古代，保甲制度的法和经济学解释[Information, Incentive and Joint Liability: An Analysis of Chinese History]." *China Social Science Quarterly* (中国社会科学), no. 3: 99–112.

Zhang, Yu. 2018. "The Credibility of Slums: Informal Housing and Urban Governance in India." *Land Use Policy* 79 (December): 876–90.

Zhang, Yufeng. 2014. "'模拟拆迁:旧城改造和谐新路径——基于F街道W路T区块综合改造工程的个案研究' [Simulated Demolition: Reconstruction of Old City Towns and a New Harmonious Path]." *Reform and Opening* (改革与开放), 19: 60–65. https://doi.org/10.16653/j.cnki.32-1034/f.2014.19.028.

Zhao, Yuezhi. 1998. *Media, Market, and Democracy in China: Between the Party Line and the Bottom Line.* Urbana, IL: University of Illinois Press.

Zhaowen Tianxia. 2012. "'走基层-曹家巷拆迁记：举步维艰的摸底' [Down to the Grassroots-Caojiaxiang Demolition: Struggling to Get to Know the Underlying Situation]." *Zhaowen Tianxia* 朝闻天下. China Central Television News Channel. http://tv.cctv.com/2012/12/31/VIDE1356911290463667.shtml.

Zhong, Raymond, and Paul Mozur. 2020. "To Tame Coronavirus, Mao-Style Social Control Blankets China." *The New York Times*, February 2020. https://www.nytimes.com/2020/02/15/business/china-coronavirus-lockdown.html.

Zhou, Kai, and Xiaojun Yan. 2014. "The Quest for Stability: Policing Popular Protest in the People's Republic of China." *Problems of Post-Communism* 6 (13): 3–17.

Zhou, Yu. 2018. "'时事大家谈: 打虎之后再"扫黑"，习近平意在何方？' ["Sweeping Black" after Beating Tigers, What Does Xi Jinping Want?]." *VOA News*, January 31, 2018. https://www.voachinese.com/a/voaweishi-20180130-io-/4231266.html.

Zhu, Jiangnan. 2012. "The Shadow of the Skyscrapers: Real Estate Corruption in China." *Journal of Contemporary China* 21 (74): 243–60. https://doi.org/10.1080/10670564.2012.635929.

Zhu, Xiaoyang. 2012. "'物的城市化与神的战争' [Urbanization of Objects and Wars between Gods]." *Law and Social Science* 10: 115–47.

Zhu, Zhihua. 2018. "'Fengqiao Experience' Two Fundamentally Different Interpretations." *CWZG*, November 13, 2018. http://www.cwzg.cn/theory/201811/45621.html.

Ziblatt, Daniel. 2006. *Structuring the State: The Formation of Italy and Germany and the Puzzle of Federalism.* Princeton, NJ: Princeton University Press.

Index